FIGHTING AUSTRALIA'S COLD WAR

THE NEXUS OF STRATEGY AND OPERATIONS
IN A MULTIPOLAR ASIA, 1945–1965

FIGHTING AUSTRALIA'S COLD WAR

THE NEXUS OF STRATEGY AND OPERATIONS
IN A MULTIPOLAR ASIA, 1945–1965

EDITED BY PETER DEAN
AND TRISTAN MOSS

PRESS

Published by ANU Press
The Australian National University
Acton ACT 2601, Australia
Email: anupress@anu.edu.au

Available to download for free at press.anu.edu.au

ISBN (print): 9781760464820
ISBN (online): 9781760464837

WorldCat (print): 1285257710
WorldCat (online): 1285243113

DOI: 10.22459/FACW.2021

This title is published under a Creative Commons Attribution-NonCommercial-NoDerivatives 4.0 International (CC BY-NC-ND 4.0).

The full licence terms are available at
creativecommons.org/licenses/by-nc-nd/4.0/legalcode

Cover design and layout by ANU Press.

Cover photograph: Informal portrait of 54415 Private (Pte) Patrick T (Pat) Brookes, 3rd Battalion, The Royal Australian Regiment (3RAR), of Perth, WA, making his way through dense jungle foliage as he patrols along the Sarawak-Kalimantan border area. He is armed with a 7.62mm L4A4 Bren light machine gun (LMG) and has a 36M hand grenade attached to his webbing strap. Pte Brookes also served in Malaya and Singapore during the Indonesian Confrontation period of the early 1960s. Courtesy of the Australian War Memorial (CUN/65/0757/MC).

This book is published under the aegis of the Asia-Pacific Security Studies
Editorial Board of ANU Press.

This edition © 2021 ANU Press

Contents

Maps	vii
Acknowledgements	xi
Contributors	xiii
Abbreviations	xvii
Introduction: Fighting Australia's Cold War	1

Part 1. Strategy and the postwar military

1. Australian strategic policy in the global context of the Cold War, 1945–65 — 11
   Stephan Frühling
2. Australia's military after the Second World War: Legacies and challenges — 35
   John Blaxland
3. The 'fourth arm' of Australia's defence: ASIO and the early Cold War — 53
   David Horner
4. The Korean War — 73
   Thomas Richardson

Part 2. Planning for and fighting in Southeast Asia, 1955–65

5. Planning for war in Southeast Asia: The Far East Strategic Reserve, 1955–66 — 95
   Tristan Moss
6. The Malayan Emergency — 115
   Thomas Richardson
7. Australia's Confrontation with Indonesia and military commitment to Borneo, 1964–66 — 137
   Lachlan Grant and Michael Kelly

8. Defending Australia's land border: The Australian military in Papua New Guinea 157
   Tristan Moss

Part 3. Retrospective

9. The Australian way of war and the early Cold War 175
   Peter J Dean

Index 197

Maps

Map 1: Asia-Pacific region.
Source: CartoGIS Services, ANU College of Asia & the Pacific.

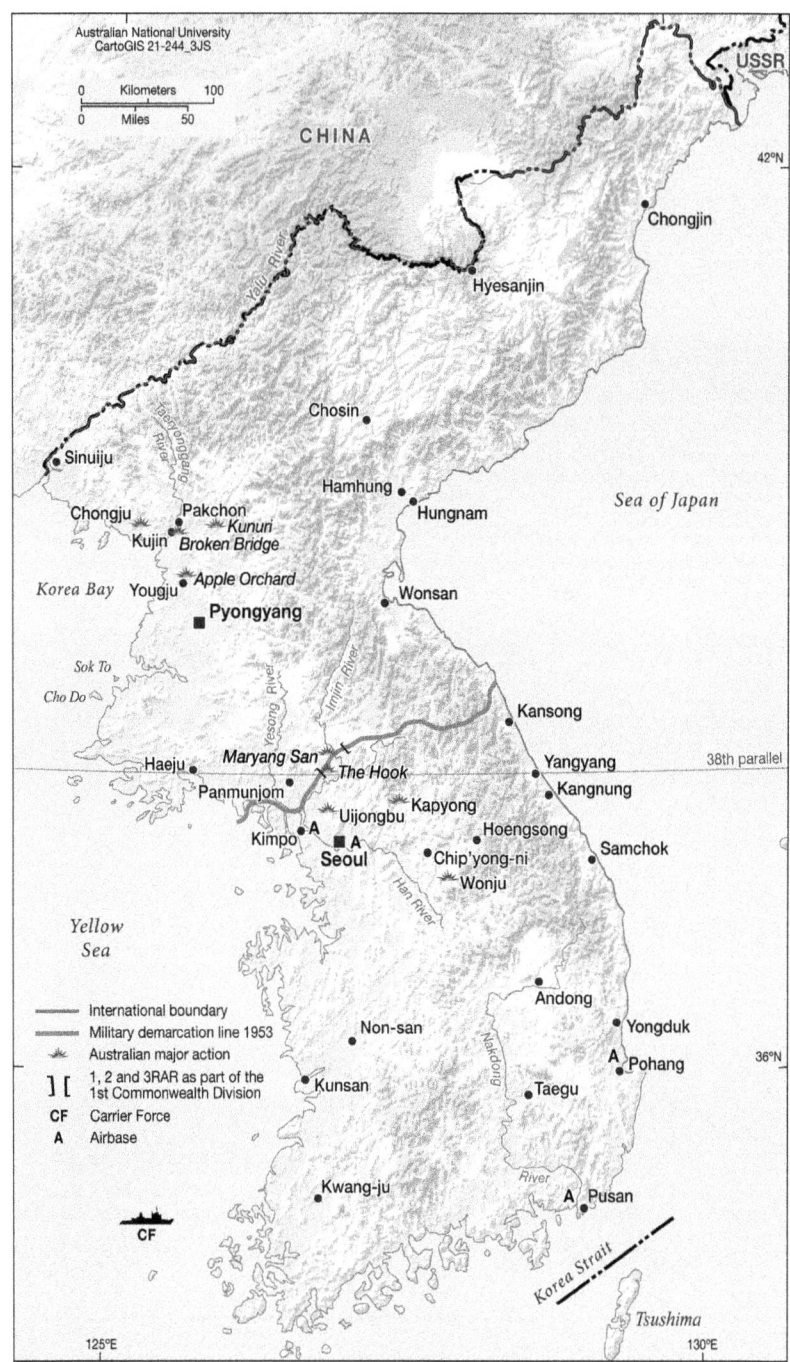

Map 2: The Korean War.
Source: CartoGIS Services, ANU College of Asia & the Pacific.

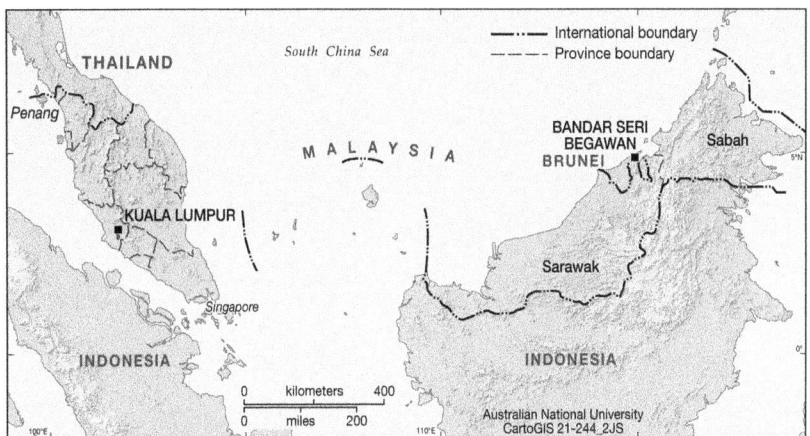

Map 3: The Malayan Emergency.
Source: CartoGIS Services, ANU College of Asia & the Pacific.

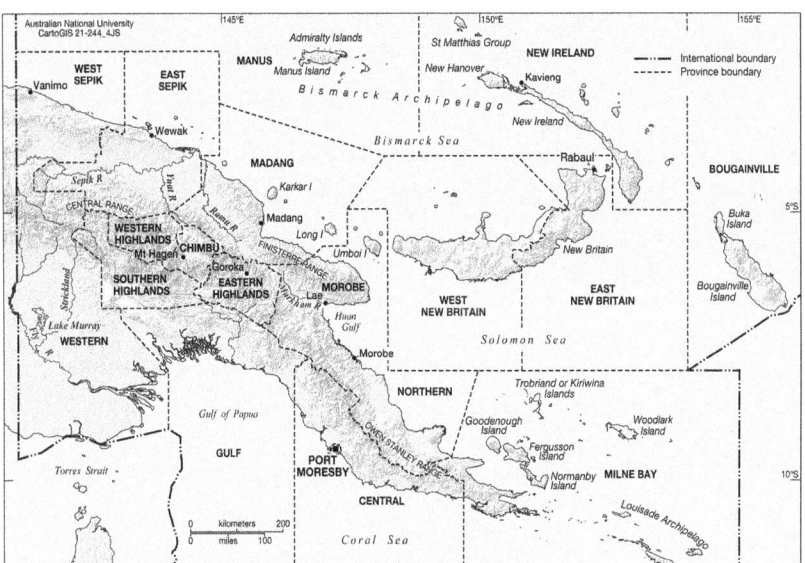

Map 4: Borneo, Indonesia and Papua New Guinea.
Source: CartoGIS Services, ANU College of Asia & the Pacific.

Acknowledgements

This book is the extension of an 'accidental' trilogy on Australia in the Pacific War that Peter edited and which was published between 2012 and 2015. At the conclusion of that series, Tristan raised an obvious question – why hasn't anyone looked at Australian strategy and operations in the early Cold War as a whole? The result of that conversation is this book.

The editors would like to thank the authors for their production of fine chapters, all of which complement each other and speak to the central focus of the book. Edited books are only as good as the faculty that is gathered around the central theme. It is their subsequent hard work that turns an idea and a theme into a book. All the authors have been a pleasure to work with and have juggled this project among the plethora of other tasks they had on their plates. They have our thanks and gratitude. Dr Greg Raymond, the editor of the ANU Press Asia-Pacific Security Studies series, was forever supportive and patient with the editors as deadlines slipped and 2020–21 had its full impact, as it has with all of us across the globe. We wish to also thank the team at ANU Press for their hard work and support. Thanks also go to the Department of Defence, whose support for the University of Western Australia Defence and Security Program through a Strategic Policy Grant made the final stages of this book possible.

Finally, thanks to family, friends and colleagues. As each of the authors in this book can attest, writing is only sometimes a solitary activity. Colleagues are crucial in the thinking process, sharing the pain and the joy of the process. Family and friends not only act as sounding boards, but also as sources of support, cajoling or advice that maybe one should just go outside for a walk.

Contributors

Professor Peter J Dean (editor) was appointed as the University of Western Australia's (UWA) first Chair of Defence Studies on 1 July 2020 and the inaugural director of the UWA Defence and Security Institute in March 2021. Prior to the commencement of this role, Peter was Pro Vice-Chancellor (Education) at UWA; he is also a Senior Fellow at the Perth USAsia Centre. Peter has an extensive background in military and defence studies. He has been a Fulbright Fellow and Endeavour Research Scholar in Australia–United States Alliance Studies as well as a non-resident fellow with the Center for Strategic and International Studies and the Center for Australia, New Zealand and Pacific Studies at Georgetown University in Washington DC. Before joining UWA, Peter was a scholar at the Strategic and Defence Studies Centre in The Australian National University's (ANU) College of Asia and the Pacific where he held numerous research, teaching and leadership positions. Peter was the founding editor of the Melbourne University Press Defence Studies Series, is a member of the editorial boards of the *Australian Army Journal*, *Global War Studies* and the *Military Studies Journal*, and is a former managing editor of the journal *Security Challenges*. He is a regular media commentator on Australian, United States and regional defence issues. An international award-winning author, his most recent book (with Brendan Taylor and Stephan Frühling) is *After American primacy: Imagining the future of Australia's defence* (Melbourne University Press, 2019).

Dr Tristan Moss (editor) is a senior lecturer at the Griffith Asia Institute, Griffith University, Queensland. He is the author of *Guarding the periphery: The Australian Army in Papua New Guinea, 1951–75* (Cambridge University Press, 2017), and coeditor of *Beyond combat: Australian military activity away from the battlefields* (NewSouth Books, 2018). Tristan has worked on the official history of Australian operations in Afghanistan, Iraq and East Timor at the Australian War Memorial and on the official history of peacekeeping. He is also a Fulbright Scholar and winner of a Discovery Early Career Researcher Award, working on a history of Australian space policy.

Professor Stephan Frühling is the Deputy Dean of the ANU College of Asia and the Pacific. He researches and teaches in the Strategic and Defence Studies Centre, and has widely published on Australian defence policy, defence planning and strategy, nuclear weapons and the North Atlantic Treaty Organization (NATO). Stephan was the Fulbright Professional Fellow in Australia–United States Alliance Studies at Georgetown University in Washington DC in 2017. He worked as a 'Partner across the globe' research fellow in the Research Division of the NATO Defense College in Rome in 2015, and was a member of the Australian Government's external Expert Panel on the development of the 2016 Defence White Paper. Previously, he was the Associate Dean Education of the ANU College of Asia and the Pacific (2016 to February 2020), the inaugural Director of Studies of the ANU Master in Military Studies program at the Australian Defence Force's Australian Command and Staff College (2011–13), and managing editor of the Kokoda Foundation's journal *Security Challenges* (2006–14).

Professor John Blaxland is Professor of International Security and Intelligence Studies at the Strategic and Defence Studies Centre at ANU. John holds a PhD in war studies from the Royal Military College of Canada, an MA in history from ANU and a BA(Hons) from UNSW. A former Army Intelligence Corps officer and defence attaché to Thailand and Myanmar, he is also a graduate of the Royal Thai Army Command and General Staff College and the Royal Military College, Duntroon. In addition to a range of chapters and articles on intelligence, military history and regional security issues, his publications include *The US–Thai alliance and international relations* (with Greg Raymond, Routledge, 2021); *Niche wars: Australia in Afghanistan and Iraq, 2001–2014* (ANU Press, 2020); *In from the cold: Reflections on Australia's Korean War* (ANU Press, 2020); *A geostrategic SWOT analysis for Australia* (ANU Strategic and Defence Studies Centre, 2019); *Tipping the balance in Southeast Asia?* (ANU Strategic and Defence Studies Centre, 2017); *The secret Cold War* (Allen & Unwin, 2016); *Manis: Time for a new forum to sweeten regional cooperation* (ANU Strategic and Defence Studies Centre, 2016); *East Timor intervention* (Melbourne University Press, 2015); *The protest years* (Allen & Unwin, 2015); *The Australian Army from*

Whitlam to Howard (Cambridge University Press, 2014); *Strategic cousins* (McGill-Queens University Press, 2006); and *Signals swift and sure* (Royal Australian Corps of Signals Corps Committee, 1998).

Professor David Horner is Emeritus Professor of Australian Defence History in the Strategic and Defence Studies Centre at ANU. He graduated from the Royal Military College, Duntroon, in 1969 and served as an infantry platoon commander in Vietnam in 1971, before retiring from the Regular Army as lieutenant colonel in 1990. David is the Official Historian of Australian Peacekeeping, Humanitarian and Post-Cold War Operations and the Official Historian for the Australian Security Intelligence Organisation. He has written or edited 37 books on Australian military history, strategy, intelligence and defence policy, is a Member of the Order of Australia and a Fellow of the Academy of Social Sciences in Australia.

Dr Thomas Richardson graduated from Monash University with a BA(Hons) in 2009 and completed his doctorate, 'As if we'd never really been there? Pacification in Phuoc Tuy Province, Republic of Vietnam, 1966–1972', at UNSW Canberra in 2014. Between then and assuming his current position at UNSW Canberra in July 2018 he worked as a tutor and lecturer at UNSW Canberra (2015–16), as a researcher on the official history of Australian peacekeeping (2015) and as a researcher on the official history of Australian operations in East Timor, Iraq and Afghanistan (2016–18). Thomas's first book, *Destroy and build: Pacification in Phuoc Tuy, 1966–1972*, was published by Cambridge University Press in 2017. He has contributed to a number of edited volumes and edited two with Tristan Moss: *New directions in war and history* (Big Sky, 2016) and *Beyond combat: Australian military activity away from the battlefield* (NewSouth, 2018). His broad research interests are Australian military history and counterinsurgency and the confluence of the two, particularly in Southeast Asia after 1945. His current project is an operational history of Australia in the Second Anglo-Boer War.

Dr Lachlan Grant is a Senior Historian at the Australian War Memorial where he was been a member of the Military History Section since 2011. He completed his PhD at Monash University in 2010 and has published widely on the Second World War and the prisoner-of-war experience. He is the author of *Australian soldiers in Asia-Pacific in World War II* (NewSouth Books, 2014) and the editor of *For county, for nation: An illustrated history of Aboriginal and Torres Strait Islander military service*

(NewSouth Books, 2018) and *The Changi book* (NewSouth Books, 2015); and coeditor, with Joan Beaumont and Aaron Pegram, of *Beyond surrender: Australian prisoners of war in the twentieth century* (Melbourne University Press, 2015); and has curated several museum exhibitions and led battlefield tours. Lachlan is currently writing a book on Australians and the battle of Normandy and is researching aircrew experiences in Bomber Command.

Michael Kelly served as a rifleman in 8/9 Battalion, Royal Australian Regiment and is a historian in the Military History Section at the Australian War Memorial. He has a special interest in Australia's role in Asia during the Cold War, with a particular focus on the Korean War, Malayan Emergency and Indonesian Confrontation. He is an editor of *In from the cold: Reflections on Australia's Korean War* (ANU Press, 2020).

Abbreviations

AATTV	Australian Army Training Team Vietnam
ACP	Australian Communist Party
AIF	Australian Imperial Force
ANZAM	Australia, New Zealand and Malaya alliance
ANZUK	Australia, New Zealand and United Kingdom alliance
ANZUS	Australia, New Zealand and United States alliance
ASIO	Australian Security Intelligence Organisation
ATOM	*The conduct of anti-terrorist operations in Malaya*
BCOF	British Commonwealth Occupation Force
CAC	Commonwealth Aircraft Corporation
CCO	Clandestine Communist Organisation
CIB	Commonwealth Investigation Branch
CIS	Commonwealth Investigation Service
CMF	Citizen Military Force
CPA	Communist Party of Australia
CT	Communist Terrorist
DoA	Defence of Australia
DOBOPs	Director of Borneo Operations
DPRK	Democratic People's Republic of Korea
FARELF	Far Eastern Land Forces
FEC	Far East Command
FESR	Far East Strategic Reserve
FOO	forward observation officer
FTC	Forces Training Centre (Far Eastern Land Forces)

GOC	General Officer Commanding
IWW	Industrial Workers of the World
JCS	Joint Chiefs of Staff
JTC	Jungle Training Centre
KPA	Korean People's Army
MCP	Malayan Communist Party
MPAJA	Malayan Peoples' Anti-Japanese Army
MRLA	Malayan Races Liberation Army
NATO	North Atlantic Treaty Organization
PIR	Pacific Islands Regiment
PMF	Permanent Military Force
PNG	Papua New Guinea
RAAF	Royal Australian Air Force
RAF	Royal Air Force
RAN	Royal Australian Navy
RAR	Royal Australian Regiment
ROK	Republic of Korea
ROKA	Republic of Korea Army
RVN	Republic of Vietnam
SAC	Strategic Air Command
SAS	Special Air Service
SEATO	Southeast Asia Treaty Organization
SIB	Special Intelligence Bureau
SWPA	Southwest Pacific Area
UNSC	United Nations Security Council
USAF	United States Air Force

Introduction: Fighting Australia's Cold War

For two decades after the end of the Second World War, Australia actively sought to ensure its security through the deployment of its forces at home and abroad. While the Australian military had drastically shrunk in size after 1945, during the 1950s and 1960s it was persistently engaged in conflict, while simultaneously preparing for the possibility of a broader world conflagration. Indeed, there was no time in the two decades after the Second World War in which Australian forces were not deployed overseas. After contributing to the occupation of Japan from 1945, only five years after the Second World War Australia was again engaged in conflict, in support of its allies in Korea and in the form of aircraft in support of Commonwealth operations in the Malayan Emergency. In 1955, Australia committed ground forces to the Emergency to form a part of the Far East Strategic Reserve (FESR) alongside Britain and New Zealand. It was from the forces serving with FESR that Australia deployed to a third conflict against Indonesia in Borneo. While these three conflicts marked the clearest examples of Australia's efforts to maintain its security during the early Cold War, between these deployments the country also prepared to fight wider conflicts and maintained vigilance at home against internal threats. These preparations were not trivial commitments: they dominated the allocation of resources, shaped training and framed force structure. Moreover, the threats for which Australian prepared during this period were not abstract ones but were instead considered likely and highly dangerous.

While Australia fought in four conflicts during the Cold War, and prepared for others, the history of this period is dominated by the war in Vietnam, on which so much of the public memory focuses. That war is at the forefront of public imagining of the period after the Second World War, and was the catalyst and symbol for many social, political and strategic shifts of that era. The strong focus on Vietnam relative to other Cold War conflicts is reflected in the wealth of histories on that war compared with others, and the consistent use of the Vietnam War to periodise Australia's military history. The 1950s and early 1960s are often seen as the lead-up to the Australian deployment of troops to Vietnam, whereas 1975 is firmly perceived as the end of an era for the Australian military. Yet this focus belies the fact that for the 20 years prior to the deployment of Australian combat troops to Vietnam, Australia was actively engaged in conflicts with their own contexts, during which the Australian military grew and developed in response to the demands placed on it by a changing strategic environment. During this time, the Australian armed forces underwent significant expansion and, in the case of the army in particular, professionalisation. Much of the equipment, tactics and doctrine developed during the 20 years after the Second World War remained in place until the 1990s; it was also these first conflicts of the Cold War that shaped how Australia fought in Vietnam. Equally, contrary to a popular imagination that often foregrounds Curtin's 1942 'turn to America', Australian forces spent the two decades after the Second World War closely integrated with the British and the wider Commonwealth, marking them out from the 'norm' of working closely alongside the United States in Vietnam, which is so powerfully embedded into the public consciousness.

The period between the Second World War and the Vietnam War features only briefly in Australia's military history.[1] Within the popular imagining, as Australia's largest and most controversial post–Second World War conflict, Vietnam has attracted the lion's share of historical writing, overshadowing the years that preceded it. The Korean War is perhaps the best studied, with its own official history and a body of memoirs and studies.[2] This was a conventional conflict, with Australia participating in a handful of hard-fought battles, around which a narrative could be established. Later conflicts are less well served by histories, scholarly or otherwise.

---

1   Jeffrey Grey, *A military history of Australia*, 3rd ed. (Cambridge: Cambridge University Press, 2008), 317.
2   Robert O'Neill, *Australia in the Korean War 1950–53*, vol. 1, *Strategy and diplomacy* (Canberra: Australian War Memorial and the Australian Government Publishing Service, 1981). For the most recent discussion of the Korean War in the Australian context, see John Blaxland, Michael Kelly and Liam Higgins, *In from the cold: Reflections on Australia's Korean War* (Canberra: ANU Press, 2020), doi.org/10.22459/iftc.2019.

Beyond a small handful of memoirs and narrative histories, a notable feature of the writing on the conflicts in Malaya and Borneo and the preparations for war in Southeast Asia is the interconnected nature of the history. The structure of the official histories, which examine conflicts and crises in Southeast Asia rather than treating the conflicts as individual events, is the clearest example of the way that these conflicts should be understood as part of one overall effort by Australia to ensure its own security through collective defence in the region. Each commitment, therefore, is treated as one part of a broader strategic aim by the Official Historian, Peter Edwards.[3] That some of the most useful military histories of this period are biographies, following key officers across multiple deployments and through the period's major changes within the military, is a further indicator of the way in which this early period can be viewed as a whole, and as important in and of itself. This is notable in the biographies of key military figures during this period, such as David Horner's biography of Chief of General Staff Lieutenant General John Wilton, and Jeffrey Grey's of Lieutenant General Thomas Daly, Wilton's successor.[4]

There are significant gaps in the historical understanding of this period, however, once one ventures beyond the official histories and the general histories of Australia's military past. The wars themselves, and the preparations for conflicts not fought, have attracted little in the way of Australian historical writing compared with, for instance, the campaigns of the First World War. Discounting contemporary accounts or memoirs, only Korea sees a handful of studies on the conflict.[5] There are no Australian-focused histories of either Malaya or Confrontation. Similarly, the non-operational aspects of this period in Australia's military past are often ill-studied. This time period could be a rich vein for historians, with significant institutional changes within an Australian military adapting to

---

3 Edwards's two studies of the strategic and diplomatic contexts reflect the interrelated nature of the conflicts in Southeast Asia. However, the 10 volumes of the *Official history of Australia's involvement in Southeast Asian conflicts, 1948–1975* are dominated by Vietnam, while the Malayan Emergency and Borneo conflicts share one book.

4 DM Horner, *Strategic command: General Sir John Wilton and Australia's Asian wars* (Melbourne: Oxford University Press, 2005); Jeffrey Grey, *A soldier's soldier: A biography of Lieutenant General Sir Thomas Daly* (Cambridge; Port Melbourne: Cambridge University Press, 2012), doi.org/10.1017/cbo9781107294240. Memoirs of other officers follow this trend. See for instance Brian W McFarlane, *We band of brothers: A true Australian adventure story* (Bowral: BW McFarlane, 2000); Pat Beale, *Operation orders: The experiences of an infantry officer* (Loftus: Australian Military History Publications, 2003).

5 For a literature review of the Korean War from the Australian perspective, see Blaxland, Kelly and Higgins, *In from the cold*, 6–12.

new technological conditions, social and racial change at home, profound strategic shifts and the need, for the first time, to maintain forces overseas for decades at a time.[6] Yet there is nothing in Australian literature that examines the services during the crucial, fast-changing period of the 1950s and 1960s, in the style of, for instance, Brian McAlister Linn's *Elvis's army*, which explores the social, technological and institutional changes with the US Army.[7]

More broadly, the gaps in the literature that this book seeks to address reflect some of the broader problems in Australian military history. The body of literature is small and is focused on a handful of notable conflicts, rather than the broad sweep of *military* (rather than war) history. Australian historians, whether they define themselves as military historians or not, overwhelmingly focus on the First World War, and to a lesser extent the Second World War and Vietnam War. Discussions of well-known campaigns or battles dominate military historians' attentions, while social histories dominate the interests of Australian scholars examining Australia's military past.

Undoubtedly, this is the product of a small number of historians working on Australian military history topics; the number of Australian historians more broadly is similarly small compared with the United Kingdom or United States. Who is doing military history in Australia is also an issue that warrants ongoing discussion. The average Australian military historian is a man, of European descent and based in Canberra, either at The Australian National University, the Australian War Memorial or the University of New South Wales Canberra; this collection, as the editors acknowledge, is no exception. The absence of women and people from diverse backgrounds, including those who speak languages other than English and who approach military history from different cultural

---

6   There have been a handful of excellent studies on some of these topics in the last decade. See for instance Christina Twomey, 'Bring the family: Australian overseas military communities and regional engagement, 1945–1988', in *Beyond combat: Australian military activity away from the battlefield*, ed. Tristan Moss and Tom Richardson (Sydney: NewSouth Books, 2018), 10–28; Mathew Radcliffe, 'In defence of White Australia: Discouraging "Asian marriage" in post war South-East Asia', *Australian Historical Studies* 45, no. 2 (2014): 184–201, doi.org/10.1080/1031461x.2014.911761; Noah Riseman, Shirleene Robinson and Graham Willett, *Serving in silence?* (Sydney: NewSouth Books, 2018); Noah Riseman, 'Racism, Indigenous people and the Australian armed forces in the post-Second World War era', *History Australia* 10, no. 2 (2013): 159–79, doi.org/10.1080/1449085 4.2013.11668466.
7   Brian McAllister Linn, *Elvis's army: Cold War GIs and the atomic battlefield*, illustrated ed. (Cambridge, Massachusetts: Harvard University Press, 2016), doi.org/10.4159/9780674973732.

perspectives, represents a significant gap in Australian military history. The data shows that, depending on level of appointment, there is rough parity between men and women in Australian history faculties across the country.[8] Anecdotally, this is not the case in military history, particularly at more senior levels. Historians across the discipline should ask why, and how to change this. One feature of this discussion is the reticence of many to define themselves as military historians or to encourage others to do so, which is a symptom of the sometimes poor reputation that military history has in Australia as conservative and theory-averse; not all of this reputation is ill-deserved. Equally, there is a tendency to judge military history by its weakest examples, including popular histories not written by academics. While there are excellent military historians working on issues such as race, gender and military cultures, to name a few, one result of the narrowness of the field and those in it can be a skewing of historical work towards Australia's major and most publicly recognised conflicts, and away from other themes, military activities and historical periods.

This book seeks to address one such understudied period by bringing together Australia's Cold War military history prior to Vietnam in one coherent narrative. Crucially, it does not focus on the conflicts of Korea, Malaya and Borneo alone. To do so would be to ignore the broader context in which these occurred and the intense Australian focus on defending itself through collective security, comprehensive planning for possible wars, and the fight against threats at home. At the heart of this book is an examination of the way in which Australian strategy was translated into action 'on the ground', not just through combat, but through the commitment of armed forces throughout the region to deter conflict while preparing for it to break out. This is a classic strategic studies approach focused on the use of armed force in international affairs.

The book is divided into two main content parts and a concluding third part. The first examines the strategic shifts facing Australia in the immediate postwar period, and the way in which the military was structured to meet them. The first 20 years of Australia's Cold War were characterised by a series of strategic challenges, marked as much by their significant threat to Australia's security as their changing nature. In the first chapter, Stephan Frühling shows that there were few certainties for

---

8   See Martin Crotty and Paul Sendziuk, 'The numbers game: History staffing in Australian and New Zealand universities', *Australian Historical Studies* 50, no. 3 (July 3, 2019): 365–69, doi.org/10.1080/1031461X.2019.1601750.

Australia during this period, as the nation dealt with decolonisation, the shift of Australian defence focus to Asia from the Middle East, the threats of nationalism and communism in the region and the need to manage collective security arrangements with allies and regional partners.

Frühling's insight at the strategic policy level is buttressed by John Blaxland's assessment of the effects of Australia's largest ever conflict, the Second World War, on Australia's military forces in the early Cold War period. This chapter is critical in setting up the legacies of this conflict, its impact on a radically reduced military force in Australia and the interaction between the United States and the United Kingdom, which dominate Australia's strategic relations in Asia during this period. The next chapter focuses on an aspect rarely integrated into military history: internal security. The Cold War was not seen by Australia as merely a military conflict; it was also a war of ideas, of culture, of economic structures and methods of government. The Cold War was also fought at home, albeit far less violently than in the jungles of Southeast Asia. David Horner examines the role played by the Australian Security Intelligence Organisation, newly created after the Second World War, in defending Australia from foreign and domestic threats.

Often termed the 'Forgotten War', Australia's participation in the Korean War sat directly between two different periods of the early Cold War. Largely fought with Second World War equipment and tactics, the war more resembled those conflicts that went before it than those that came after. However, in the clear linking of Australia's strategic interests with the judicious deployment of a small number of troops in support of allies, the Korean War had the hallmarks of later Cold War conflicts. Militarily, as Thomas Richardson shows in Chapter 4, Australia was keenly aware of the way in which the commitment of forces to the Korean peninsula might help secure not only that country from communism, but also ensure a security arrangement with the United States. Yet, in order to do this, the Australian Government recognised that its soldiers, sailors and airmen had to make a meaningful contribution to the war; for the Australian forces deployed, therefore, the war was an intense one.

The second part of the book focuses on the shift of Australia's armed forces from fighting and preparing for conventional war to counterinsurgency warfighting after 1955. During this period, Australian forces were integrated with British Commonwealth organisations under the FESR, based in Malaya and Singapore, which is explored by Tristan Moss in

Chapter 5. The deployment of a battalion of Australian infantry in 1955 reflected Australia's commitment to collective defence with the British Commonwealth in the face of the threat of another global war. As part of 28 Commonwealth Brigade, in the British Far East Air Forces and as a significant part of the British-led naval presence in the region, Australian forces made a substantial contribution to the Commonwealth's first response should war have broken out, while Australia was also closely involved in planning and training for these possible wars.

While ostensibly based in Malaysia as part of the FESR, Australian forces, particularly those from the army, spent a great deal of their time fighting insurgents during the Malayan Emergency. Richardson details this frustrating war, in which Australian ground forces rarely saw the enemy. The formation of Malaysia in 1957 led to Australia's third Cold War conflict, against Indonesian Confrontation. Lachlan Grant and Michael Kelly's chapter on operations in Borneo details how, even before the deployment to Vietnam, Australian forces had gained significant experience in jungle warfare, working alongside British forces to defeat the policy of Indonesian Confrontation.

At the same time, Australia's Papua New Guinea–based force – the Pacific Islands Regiment – prepared to defend the Australian territory of Papua New Guinea (PNG). Rather than an overlooked outpost of the Australian Army, PNG was an important part of Australia's defence. Given the tensions with Indonesia elsewhere – which erupted into a low-level conflict in Borneo – Australian planners worried that the war would reach Australian territory. In Chapter 8, Moss explores how the Australian Army's series of deep patrols on the border complemented broader Commonwealth plans to defeat Indonesia in the case of conventional war.

The period 1945–66 was one of change, in which Australia reorientated its defence forces and strategic outlook to address a threat arising in its region in the context of the Cold War. It was this period that laid the foundations for the military that would go to war in Vietnam. Peter Dean's final chapter, and the concluding part of the book, draws together the strategic, doctrinal and tactical influences on the Australian armed forces preparation and conduct of its roles in Southeast Asia, asking how the strategy evolved, the military adapted and to what extent these changes were reflective of an 'Australian way of war'.

Part 1. Strategy and the postwar military

1

Australian strategic policy in the global context of the Cold War, 1945–65

Stephan Frühling

It is difficult to understate the strategic challenges that Australian governments were confronted with in the two decades after the Second World War. The period from 1945 to 1965 includes the 'first Cold War', in which the Western and communist blocs were locked in an existential strategic competition that was as yet unmitigated by any notion of détente. Moreover, for Australia this era of the 'Cold War' was very much a hot one, as its forces were continuously engaged in combat operations in different parts of Asia from 1950 to 1971. The interplay of decolonisation in Australia's neighbourhood, of threats of nationalism and communism, of the conditional nature of allies' commitment to Australia's security, and even of the revolutionary change in weapons technology, made the two decades after the Second World War a period where few certainties seemed to exist as Australia navigated its own particular version of the Cold War.

In the midst of global and regional turmoil and conflict, Australia had again to solve the basic problem of Australia's defence policy: how to defend a thinly populated continent, off the archipelago of Southeast Asia and far removed from its allied great powers, whose strategic interests and priorities by necessity lay elsewhere. The quest to solve this problem led Australia to seek close cooperation and even integration with the defence planning and posture of both Britain and the United States in Southeast

Asia, and to play its role in the global fight against communism. At the same time, however, the consequences of decolonisation and nationalism in Indonesia presented particular challenges for Australia's strategic policy, exactly because its allies were primarily focused on the communist threat, and the centre of gravity of the global Cold War lay elsewhere.

Australia's (and New Zealand's) Cold War operations in Southeast Asia focused on a region where the Cold War was 'hot' for longest, but which was nonetheless only of third-rate importance for Australia's allies. With the notable exception of the Vietnam War, US engagement in Southeast Asia was always framed within a global strategy focused on conflict with the Soviet Union. In the 1950s in particular, the near-singular US focus on the strategic nuclear offensive as the basis of Western security was a particularly poor fit for Australia's regionally focused defence policy. By the end of the period under examination in this collection, the Kennedy Administration's new strategy of 'flexible response' proved more amenable to address Australia's concerns – and would set both countries on the fateful road to escalation in Vietnam.

The origins of the Cold War

The Cold War, between the Soviet Union and its vassal states on the one side and the free world united in a series of alliances and led by the United States on the other, began to divide the victorious coalition of the Second World War within months of the end of that momentous conflict. Demobilisation by the United States had left the Soviet Army as the dominant military power in Europe. In 1946, former British prime minister Winston Churchill warned the United States of an 'iron curtain' that had descended through the middle of Europe,[1] as non-communist parties were persecuted in Poland and elsewhere in the Soviet sphere of influence. The same year, George Kennan sent his 'long telegram' from Moscow, warning of the existential and implacable threat that Soviet expansion posed for the free world.[2]

---

1   John Ramsden, 'Mr Churchill goes to Fulton', in *Churchill's Iron Curtain speech fifty years later*, ed. James Muller (Missouri: University of Missouri Press, 1999), 15.
2   Telegram, George Kennan to George Marshall (the 'Long Telegram'), 22 February 1946, Truman Library, Harry Truman Administration File, Elsey Papers, www.trumanlibraryinstitute.org/this-day-in-history-2/ (accessed November 2021).

1. AUSTRALIAN STRATEGIC POLICY IN THE GLOBAL CONTEXT OF THE COLD WAR, 1945–65

In 1947, the United Kingdom and France renewed their alliance in the Dunkirk Treaty, and the Truman Administration replaced Britain as the sponsor of anti-communist forces in Greece and Turkey. The threat was not confined to the Atlantic area, as communist movements also took up arms in China, Tonkin, Malaya and the Dutch East Indies. But what really focused the minds of governments in London, Paris and the Hague was the impending danger to their homelands in Europe. The year 1948 saw the communist coup in Czechoslovakia, and the conclusion of the Brussels Pact between France, Britain and the Benelux countries. Even together, however, these five countries had little hope of resisting a Soviet invasion on their own. Their defence cooperation was an invitation (and plea) for the United States to overturn its adherence to George Washington's old exhortation to 'to steer clear of permanent Alliances, with any portion of the foreign World',[3] and to commit its economic and military resources to the defence of Western Europe.[4] The same year, the United States committed the US Air Force to defy the Soviet blockade of Berlin. One year later, it then finally pledged itself in the 1949 Washington Treaty to the defence of the members of the Brussels Pact, of Italy (as the key to the Mediterranean) and of the 'stepping stone countries' of Norway, Denmark and Portugal, which controlled vital islands in the North Atlantic: the North Atlantic Treaty Organization (NATO) was born.

America's new political commitments were translated into national defence mobilisation in 1950. In September, the Truman Administration endorsed NSC-68, which was in a sense the founding document of US and NATO strategy for the conflict with global communism. To win the Cold War, the United States would have to build up sufficient conventional and nuclear military capabilities to deter, and if necessary to defeat, Soviet attacks against the main population and industrial centres of Western Europe and East Asia. Moreover, it would need to maintain this unprecedented peacetime effort indefinitely, until the Soviet political system would eventually collapse under the weight of its internal contradictions.[5]

---

3   George Washington, 'Friends & fellow citizens', farewell address, United States, 19 September 1796. Transcript: gwpapers.virginia.edu/documents_gw/farewell/transcript.html (accessed April 2018), p. 27.
4   David Millar, *The Cold War: A military history* (London: John Murray, 1997), 10–13, 16–24.
5   'A report to the National Security Council – NSC 68', 12 April 1950, Truman Library, Truman Papers, www.trumanlibrary.gov/library/research-files/report-national-security-council-nsc-68?document id=NA&pagenumber=1 (accessed November 2021).

During the final days of deliberation of NSC-68, North Korea attacked and nearly defeated the forces defending the Republic of Korea, including a small and ill-equipped US constabulary force. The Cold War had become hot, as the Korean War seemed a likely feint before the onset of global war. The United States declared a state of national emergency to assist defence mobilisation in December 1950. Even as it fought in Korea, it undertook a rapid and massive effort to create the alliance forces, standing commands, logistics and supply infrastructure that would be required for NATO to fight off the Soviet Army in Europe.[6]

For the following four decades, the United States would lead – and in many ways create and shape – the free world through the concerted military, economic and ideological efforts through which the Cold War was fought. The early Cold War gave rise not only to military alliances across the globe that persist to this day, including the ANZUS alliance between Australia, New Zealand and the United States, but also to the institutional underpinnings of what is today called the 'global rules-based order': the International Bank for Reconstruction and Development (today's World Bank), the International Monetary Fund, the Global Agreement on Tariffs and Trade (which became the World Trade Organization) and the Organisation for Economic Co-operation and Development that emerged from the Organisation for European Economic Cooperation to administer the US and Canadian Marshall Plan aid to Europe.[7] But as these new global institutions took shape in the North Atlantic area, Britain's faraway, antipodean dominions had to navigate their own particular challenges of the Cold War.

---

6   Terrance J Gough, *U.S. Army mobilization and logistics in the Korean War: A research approach* (Washington DC: Centre of Military History, United States Army, 1987), 10; Dieter Krüger, 'Institutionalizing NATO's military bureaucracy: The making of an integrated chain of command', in *NATO's post–Cold War politics: The changing provision of security*, ed. Sebastian Mayer (New York: Palgrave Macmillan, 2014), 55.

7   While some of these institutions date to the 1944 Bretton Woods conference, they became key elements of the economic organisation of the free world. For a discussion of the interplay of economic and military institutions in US grand strategy during the Cold War see Richard Betts, 'U.S. national security strategy: Lenses and landmarks' (paper presented for the launch conference of the Princeton Project: Toward a New National Security Strategy, November 2004).

Australian strategic policy between Commonwealth defence and the US alliance

As the confusing aftermath of the Second World War settled into the Cold War conflict in the northern hemisphere, Australia too was faced with disorder and uncertainty about its own security. Until the mid-1950s, its main strategic challenge in this new environment was how to reconcile four different, sometimes conflicting and sometimes reinforcing, considerations: its desire for defence relations with Britain and with the United States, and whether to determine the geographic focus of its defence priorities from considerations at the global or the regional level. None of these considerations arose from a direct communist threat to Australia itself, but the way Australia responded to them would shape the way it engaged (and fought) in the Cold War during the 1950s and into the 1960s.

Before the Second World War, Australia had rested its defence on Britain's promise to send the Royal Navy to Asia in wartime. The abject failure of this 'Singapore strategy' in 1942 had demonstrated the inability of Britain to guarantee the security of Australia. But in the immediate aftermath of the war, the United States only kept a token military presence in Europe as well as Asia. While it had returned to the Philippines, Washington left the reimposition of order in the rest of Southeast Asia to the exhausted colonial powers of Britain, France and the Netherlands.[8] In 1946 the Chifley Government attempted to leverage the US' interest in its wartime base on Manus Island. Australia tried, with only little chance of success, to broker a deal for ongoing use of this base on the north coast of New Guinea in return for an enduring US defence commitment to Australia. The United States preferred to divest itself of the base, rather than remain bound to a wartime coalition partner whose main asset – its geographic importance after the 1942 retreat from the Philippines – had only been of temporary relevance.[9]

---

8   Peter Dennis, 'Major and minor: The defense of Southeast Asia and the Cold War', in *The Cold War and defense*, ed. K Neilson and R Haycock (New York: Praeger, 1990), 138–40.
9   Roger Bell, 'Australian–American discord: Negotiations for post-war bases and security arrangements in the Pacific 1944–1946', *Australian Outlook* 27, no. 1 (2008): 12–33, doi.org/10.1080/10357717308444457.

In the immediate aftermath of the war, there was thus little else to fall back on for Australia's strategic policy other than to look, once more, to concerted efforts of Britain and its dominions in preparing for the common defence. The 1946 Commonwealth Prime Ministers' Conference decided that the dominions should take greater responsibility for the defence of areas of strategic importance in their respective regions. The Australian Chiefs of Staff Committee proposed, in its 1947 *Appreciation of the strategical position of Australia*, to define Australia's region by the areas that would allow an enemy to mount air attacks against the country, which led to a focus on defending the two major access routes into Southeast Asia that the Japanese had also taken in 1942: the Philippines, to whose defence the United States remained committed, and the Malay Peninsula.[10]

However, the Chifley Government was far more reluctant than its military advisers to adopt Britain's threat assessments as its own – or to accept that Australia's area of strategic responsibility should be conceived of as part of the overall defence of the Empire (and hence potentially of lesser importance than the Middle East), rather than as an expression of Australia's own priorities. Britain's main possession in Southeast Asia, the Malay Peninsula, mattered for Australia primarily because of its strategic location in wartime. To Britain, however, it was the (peacetime) dollar revenues of Malaya's tin and rubber exports that made it of prime importance. London was thus careful to curtail Australia's leadership in regional security planning to the defence of sea lines of communication[11] – an issue whose importance had, however, also been reinforced to Australia by its recent wartime experience.

In 1948, Australia's Council of Defence, which comprised relevant members of the Cabinet as well as their main advisers, remarked that 'the designation of a potential enemy at this stage is not consistent with' government policy, and noted that 'political agreement between members of the British Commonwealth on joint strategic plans is impossible of attainment at the present time'.[12] Chifley decided against Britain's requests to reinforce its forces in Hong Kong, which was threatened by communist

---

10 Chiefs of Staff Committee, *Appreciation of the strategical position of Australia* (28 October 1947). Unless referenced to the National Archives of Australia, all strategic guidance documents by the Chiefs of Staff and Defence Committees cited in this chapter are reproduced in Stephan Frühling (ed.), *A history of Australian strategic policy since 1945* (Canberra: Defence Publishing Service, 2009).
11 Dennis, 'Major and minor', 140, 145.
12 *Conclusions of the Council of Defence*, 20 April 1948, National Archives of Australia (NAA): A816, 14/301/321.

armies in the Chinese Civil War, or in Malaya where the 'Emergency' of communist insurrection had started the same year. Australia likewise remained very cool about Britain's request for a commitment to the defence of the Middle East.[13]

In December 1949, Robert Menzies returned to the prime ministership, heading a Coalition Government whose views on global security were more sympathetic with those of Britain. The Council of Defence decided that Australia was now:

> to join with the other Commonwealth countries, the United States and the countries of Western Europe in organising essential deterrent forces, in building up effective defences and in working out the necessary plans, preferably on a regional basis ... [and] to resist the spread of communism by all means short of war.[14]

Australia should take responsibility for its home defence, for 'the overall direction and control of operations' for the defence of the ANZAM (Australia, New Zealand and Malaya) region in Southeast Asia, but its effort should conform with overall Commonwealth strategy. Hence, the government left open whether Australian forces would first be sent to the Middle East or to Southeast Asia.[15]

At the outbreak of the Korean War, Australia initially followed Britain's lead and did not commit forces to the conflict, but also saw an opportunity once again to seek a direct US commitment to the defence of Australia. Australia thus decided to join the war once Britain did, but exploited time zone differences to announce its decision to the United States before the government in London. The Korean War made it more urgent to settle the US–Japanese relationship through a formal peace treaty; Australia made clear the price for its agreement would be a formal US security guarantee; and hence the ANZUS Treaty was concluded in September 1951 between Washington, Canberra and Wellington – alas, with a much vaguer mutual assistance commitment than that of the Washington Treaty that had created NATO, and with little interest on the part of the United States to establish any of the joint planning or command arrangements that

---

13 Dennis, 'Major and minor', 144–45.
14 Defence Committee, *The basic objectives of British Commonwealth defence policy and general strategy*, Minute No. 86/1950, 15 June 1950, para 7.
15 Defence Committee, *A suitable basis for the distribution of strategic responsibility and war effort*, Minute No. 89/150, 15 June 1950, paras 8, 16.

then developed in that alliance.[16] While the State Department convinced the US Joint Chiefs of Staff (JCS) to agree to staff talks, Chairman of the JCS General Omar Bradley suggested that these be held in Hawai'i, expressing the hope that the Australians 'will get tired of hanging around with nothing to do'.[17]

Somewhat ironically, the conclusion of the ANZUS Treaty thus actually reinforced Australia's focus on the defence of and through the British Commonwealth. Tensions between London, Washington and Canberra over the possibility of a US treaty with Britain's antipodean dominions that would not involve Britain itself had been ameliorated by Australia's decision in 1950 to send Royal Australian Air Force (RAAF) aircraft to Malaya to support British forces in the 'Emergency' there.[18] The 1951 Radford–Collins agreement between the US and Australian navies formalised the geographic and organisational separation of peacetime surveillance and wartime protection of shipping between the Commonwealth's ANZAM area on the one hand, and the US national effort in the Pacific on the other.[19] Australia sought joint planning with the United States in ANZUS, but since that was not on offer, it continued its close relationship with Britain in the hope that the United States could be brought, formally or informally, to that table.

In 1951, London also brought up again the question of an Australian commitment to the defence of the Middle East. The Menzies Cabinet decided that in wartime Australia would send the first Army and Air Force units ready for deployment to that region, and also agreed to send two understrength squadrons and ground crews to Malta in early 1952. Britain's interest in having Australian forces in the Mediterranean occurred in the context of another diplomatic tug-of-war between London and Washington: both Britain and the United States sought leadership of a new major command on NATO's southern flank, and their arguments rested on the relative size of the forces they could contribute to the region. When the RAAF units arrived in Malta, London had already accepted

---

16 Dennis, 'Major and minor', 144–45.
17 Henry Brands Jr, 'From ANZUS to SEATO: United States strategic policy towards Australia and New Zealand, 1952–1954', *The International History Review* 9, no. 2 (May 1987): 254, doi.org/10.1080/07075332.1987.9640442.
18 Dennis, 'Major and minor', 145.
19 Andrew Brown, 'The history of the Radford-Collins Agreement', Royal Australian Navy, Sea Power Centre, www.navy.gov.au/history/feature-histories/history-radford-collins-agreement (accessed 2018).

that NATO's new Mediterranean Command would be headed by a US officer.[20] The Australians thus served for two years as part of NATO's force structure dedicated to the defence of Europe, and notably participated in the massive 1953 air exercise 'Coronet', during which they flew from an Australian-manned improvised airfield outside Cologne.[21]

This was not exactly what Australia had in mind for its limited available forces. In particular, the government was conscious of the long-term strategic consequences for Australia of sacrificing the defence of the Malay Peninsula in wartime.[22] Hence, Menzies asked for plans to be drawn up to send troops to Southeast Asia rather than the Middle East as early as July 1952, and for the Defence Committee to examine commitments to both regions in its first *Strategic basis of Australian defence policy* paper of 1953. Ultimately, the question of where to place Australia's priority rested on judgements about the likelihood of global war – in which the Middle East would have been more important than Malaya from a global perspective – and about the long-term cost for Australia of possibly losing Malaya to communism. The government accepted the committee's recommendation to give priority to ongoing 'Cold War' commitments in Southeast Asia in Australia's defence program over preparations for the possibility of global war. Moreover, Australia from now made the case to Britain for the importance of defending Malaya even in global war.[23]

From 1953, it was thus decided that a Third World War would not see a third Australian Imperial Force go off to fight in the Middle East. Instead, Australia sought to commit Britain and the United States to fend off a communist invasion in Southeast Asia, even in global war. Alas, here again Australia was confronted with the difficulty of managing different US and British expectations. In general, Britain was reluctant to commit to direct action against China, for fear of overcommitting Western forces and because of the vulnerability of Hong Kong. It

---

20   Dionysios Chourchoulis, 'High hopes, bold aims, limited results: Britain and the establishment of the NATO Mediterranean Command, 1950–1953', *Diplomacy & Statecraft* 20, no. 3 (2009): 434–52, doi.org/10.1080/09592290903293779.
21   Air Power Development Centre, 'The RAAF's Malta deployment 1952–1954', *Pathfinder* 192 (January 2013), reproduced in *Pathfinder collection* 6 (2014): 105–8, at: airpower.airforce.gov.au/sites/default/files/2021-03/PFV06-Pathfinder-Collection-Volume-6.pdf; 'R.A.A.F. wing in arduous, revealing Ruhr exercises', *Sydney Morning Herald*, 4 August 1953, 2.
22   Letter, McBride to Prime Minister, 6 June 1952, NAA: A816, 14/301/447.
23   Defence Committee, *Strategic basis of Australian defence policy*, 8 January 1953, paras 16, 20, 51; David Horner, *Defence supremo: Sir Frederick Shedden and the making of Australian defence policy* (St Leonards: Allen & Unwin, 2000), 311–414.

preferred to find accommodation with Peking over East Asian security, and refused to support joint action with the United States to support the French in Indochina. The same French difficulties did, however, also raise British concerns about the security of the Malay Peninsula. Britain did not have available in global war the three divisions that were seen as sufficient for a defence of Malaya against a full-scale invasion. But in any case, the ability to quickly occupy a defensive position at the narrow isthmus of Songkhla in southern Thailand was seen as necessary for any successful defence of the peninsula. For this task, forces had to be available in Malaya. Hence, in 1953, Australia, New Zealand and Britain agreed in principle to deploy forces from all three countries and services to form the permanent Commonwealth Strategic Reserve in Malaya.[24]

In contrast, the US JCS were loath to commit to the defence of any particular area in the region, preferring instead to respond to Chinese aggression with mobile air and naval forces and strikes on the Chinese mainland – and also to encourage its allies into joint action to help the French in their fight against the communist Viet Minh in Indochina, so as to prevent British pressures for assistance in the defence of Malaya later on. Hence, although the 'Five Power' talks that started in 1952 between the United States, Britain, France, Australia and New Zealand could not agree on a basic strategy for the defence of Southeast Asia, they all were interested for different reasons in a defensive arrangement for the region. The capitulation of French forces at Dien Bien Phu in 1954 made such an arrangement much less useful militarily than originally intended. But the idea retained political utility for the United States, since it would include regional countries and give Washington political cover both domestically and internationally to respond to communist aggression in the way it saw fit. Hence, Britain, Australia, New Zealand and France agreed to join the United States, Pakistan (which then included today's Bangladesh), Thailand and the Philippines as members of the Southeast Asia Treaty Organization (SEATO) in 1954, and agreed in a protocol to also consider the formally neutral countries of Laos, Cambodia and South Vietnam as relevant to their treaty commitment.[25]

---

24 David Lee, 'Australia and allied strategy in the Far East, 1952–1957', *Journal of Strategic Studies* 16, no. 4 (2008): 514–16.
25 Lee, 'Australia and allied strategy in the Far East', 516–22.

Within just four years, Australia had thus become part of three formal alliance arrangements with Britain and the United States – ANZAM, ANZUS and SEATO – as well as the Five Power talks. None of them, however, achieved what it really sought: a US commitment to the defence of Southeast Asia that was underpinned by joint planning and actual force allocation. To Australia's dismay, the United States refused to use SEATO to develop the permanent alliance commands, infrastructure and plans it was creating in NATO for the defence of Europe. Moreover, Australia's commitments under SEATO were even more extensive than those of the United States, which had limited its obligations to the defence against communist threats alone.[26] The only framework that resulted in genuine planning and preparations for the defence of the region remained ANZAM, but lack of US support for those arrangements would shortly cause significant embarrassment for the Australian Government. Ultimately, Australia's strategic problem was that the US defence commitment to Southeast Asia that it so much desired ran counter to the overall US strategy for the Cold War as a whole.

Australian strategic policy and the Eisenhower 'New Look' strategy

When the Eisenhower Administration assumed office in 1953, it was very concerned about the economic cost of the US defence effort in Europe and Korea. NATO had set itself significant conventional force-level goals at the Lisbon summit in 1952, which also proved beyond the means of Europe's still recovering economies. The Cold War was a global challenge, but the Soviet Union was the main adversary, and Eisenhower was looking for a better way to meet the Soviet threat that would not reduce deterrence in the short term, nor bankrupt the United States in the long term.

In a rather fortuitous coincidence, the solution to this challenge also appeared at the same time: rapid advances in almost all aspects of nuclear weapons technology. In the late 1940s, nuclear weapons had still been scarce, expensive and bulky, and the expectation was that the battles of the Third World War would be not too different from those of the second one, with atomic munitions merely providing a somewhat faster and more efficient way of conducting the strategic bomber offensive. This changed, however,

---

26 Dennis, 'Major and minor', 148.

as the cost of fissile material dropped with new gaseous diffusion plants for uranium enrichment and plutonium production reactors; breakthroughs in miniaturisation made it possible to shrink nuclear warheads from the size of a small car to that of an artillery shell; and Edward Teller and Stanislaw Ulam conceived of radiation pressure as the key to engineering a nuclear weapon primarily based on nuclear fusion, not fission: the 'thermonuclear' or 'hydrogen' bomb, first tested in 1952, opened up an age of nuclear plenty in munition numbers, warhead yields and engineering opportunities. In strategic terms, it was the early 1950s rather than the Second World War's Manhattan project that really brought about revolutionary change through nuclear weapons,[27] and Eisenhower's 'New Look' strategy embraced them fully to fight the Cold War.

The long-range heavy bombers of the US Air Force's Strategic Air Command (SAC) became the main Western deterrence and warfighting instrument: a large-scale thermonuclear attack would destroy the Soviet Union as a functioning society within the first days of a new conflict.[28] SAC bomber bases began to ring the Soviet Union and Eastern bloc from Greenland, over the British Isles and French Morocco, to the Eastern Mediterranean. But whereas SAC's base demands significantly expanded the geographic areas of military interest to the United States on the Soviet Union's Arctic and south-western flanks, SAC's presence in Asia was concentrated between Alaska and Guam,[29] and Southeast Asia was of little relevance to the strategic bomber force.

The defence of Western Europe posed a separate problem. Thermonuclear destruction of the Soviet Union itself would not necessarily stem an attack by the Soviet Army into West Germany and beyond, and Washington had already committed to a NATO strategy of 'forward defence' as close to the Iron Curtain as possible. The solution to this particular challenge was to embrace cheap, 'tactical' nuclear weapons as a substitute for expensive, conventional manoeuvre forces. The US Army reorganised itself based on the 'Pentomic division', a structure thought to be best suited to employ nuclear weapons, and to survive on the atomic battlefield.[30] Support

---

27   Colin Gray, *Strategy for chaos: Revolutions in military affairs and the evidence of history* (London: Frank Cass Publishers, 2002), 222–69.
28   Edward Kaplan, *To kill nations: American strategy in the air-atomic age and the rise of mutually assured destruction* (Ithaca: Cornell University Press, 2015), doi.org/10.7591/cornell/9780801452482.003.0006.
29   Kurt Wayne Schake, 'Strategic frontier: American bomber bases overseas, 1950–1960' (PhD dissertation, Norwegian University of Science and Technology, 1998).
30   Richard W Kedzior, *Evolution and endurance: The U.S. Army division in the twentieth century* (Santa Monica: RAND, 2000), 25.

to NATO regional commanders' atomic strike plans assumed a higher priority for NATO air forces than defence of allied territory.[31] The first nuclear-armed US Army units appeared in Germany in 1954, and nuclear cannon and missile artillery, gravity bombs, air defence missiles and landmines quickly spread throughout the force. In 1957, the United States argued for a 'nuclear stockpile' approach where US nuclear weapons would be made available to all NATO allies, so that their artillery and air defence forces could be structured for the use of nuclear firepower as well. Given US preponderance in military and political terms in the alliance at the time, NATO agreed to embrace nuclear weapons as a substitute for conventional forces.[32] Hold-outs such as Norway and Denmark, which refused to allow basing of nuclear warheads on their territory in peacetime, remained under considerable US pressure for refusing to 'modernize' their forces with nuclear weapons until the early 1960s.[33]

In contrast, US military strategy in Asia was a derivative of its global posture. The defence of South Korea was a commitment that the United States had assumed almost by accident, and US ground forces there received tactical nuclear weapons from 1958, largely consisting of older systems that were being phased out in Europe.[34] But in general there were no positions in Asia that were both as important and as immediately vulnerable as Europe was to communist invasion, before the strategic nuclear offensive would have broken the Soviet Union's back.[35] The ability to inflict devastating nuclear punishment even on a country as large as China – thus negating its traditional reliance on geographic and demographic depth against external threat – was sufficient in US eyes to manage regional threats in Asia, and Washington would issue thinly veiled nuclear threats to manage the end of the Korean War, as well as the crises over Quemoy and Matsu in 1955.[36] Given this global US strategy, it is no surprise that in the 1950s the United States looked upon planning for the local defence of the Malay

---

31   The so-called SNOWCAT (Support of Nuclear Operations With Conventional Air Tactics) missions.
32   Simon J Moody, 'Enhancing political cohesion in NATO during the 1950s or: How it learned to stop worrying and love the (tactical) bomb', *Journal of Strategic Studies* 40, no. 6 (2015): 817–38, doi.org/10.1080/01402390.2015.1035434.
33   Rolf Tamnes, *The United States and the Cold War in the high north* (Dartmouth: Aldershot, 1991), 164.
34   Lee Jae-Bong, 'US deployment of nuclear weapons in 1950s South Korea & North Korea's nuclear development', *The Asia-Pacific Journal* 7, issue 8, no. 3 (2009): 1–17.
35   A not completely inappropriate metaphor as 'broken-backed warfare' became the term commonly used in the late 1950s for a possible phase of sporadic warfare after both Western and Communist forces would have received devastating damage from widespread use of nuclear weapons.
36   John Lewis Gaddis, *Strategies of containment* (Oxford: Oxford University Press, 1982), 168–71.

Peninsula, especially if it was to only employ conventionally armed forces, as something that would be of little relevance for global war, and should not distract US or allied forces from higher priorities.

In 1953, the ANZAM powers had agreed in principle on the deployment of the Commonwealth Strategic Reserve, but detailed planning still required knowledge of US atomic strike plans. These the United States would not provide, neither directly nor through SEATO. Prime Minister Menzies, however, was reluctant to announce the peacetime commitment of ground forces to the defence of Malaya without US agreement to publicly link the deployment to SEATO, and a private commitment of US military support. At a visit to the White House in March 1955, he thought he had obtained both, and soon thereafter made public Australia's commitment to the Strategic Reserve. In July 1955, however, the US chair of the JCS, Admiral Radford, provided a reply to the ANZAM plans that caused significant consternation among the Australian Government, as he reiterated that the United States would not commit specific forces to the region, that Indochina and Thailand rather than Malaya should be the first line of defence, that the United States would not exclude SEATO's Asian members from regional planning with Australia and Britain, and that given US nuclear preponderance, subversion and insurrection, rather than outright invasion, would be more likely threats in Southeast Asia.[37] In effect, the United States told Australia it was preparing for the wrong war, in the wrong place and through the wrong arrangements.

Trying to use SEATO to link the United States to the ANZAM framework had failed. But although US commitment to SEATO was primarily political rather than military, the United States around the same time grew increasingly concerned about the view of the alliance's Asian members that they were being shut out from actual planning by the Anglo-Saxon powers. From late 1955, the United States thus started to share more information on its nuclear strike plans within the organisation, and agreed to increased SEATO planning activities.[38] This was of course welcome to Australia, which decided to shift its focus from ANZAM and informal four-power planning to the SEATO framework, and informed Britain that it would no longer commit its forces in Malaya to the defence of the Songkhla position.[39]

---

37 Lee, 'Australia and allied strategy in the Far East', 526–27; Mathew Jones, 'The Radford bombshell: Anglo–Australian–US relations, nuclear weapons and the defence of South East Asia, 1954–57', *Journal of Strategic Studies* 27, no. 4 (2004): 642–49, doi.org/10.1080/1362369042000314547.
38 Jones, 'The Radford bombshell', 639–42, 650–52.
39 Lee, 'Australia and allied strategy in the Far East', 527–28.

Britain also started to have second thoughts. As the British nuclear weapons program began to deliver operational capability, London also looked to use nuclear weapons to make economic savings in its overall defence effort. Australian planners acknowledged the usefulness of nuclear weapons for interdiction and long-range bombing, but were less convinced that they could directly substitute for conventional forces in Southeast Asia's geographic context. Nonetheless, the British 1957 Defence White Paper cut the UK military presence in Malaya by half, while promising to deploy three squadrons of nuclear-capable V bombers in times of crisis instead – a posture whose strong parallels to the failed Singapore strategy of the interwar years was not lost on the Australians.[40]

When Australia rethought its defence strategy in 1956, it thus did so in the context of the US reliance on the strategic nuclear offensive to deter global war, increased US willingness to engage in some forms of SEATO planning, the reduction of British forces in the Far East and increased allied reliance on nuclear weapons for doubtful tactical economies. Menzies travelled to London and Washington to discuss global and regional defence strategy, and the Defence Committee argued in a new *Strategic basis* paper that thermonuclear deterrence had increased the likelihood of limited war, especially involving client states such as could be found in Southeast Asia. Hence, Australia decided to adopt a 'fire brigade' posture of strategic mobility that would be able to cover its SEATO commitments beyond Malaya, shorter timelines for the mobilisation of forces for limited war and greater commonality of equipment through purchases with the United States, rather than Britain.[41]

The *Strategic basis* paper argued:

> If … adequate conventional forces are not maintained by the Western Powers to meet the requirements of cold and limited war, it may be possible for the Communist powers to achieve their aims despite the maintenance by the Western Powers of the thermonuclear deterrent.[42]

Australia's main contribution to the global defence effort would thus be in the form of conventional forces, but in classified guidance and public statements, the government continued to hold on to the possibility

---

40 Jones, 'The Radford bombshell', 653–56.
41 Lee, 'Australia and allied strategy in the Far East', 529; Jones, 'The Radford bombshell', 645–58.
42 Defence Committee, *Strategic basis of Australian defence policy*, 11 October 1956.

of acquiring nuclear weapons from Australia's allies. Australia's Canberra bombers in Malaya could have deployed the new British atomic bombs. But Britain's nuclear strategy was becoming more firmly embedded in the political context of NATO and, at the 1957 Bermuda summit, in its 'special relationship' with the United States. The United States had adopted legislation to make available nuclear warheads to NATO, but Australia remained a fourth-tier ally insofar as US nuclear cooperation was concerned: after Britain, NATO members 'sharing' US warheads, and the rest of that alliance. The prospect of obtaining British or US commitments to provide Australia with nuclear charges was thus slipping even as their role increased in UK and SEATO planning for Southeast Asia,[43] and in announcing the changed posture, Menzies told parliament that 'the chances are that jungle fighting will be involved'.[44] National service was suspended in 1959 to release active duty personnel for deployment of the Army's new 'Pentropic' division concept – a scheme modelled on the US 'Pentomic' organisation that mostly served to provide independent confirmation of the US conclusion that this was indeed an idea more convincing in theory than in practice.[45]

Australia had thus settled on a defence posture that it thought more relevant to likely threats and to US policy. What remained was to pay for it. Australia's defence expenditure continued to decline as a share of GDP as the government prioritised national economic development, and the Citizen Military Forces consumed significant resources even though they were not eligible to serve beyond Australian territory. A high-ranking delegation led by the Defence Minister travelled to Washington in 1957 to request US defence assistance and industrial support. Alas, at a time when the US treasury was covering a substantial part of NATO and other allies' equipment purchases, the US National Security Council declined to do the same for Australia, as it was not seen as necessary for US global strategy to develop Australian defence or industrial capability.[46]

---

43 Wayne Reynolds, 'The wars that were planned: Australia's forward defence posture in Asia and the role of tactical nuclear weapons, 1945–1967', *Australian Journal of International Affairs* 53, no. 3 (1999): 297–306, doi.org/10.1080/00049919993872.
44 Commonwealth, *Parliamentary Debates*, House of Representatives, 19 September 1957, para 29 (Robert Menzies).
45 Jeffrey Grey, *A military history of Australia*, 3rd ed. (Cambridge: Cambridge University Press, 2008), 227–28.
46 Lee, 'Australia and allied strategy in the Far East', 530.

Time, however, was on Australia's side. By accident more than by design, Australia had settled on a strategic posture that was a congruent fit with the emphasis on conventional forces that began to be advocated in the United States by General Maxwell Taylor and others, and would become an integral part of the new strategy of 'flexible response' under the new Kennedy Administration in 1961. What remained to be seen, however, was whether the increased US engagement in Southeast Asia that Australia promoted, prepared for and would soon see develop would really bring about the enduring and broad US commitment to the security of Australia and its region that it ultimately sought. In 1957, Menzies had confidently stated that 'in time of war it is quite certain that SEATO will establish overall commands and that our forces, by suitable arrangements, will be under them'.[47] But as one prescient observer cautioned a year later:

> SEATO's potential military strength depends almost wholly on American policy in a given situation, and it is difficult to see how the existence of SEATO can have material influence on that policy.[48]

Conventional escalation: Australian strategic policy between the Communist and Indonesian threats

In the second half of the 1950s, the main challenge for Australia's strategic policy had thus been the distance between its own concerns and US global strategy. The Malayan 'Emergency' was the only real operation, however, and Australia's defence preparations focused on limited and global wars that never happened. Writing in 1962, one particularly acerbic writer observed that Australia's defence effort was characterised by its 'sheer lack of dimension' at the global scale, 'high enough to be a burden on the economy but not high enough to provide a worthwhile defense at all'.[49] By that time, however, the strategic demands on Australia had changed quite substantially compared to 1957. Conflict with Indonesia had become an urgent concern, and the limits of direct support from the

---

47 Commonwealth, *Parliamentary Debates*, House of Representatives, 19 September 1957, para 8 (Robert Menzies).
48 W Macmahon Ball, 'A political re-examination of SEATO', *International Organization* 12, no. 1 (1958): 21.
49 BB Schaffer, 'Policy and system in defense: The Australian case', *World Politics* 15, no. 2 (January 1963): 237, 239.

United States were made distressingly explicit, even as both Britain and the Americans looked to greater Australian contributions to security in Southeast Asia.

The first major reckoning for government of the weaknesses in the new defence posture came only two years later, when the Defence Committee submitted its 1959 version of the *Strategic basis*. In the intervening years, the United States had seemingly ruthlessly refused to support its close allies Britain and France in the Suez Crisis, and the Eisenhower Administration's lack of genuine military (as opposed to political) commitment to SEATO had become increasingly apparent. Both developments were particularly ominous in light of Indonesia's political–military pressure to gain control of Dutch West Papua, which still provided a geographic buffer to Australia's New Guinea territory. Jakarta skilfully toyed with Chinese and Soviet alignment, and Australia found little support from its allies as it attempted to support the Dutch.[50] The Defence Committee thus recommended that Australia 'should be prepared to act independently at least for a time' in limited war against Indonesia or following global war,[51] and that 'our forces … should be designed primarily with the ability to act independently of allies'.[52] For the first time, it included a statement of specifically Australian 'National Policy Objectives'.[53]

This was a radical shift. Since the Second World War – indeed, since Federation – it had been Australia's aim to maximise its allies' commitment of forces to Australia's region, but this was always conceived of as a problem of how to best distribute limited resources in a global conflict – be it hot or cold. Now Canberra had to face the prospect of being in a significant conflict all alone. How difficult this was to contemplate can be gleaned from the Cabinet's repeated deliberations on the 1959 *Strategic basis*, in which the government could not bring itself to endorse the paper, even as it ultimately accepted its substantive conclusions.[54]

---

50   Peter Edwards with Gregory Pemberton, *The official history of Australia's involvement in Southeast Asian conflicts 1948–1975*, vol. 1, *Crises and commitments: The politics and diplomacy of Australia's involvement in Southeast Asian conflicts 1948–1965* (North Sydney: Allen & Unwin and the Australian War Memorial, 1992), 182–207; JAC Mackie, 'Australia and Indonesia, 1945–1960', in *Australia in world affairs 1956–1960*, ed. Gordon Greenwood and Norman Harper (Melbourne: F.W. Cheshire, 1963), 296–304.
51   Defence Committee, *Strategic basis of Australian defence policy*, 12 January 1959, para 43.
52   Ibid., para 44.
53   Defence Committee, *Strategic basis of Australian defence policy*, 12 January 1959, para 5.
54   Frühling, *A history of Australian strategic policy since 1945*, 17–18.

As it turned out, Australia's allies substantially increased their engagement in the region in the 1960s. Alas, the reasons for their engagement, and their expectations of Australian support, made Australia's challenges even more acute. The new Kennedy Administration had radically different ideas about global strategy than its predecessor. In a situation of mutually assured destruction, immediate and massive nuclear escalation ceased to be a viable approach to global war. Under the strategy of 'flexible response', Washington now sought to build up conventional forces to avoid nuclear escalation, and to keep global as well as limited war below the 'nuclear threshold' as long as possible. Moreover, communist expansion had shifted to encompass much of the developing world, including the Caribbean and Southeast Asia, and the Kennedy Administration was determined to stem this trend, including through the use of force.[55] Echoing Australia's 1957 'fire brigade' posture, the Pentagon stood up a new 'Strike Command' in 1961 to provide conventional forces based in North America to regional commanders for limited war scenarios,[56] and the central reserve as well as sea and airlift capabilities for rapid deployment were increased in US conventional force planning.[57]

Finally, Australia thus had a US Administration willing to commit forces to Southeast Asia, but this brought with it US demands to make good on Canberra's commitments under SEATO. In 1959, the communist Pathet Lao had taken up arms in Laos, and North Vietnam began its fight against the South. As SEATO discussed intervention in Laos during the first half of 1961, the Menzies Government decided on several occasions that Australia would in principle contribute forces to such an operation. By late 1961, the United States had deployed several thousand advisers to South Vietnam.[58] Australia's own military involvement in the Indochina conflict began the following year, as it deployed the first advisers to Vietnam, and a squadron of Sabre fighters to its SEATO ally Thailand to deter North Vietnamese attack.[59]

---

55 Gaddis, *Strategies of containment*, 198–236.
56 Robert Haffa, *Rational methods, prudent choices: Planning U.S. forces* (Washington DC: National Defense University Press, 1988), 75–101.
57 William W Kaufman, *Planning conventional forces 1950–1980* (Washington DC: The Brookings Institution, 1982), 6–11.
58 Edwards with Pemberton, *Crises and commitments*, 208–36.
59 Ibid., 242.

That same year, the West Papua crisis escalated with significant loss of life in skirmishes between Dutch and Indonesian forces. By 1962, Indonesia had become the largest non-communist recipient of Soviet arms. From Russian sources available since the end of the Cold War, it has now become apparent that the Soviet Union sent Soviet submarines and TU-16 bomber crews to participate in a large assault on the Dutch in West Papua, and to help with the planning of that operation.[60] Lacking international support, the Dutch caved before this could happen, and Indonesia took control of the territory in 1963 – the same year that it began cross-border raids onto the Malay Peninsula as part of its campaign of 'Confrontation' against the creation of Malaysia.

Britain was understandably eager to employ the Commonwealth Strategic Reserve in Malaya against this threat. While Australia agreed that its forces could contribute to the defence of the Malay Peninsula against open, external attack, it also feared direct conflict with Indonesia on New Guinea, and was reluctant to expand its involvement in 'Confrontation'. The old question of whether the United States would be willing to militarily support Australia's ANZAM defence efforts, and how it would interpret its commitments under ANZUS, thus reappeared in a more urgent and immediate form. After repeated enquiries by Australia, President Kennedy and Secretary of State Dean Rusk clarified in late 1963 that the ANZUS Treaty would apply in case of open aggression by Indonesia against Australian forces in Malaysia, but that US military support would even then not necessarily be forthcoming and that it would, in any case, be limited to sea and air forces and logistic support. In addition, the United States expected Australia to consult before any Australian commitment of forces, and to avoid any measures that could be perceived as provocative.[61]

Faced with the need to potentially fight on three fronts – alongside Britain in 'Confrontation', to defend New Guinea against Indonesian attack, and alongside the United States in Vietnam – the limits of Australia's defence effort became painfully obvious. As early as January 1962, the Defence Committee's new *Strategic basis* advised the government that direct intervention in Indochina alone might require a deployment larger

---

60   David Easter, 'Active Soviet military support for Indonesia during the 1962 West New Guinea crisis', *Cold War History* 15, no. 2 (2015): 202.
61   Letter, Barwick to Menzies, 22 October 1963, 'ANZUS Treaty – United States obligations under', NAA: A7942.

than could be sustained from Australia's regular forces.[62] By September, the government asked for a reconsideration in light of the deteriorating strategic situation. A key issue was the relationship between the 'forward defence' commitment against communist expansion in Southeast Asia, which still centred on the Commonwealth Strategic Reserve in Malaya, and the possibility of conflict with Indonesia. In the 1963 paper on *Australia's strategic position*, the Defence Committee advised that the commitment to the former would increase the risk of the latter,[63] but at the same time 'the degree of obligation which America feels to Australia under ANZUS could be influenced by the contributions which Australia makes to the common defence'.[64]

Hence, Australia's defence integration through ANZAM was a main reason for conflict with Indonesia; Australia's hope for US support based on the ANZUS Treaty rested on its willingness to support SEATO; to which Australia's ANZAM commitment was still its most important contribution. Australian strategic policy was caught in a dilemma from which there seemed to be no obvious way out. Cabinet thus confirmed that

> Australia's military strategy is based on the maintenance of a forward position in South-East Asia … and [decided] to accept the risk that thereby we may cause tension in our relations with Indonesia.[65]

As a consequence, it

> agreed that there should be an increase in the present scale of defence programming … not only to ensure the security of the Australian mainland and East New Guinea, but also to enable us to make an effective and sustained contribution in South-East Asia and to present a deterrent to possible activities by Indonesia inimical to our strategic interests.[66]

Military expenditure was increased, the strength of the Army was raised, Australia purchased additional helicopters and transport aircraft, 40 additional Mirage fighters, and ordered 24 F-111 to replace the ageing

---

62 Defence Committee, *Strategic basis of Australian defence policy*, 25 January 1962, paras 22, 54.
63 Defence Committee, *Australia's strategic position*, 4 February 1963, paras 17, 18, 30.
64 Ibid., para 25.
65 Cabinet Decision No. 675, 5 March 1963, NAA: A1945, 83/2/8.
66 Ibid.

Canberra bombers.[67] It also ordered a third guided missile destroyer which the new US Administration now agreed to subsidise with interest-free loans, as it had done with the previous two ships in 1961.[68]

The next *Strategic basis* paper of October 1964 followed more substantial Indonesian landings in Malaya, as well as the Gulf of Tonkin incident. It foreshadowed commitments in Vietnam 'on a scale which could approach the proportions of a limited war', concomitant with the need to potentially fight and deter Indonesia in Malaysia as well as in New Guinea, and recommended further increases in the size and capability of the defence force.[69] Decades later, then Secretary of the Department of External Affairs Sir Arthur Tange would recall the pressures facing Australia's ministers at the time:

> I retained a memory of the blunt warning that I heard [US Secretary of State] Dean Rusk give to [Foreign Minister] Hasluck in 1964. During the discussion of worsening relations between Malaysia and Indonesia, Hasluck volunteered to inform the Americans before committing Australian forces in support of Malaysia. Responding to the inherent assumption that such a deployment would trigger an expectation of American military support, Rusk pointedly said that the United States would expect that Australia would have introduced conscription and full mobilisation, and added 'there is no residuum of responsibility falling on the United States that is reached at a certain point'.[70]

Within weeks of considering the 1964 *Strategic basis*, the government reintroduced conscription, for the second time since the Second World War. In January 1965, it deployed one battalion to counter Indonesian incursions in Borneo and, in June 1965, the first battalion went into Vietnam. Australia's Cold War had well and truly become a hot one.

---

67   Alan Stephens, *Going solo: The Royal Australian Air Force, 1946–1971* (Canberra: Australian Government Publishing Service, 1995), 47–48; Grey, *A military history of Australia*, 229.
68   Steven Paget, 'On a new bearing: The reorganized Royal Australian Navy at war in Vietnam', *The Mariner's Mirror* 101, no. 3 (2015): 288–90, doi.org/10.1080/00253359.2015.1054686.
69   Defence Committee, *Strategic basis of Australian defence policy*, 15 October 1964, paras 45, 67, 70, 78.
70   Sir Arthur Tange, *Defence policy-making: A close-up view, 1950–1980*, ed. Peter Edwards (Canberra: ANU E Press, 2008), 40, doi.org/10.22459/DPM.07.2008.

Conclusion

In 1965, the heaviest fighting and most Australian casualties in Vietnam had yet to occur. And yet, the replacement of Indonesia's President Sukarno by General Suharto late that year meant that the nightmares of a three-front conflict, which had occupied Australia's government and senior defence advisers in the early 1960s, did not come to pass. The end of 'Confrontation' also spelled the end of Britain's military commitment to Southeast Asia, which the conflict with Indonesia had given an unexpected but temporary reprieve. The logic of Australia's 'forward defence' now solely rested on the policy of the United States, but Washington's decision not to burden itself with the SEATO framework in Vietnam made clear that Australia's hope for an enduring US commitment to the region was as misplaced as before.

As early as November 1966, the Defence Committee endorsed the view that Southeast Asia would not quickly fall to communism, that there would be warning time available of a significant threat, and that within a force structure designed for limited war a 'potential for expansion' should now also be provided.[71] In 1968, a new *Strategic basis* paper broke with the 'domino theory' that the fall of one country to communism would inexorably bring the communist threat to Australia's doorstep, and started to make numerous references to the 'defence of Australia' as a future consideration. As the spectre of the communist threat receded, so did the need for, and viability of, Australia's posture of 'forward defence'. What remained was to prepare for the possibility of future conflict with Indonesia, which would become the main preoccupation for Australian defence policy in the era of 'self-reliance' after Vietnam. Australia continued to support its allies politically in the Cold War, through the Joint Facilities, and through maritime surveillance in the Indian Ocean, South Pacific and Southeast Asia; but as the central focus of strategic policy, Australia's Cold War ended with the war in Vietnam.

When the Menzies Government committed to the forward defence policy in the 1950s, it was not doing the bidding of its 'great and powerful friends'. Indeed, Britain had good reason to gripe about the limitations and conditions that Australia placed on its commitment to the defence

---

71 Defence Committee, *Interim review of the Strategic basis of Australian defence policy*, 24 November 1966, NAA: A1838, TS677/3 PART 10, paras 39, 41, 42, 51.

of Malaya at Sogkhla in the 1950s, and against Indonesia in the 1960s. Until the commitment of major Australian forces to Vietnam, the way in which Australia went about trying to prepare for the defence of Southeast Asia, politically as well as militarily in the ANZAM and SEATO frameworks, also never aligned with US preferences and perspectives. Australia sought a US strategic commitment to the region that was institutionally embedded and enduring, as well as politically significant and militarily meaningful. In the 1950s it achieved the former but not the latter, in Vietnam the latter but not the former. Was Australia's strategic policy between 1945 and 1965 an abject failure?

It is not difficult, but also ultimately irrelevant, to poke holes in the perception by Australian leaders of the time that Southeast Asia was in direct and immediate danger of falling to communism through outright invasion, or through an inexorable fall of the 'dominos' to communist insurrection. What matters is that this perception was real, and that the British and US priority on Europe and Northeast Asia meant that Australia was faced, throughout this time, with a strategic problem to which there were no good solutions. Some aspects of Australia's attempts to bind Britain and the United States to the defence of Southeast Asia seem almost quixotic when placed in the global context of their time. But the Australians of the 1950s and early 1960s were battling not just the threat of contemporary communism, but also the spectre of 1942 and the fall of Singapore. The war in Vietnam would vanquish both, through its regional–strategic as well as domestic–political consequences. In that sense, for Australia's strategic policy the year of 1965 marked not just the beginning of the end of Australia's Cold War, but also of the war that had come before.

2

Australia's military after the Second World War: Legacies and challenges

John Blaxland

This chapter provides a brief overview of the challenges faced by the Australian armed services as they emerged from the Second World War. It looks at how they adjusted to the changed regional dynamics after the war, the massive shrinkages in size, the new missions that emerged including the provision of occupation forces in Japan and rehabilitation at home, and the fluid security dynamics as the postwar order settled into the confrontation of the Cold War. The legacies of war for the armed services and the veterans themselves are also considered. The chapter illustrates that while the United States had played an enormous role in helping to defend Australia during the Second World War, the Australian armed forces retained their distinctive British-derived practices, procedures, equipment and orientation. This legacy would endure for decades.

The Second World War left an indelible impression on Australia's military. The three armed services, the Royal Australian Navy (RAN), the Australian Military Forces (now known as the Australian Army) and the Royal Australian Air Force (RAAF), were transformed into professional, proven and well-equipped defenders of Australia and contributors to allied military operations abroad. Australians had fought across the globe alongside other British Empire forces in the European and Mediterranean theatres as well as the Pacific and Indian Oceans.

They had also fought alongside US forces, notably in the South West Pacific Area under the command of US General Douglas MacArthur, while retaining British-derived equipment and practices.

The British influence would prove remarkably resilient in terms of policy orientation, military doctrine, procedures, equipment and uniforms. Rank insignia, for instance, remained distinctly British, albeit with some noticeable local variants, and RAAF and RAN contingents evinced few distinctive features in their uniforms, apart from the iconic slouch hat. For the RAN, practices and standards remained closely UK-aligned. The same was the case for the RAAF, even though increasingly US-sourced aircraft were in use. During the war the Army had published and promulgated training bulletins reflecting both home-grown tactical innovations and shared notes and lessons learned from other parts of the British Empire.

Along the way, the three armed services had grown almost exponentially to meet the wartime demand for specialisations inherent in self-reliant armed forces. Schools, for instance, proliferated to cover a wide range of military specialisations, including engineering and military intelligence, and a wide range of combat-related skills. A unique Australian military identity, metaphorically born in 1915, developed and matured to become more capable and more reliant on its own capabilities, albeit within the context of a grand alliance encompassing the United States and Britain's empire.

In essence, the Australian armed services at the end of the war were world-class and among the largest in the world. The RAAF briefly was the world's fourth largest air force.[1] Australia's land forces ranked about 16th in the world at their peak, with a force of 464,000 troops.[2] The RAN, with about 680 ships in 1945, was still enormous, but it was dwarfed

---

1   At the end of the Second World War, the United States, the Soviet Union and Britain were the three major air powers in the world. At its peak in 1944, the Royal Canadian Air Force provided the fourth largest allied air force, but after Germany's defeat it began a process of rapid reduction. On Japan's surrender, the RAAF stood as the fourth largest air force in the world, but did not remain so for long. 'World's fourth largest air force?', *Pathfinder* 119 (September 2009), reproduced in *Pathfinder collection* 4 (2010): 123–26, at: airpower.airforce.gov.au/sites/default/files/2021-03/PFV04-Pathfinder-Collection-Volume-4.pdf.

2   Albert Palazzo, *The Australian Army: A history of its organisation, 1901–2001* (Melbourne: Oxford University Press, 2001), 176; Tom Gargaro, 'What country had the largest army in World War II?', Quora post, at: www.quora.com/What-country-had-the-largest-army-in-World-War-II (accessed 16 September 2020).

by the 6,768-ship US Navy.³ With the euphoria of the war's end and the demand for labour to be made available to redevelop the economy, however, they dramatically shrank back close to their prewar levels in a remarkably short time frame, mostly over the course of 1945 and 1946.

With much of the force raised specifically for wartime and with demobilisation tied to the end of the war, an interim arrangement to maintain forces was devised in early 1945. The interim arrangements were necessary to enable the initial postwar requirements to be met – including the occupation of Japan, repatriation of prisoners of war and internees, maintenance of order until restoration of civil rule in occupied territories and the removal and disposal of large quantities of surplus military supplies and equipment. By February 1946, the Interim Army would come to include those members of the Australian Military Forces who were on continuous full-time duty on 1 October 1945 and personnel who joined after that date.[4]

Postwar repatriation and peacekeeping challenges

The task of repatriating over 150,000 soldiers back home, including 20,000 former prisoners of war in parts of Southeast Asia and Japan, presented the Australian forces and the Commonwealth Government with major logistical challenges. Shipping tonnage was at a premium and much work was required for moving people, as well as facilitating the return of the former colonial authorities and assisting with reconstruction. Japanese forces in much of the eastern end of the Netherlands East Indies, now Indonesia, surrendered to Australian forces. Administering this force of more than 300,000 military personnel while working to arrange a handover of authority to the postwar rulers proved challenging. With Indonesia's independence leaders having declared independence as Japan surrendered, there was considerable conjecture over to whom Australian forces should ultimately hand over authority.

---

3   'US ship force levels 1866–present', Naval History and Heritage Command, at: www.history.navy.mil/research/histories/ship-histories/us-ship-force-levels.html (accessed 18 September 2020).
4   Palazzo, *The Australian Army*, 197.

The Australian Government under Ben Chifley played an advocacy role on behalf of the Indonesians. Mindful of Australia's sympathetic position towards the Indonesians, Australian advocacy was welcomed by the Indonesian independence leaders. Eager to play a constructive role, Australia volunteered to send peacekeepers. In the end, Dutch authorities resumed their place as colonial masters – at least on an interim basis – and their rule was resisted by the newly declared Republic of Indonesia. Australia followed Britain's lead and complied with Dutch demands, but this was a fraught enterprise. By August 1947 Australian staff were seconded to the UN Good Offices Committee for Indonesia, including four Australian military observers – the world's first UN peacekeepers. These were Australian Army Brigadier LGH Dyke and Major DL Campbell, Commander HS Chesterman (RAN), and Squadron Leader DT Spence (RAAF). Ongoing fighting occurred through to the Dutch withdrawal from Indonesia in 1949, but by then Australian troops were well and truly out of the picture.[5]

Prior to that, however, many of the Japanese captives were subject to war crimes trials that endured for many months after the war. Australian lawyers, interpreters, guards and support staff played a critical role in prosecuting war criminals. Australian forces were also instrumental in facilitating the repatriation of tens of thousands of Japanese soldiers back to Japan. In fact, with competing pressures to repatriate and demobilise Australian soldiers, while handing over governance arrangements to Dutch authorities, these tasks proved increasingly challenging as the months passed after the cessation of hostilities and the number of Australians remaining in uniform dwindled.

Postwar security concerns

While only a fraction of the force would be maintained after the war, that which was retained reflected a broad range of capabilities that had been developed in the intervening years of war. This was largely because the postwar Australian armed forces that emerged by the late 1940s were not just a repeat of those that remained after demobilisation in the aftermath of the First World War. The RAAF, for instance, had not

---

5   'United Nations Good Offices Committee Indonesia (UNGOC) 1947–1951', Australian War Memorial, at: www.awm.gov.au/collection/CN500115 (accessed 18 September 2020).

existed in 1918 and the range and sophistication of aircraft types and the accompanying support requirements to maintain them had grown exponentially in the intervening years. Naval platforms had evolved considerably as well, with entire new classes of vessels, equipped with previously unheard-of technologies (including radar and eavesdropping equipment), incorporated or soon to be incorporated into the fleet (notably aircraft carriers).

Land forces had gone through a similar transformation. The Australian Military Forces of the interwar years had been based on militia units with a preponderance of infantry, supported by a modicum of artillery, engineers and cavalry units. The interwar militia largely ignored logistics (along with much else). Back then, though, the expectation remained that much of the logistical and technical backup for high-end warfighting would come from Britain. Yet given the focus on continental defence, how Britain might be of much help for supplies and technical matters seems to have been questionable at best. Finances were the key constraint in the interwar period and would be so again after the war.[6] By 1945, however, the Australian Army maintained relatively sophisticated capabilities ranging across the armoured, airborne, jungle, amphibious and special operations domains. What's more, many of these capabilities were supported by home-grown logistical and administrative support arrangements and training schools as well as Australian industry.[7] Admittedly, many of the weapons and equipment types remained licensed copies of British origin.

At first, Australia's postwar security concerns revolved around ensuring the former enemy states, notably Japan, were disarmed and their arsenal disabled. This was seen as fundamentally important in order to prevent them from being able to stage a repeat of their wartime actions. It soon become evident, however, that Japan and Germany were unlikely to present a significant threat in the foreseeable future. At first, there was a degree of optimism in the Chifley Government about the postwar order. Australia played a prominent role in establishing the United Nations, in part reflecting this optimism. Indeed, Australia's external affairs minister,

---

6   Palazzo, *The Australian Army*, 98.
7   See AT Ross, *Armed and ready: The industrial development and defence of Australia 1900–1945* (Wahroonga: Turton & Armstrong, 1995).

Herbert 'Doc' Evatt, was appointed President of the United Nations in 1948 in large part as recognition of Australia's enthusiasm for the United Nations as the mechanism for managing the postwar world order.

As it happens, the Chifley Government's benign view soon stood at odds with the views developing in London, Washington and Ottawa. Erstwhile wartime ally the Soviet Union soon emerged as the principal adversary of the United States and Britain. On 5 September 1945, three days after the signifying of the surrender on USS *Missouri* in Tokyo Bay, a cipher clerk from the Soviet embassy in Canada, Igor Gouzenko, defected to the West with revelations of large-scale Soviet espionage in North America. Indeed, Gouzenko's defection reverberated around the world, including in Australia, where the Soviet Union had been engaged in espionage during the war – this continued apace after the cessation of hostilities.[8]

In addition to emerging Cold War tensions, Australia emerged from the Second World War with a different mindset towards United Kingdom authorities. While there remained a strong sense of still being British, there was a marked distinction between the British of the United Kingdom and of self-governing and now more independent dominions like Australia. No longer would Australian leaders feel compelled to fall into line with directives from London-based prime ministers. Never again, for instance, would the melancholy duty of a war declaration be an automatic invocation, as had been the case when Robert Menzies was prime minister in September 1939. The appropriation of the Statute of Westminster as an Act of the Australian Commonwealth Parliament in October 1942 put an end to that. Thereafter, the relationship would remain cordial and close, but with a much sharper focus on the distinction between the national interests of the United Kingdom in contrast to those of Australia.[9]

At the same time as a closeness was re-emerging in the ties between Australia and the United Kingdom, the relationship with the United States appeared to drift as US interests and focus shifted elsewhere. While Australia had been America's wartime ally, the United States was initially not interested in extending a security guarantee to Australia after the war. The Americans understood that, despite the setbacks of 1942 with the fall of Singapore, Australia remained in Britain's orbit and as Britain returned

---

8   This is covered in some detail in David Horner, *The spy catchers: The official history of ASIO*, vol. 1, *1949–1963* (Sydney: Allen & Unwin, 2014).
9   John Blaxland, *Strategic cousins: Australian and Canadian expeditionary forces and the British and American empires* (Montreal: McGill-Queens University Press, 2006), 52.

to govern its territories in the 'Far East', Australian ties with Britain would be reinforced. Notably, Australia also remained a member of the British pound sterling economic area (made up of most British Commonwealth countries, excluding Canada), whereby Australia's currency remained fixed in value to Britain's. Britain also remained Australia's principal trading partner through the immediate postwar decade, with much of Australia's trade transiting through the Suez Canal and the Mediterranean Sea, where Britain remained influential. Australia's armed forces, therefore, maintained their wartime disposition to remain orientated towards British models, standards and equipment types, even if sometimes locally manufactured or assembled.

The ramifications of the emerging Cold War between the Soviet Union and the United States (and their respective security partners or allies) were not immediately clear at war's end. It would take some time, including a growing number of signs of Soviet–US confrontation, before American resolve to form a network of alliances crystallised in response. Australia would not sign the Australia, New Zealand and United States (ANZUS) Treaty with the United States and New Zealand until after the onset of the Korean War. Nonetheless, in the meantime, Australia remained a security partner of the United States in the occupation of Japan from 1946 to 1951, alongside other participating British Commonwealth nations.

Australia was eager to participate in the occupation of Japan as one of the victors. While eager to prevent resurgent Japanese militarism, the Australian Government demonstrated an overwhelming sense of security at the end of the Second World War. This is most evidently manifested in the pace and scale of demobilisation.

The existential fears of 1942 effectively vaporised in August 1945. It is in this context that the three services demobilised the overwhelming majority of the more than 600,000 personnel still serving in uniform at war's end. The government faced a gargantuan task, sending hundreds of thousands of their soldiers, sailors, airmen and airwomen back to their homes to return to their families, readjust, find work and get on with their lives after six years of war. Indeed, the armed services had reached nearly 1 million members at the height of the expansion by late 1942. As the tide of war turned, however, and as demands for labour in support of domestic industry and agriculture grew to meet the demands of the war itself, from as early as 1943 the government of prime minister John Curtin had set about demobilising those deemed surplus to requirements, particularly land forces. In response, each of the three armed services faced similar but distinct circumstances and challenges as they sought to demobilise and adjust to the postwar circumstances.

Postwar plans

A few months after the end of the war, in March 1946, the Chiefs of Staff Committee considered an 'Appreciation of the strategical position of Australia'. It saw Australia as protected by its geographic position and the collective security system of the United Nations, but beyond that, Australia was 'unable to defend herself unaided against a major power'. The only viable contender for the title was the Soviet Union.[10] Australian forces, the paper argued, should be organised to fulfil the following requirements:

   a. A Naval Mobile Task Unit consisting of aircraft carriers with their escorts, capable of forming part of an Empire Task Force and cooperating with the United States Navy;
   b. A Fleet Train for the maintenance of a Mobile Task Unit;
   c. A Sea Frontier Force consisting of escorts for shipping, and for the seaward defence of bases;
   d. Amphibious craft for combined operations;
   e. Standard Army formations designed for operations on normal terrain, and for amphibious operations but capable of conversion to meet the conditions of jungle warfare;
   f. Army Garrison forces for the protection of bases against sea and air raids and for internal security;
   g. Adequate maintenance provision for the Forces under (e) and (f);
   h. An Air Mobile Task Force, including units for long range missions and transportation, ready to move wherever required for strategic purposes or in support of the other Services; and
   i. Air units for the protection of bases and focal areas against sporadic raids.[11]

---

10   Stephan Frühling, *A history of Australian strategic policy since 1945* (Canberra: Defence Publishing Service, 2009), 11.
11   'An appreciation of the strategical position of Australia (February 1946)', in Frühling, *A history of Australian strategic policy since 1945*, 61–62.

Over 18 months later, reflecting the heightened concerns about the emerging Cold War, the updated 'Appreciation of the strategical position of Australia' in 1947 also added the requirement for a training and maintenance organisation for the support of the forces 'and for expansion in war'.[12] In practice, not everything on this list would be achieved in the immediate postwar years, but this guidance provided the framework that set the parameters in the early postwar years for the three armed services: the Air Force, the Army and the Navy.

The Royal Australian Navy

The RAN had grown from a strength of 5,010 personnel in 1939 to nearly 40,000 personnel at its height, operating on more than 300 vessels, consisting of dozens of warships including corvettes, frigates, destroyers and cruisers.[13] The RAN did not operate aircraft carriers or submarines during the war, but aircraft carriers would come to be acquired shortly thereafter, although submarines were not included until the late 1960s. While the fleet shrank dramatically after the cessation of hostilities, many of its duties endured, including participating in the British Commonwealth Occupation Force (BCOF) in Japan and in conducting minesweeping operations in and around the South Pacific, clearing mines laid during the war from the harbours and waterways to enable commercial and naval traffic to pass unhindered. This meant that there remained considerable scope for naval personnel to serve after the war if they wished to do so.

The RAN had been well represented at the surrender signing ceremony in Tokyo Bay, with 10 Australian warships present. Two would remain on station as part of BCOF, although that force slowly shrank as its postwar occupation obligations wound up. Still, the presence with BCOF left the RAN, along with its RAAF and army counterparts, with readily available forces that would come to be deployed following the outbreak of the Korean War in mid-1950.

---

12   'An appreciation of the strategical position of Australia (September 1947)', in Frühling, *A history of Australian strategic policy since 1945*, 131.
13   David Stevens, 'The RAN: A brief history', Navy.gov.au, at: www.navy.gov.au/history/feature-histories/ran-brief-history (accessed 4 January 2019).

The postwar RAN was, in a number of respects, a more sophisticated force, having recognised the challenges of coalition warfighting, and witnessed the transformation of naval warfare generated as a result of the air war at sea and other advances in naval technology. It was with this in mind that the RAN acquired two aircraft carriers from Britain in 1947. HMAS *Sydney* and HMAS *Melbourne* were acquired in succession, with HMAS *Sydney* ready for tasking by the time of the Korean War in late 1950.[14] For an island continent, naval forces would always play a prominent role in the nation's defence strategy. The wartime role for land forces would similarly be self-evident to many, but after the war, the fate of land forces would be subject to greater questioning.

The Australian Army

At its peak in late 1942 and early 1943, the Australian Military Forces, or what we now call the Australian Army, consisted of a force that included 14 divisions. This force included the infantry divisions of the militia, namely the 1 through 5, and 11 and 12, Australian divisions. It also included the infantry divisions of the Second Australian Imperial Force (2 AIF), namely 6, 7 and 9 Divisions, noting that 8 Division was in captivity. In addition, there were three mechanised divisions, namely 1 Armoured Division and 1 and 2 Australian Motor Divisions (later 2 and 3 Armoured Divisions).[15] The 'War establishment' (that is, the personnel planning number for the Australian Army) in September 1943 was for an organisation employing 370,300 troops.[16] Out of a population of just over 7 million people, the force that expanded dramatically from 1939 to 1942 shrank at an equally dramatic and accelerating pace as the war's end approached.

Despite the surprising scope and breadth of the Army's capabilities, it had emerged in a disparate manner that compounded the postwar arrangements. By 1945 there were three separate enlistment organisations grouped under the banner of the Australian Military Forces. These included the Permanent Military Force (PMF), the Citizen Military Force (CMF)

---

14   See Anthony Wright, *Australian carrier decisions: The acquisition of HMA Ships Albatross, Sydney and Melbourne*, Papers in Australian Maritime Affairs No. 4 (Canberra: Royal Australian Navy Maritime Studies Program, 1998), 57.
15   Chart: 'Distribution of the Australian Army, May 1942', National Archives of Australia (NAA) (Vic): MP729/6, 37/401/759, cited in Palazzo, *The Australian Army*, 170–71.
16   Palazzo, *The Australian Army*, 175.

and the all-volunteer Australian Imperial Force (AIF), which had been raised specifically for expeditionary use during the war. The disbandment and repatriation of the AIF and the CMF was a priority.[17]

Table 2.1: Australian Military Forces divisions in 1943

Division designation	Higher formation	Comments
1 Australian Division	2 Australian Army	Militia
2 Australian Division	2 Australian Army	Militia
3 Australian Division (Jungle)	New Guinea Force	Militia
4 Australian Division	Disbanded early 1943	–
5 Australian Division (Jungle)	New Guinea Force	Militia
6 Australian Division (Jungle)	New Guinea Force	2 AIF
7 Australian Division (Jungle)	New Guinea Force	2 AIF
8 Australian Division	In captivity	2 AIF
9 Australian Division (Jungle)	New Guinea Force	2 AIF
11 Australian Division (Jungle)	New Guinea Force	Militia
12 Australian Division	Northern Territory Force	Militia
1 Australian Armoured Division	HQ Reserve	Militia
2 Australian Armoured Division	Disbanded early 1943	Former 2 Australian Motor Division
3 Australian Armoured Division	–	Formerly 1 Australian Motor Division
2 Australian Corps & assorted brigade formations	1 Australian Army	NE Reinforcement Training Centre

Source: Drawn from Albert Palazzo, *The Australian Army: A history of its organisation, 1901–2001* (Melbourne: Oxford University Press, 2001), 176–79.

The 'Army Post War Plan' of 1946 provided for the establishment over five years of two brigade groups and an armoured regiment as part of the PMF, with a strength of 11,880 personnel. This was to be the first peacetime regular operational army for Australia. In addition, two divisions and an armoured brigade would be retained as the CMF, with 43,423 personnel as well as headquarters and fixed establishments of another 20,759, making a total of 76,062, including 33,641 personnel in

---

17 D Maclean, 'The development of the Australian Army: A study in policy and capabilities' (BA(Hons) thesis, University of New South Wales Canberra), 3.

the PMF.[18] In the end, these numbers were aspirational and never quite realised, but most of the forces that were maintained as part of the PMF would be retained overseas as part of BCOF in Japan.

Australia's land force contributions to BCOF formed the basis for the Australian Regular Army that emerged from the 1947 'Army Post War Plan'.[19] Notably, this included the conversion of the 65, 66 and 67 Australian Infantry Battalions, which had been raised at the end of the war for special service with BCOF, into the 1, 2 and 3 Battalions of the Royal Australian Regiment (otherwise known as 1RAR, 2RAR and 3RAR).[20] British-pattern equipment, insignia and procedures endured, with many conscious of their status as members of a force nominally identified as British as much as it was, in practice, substantively Australian.

The Royal Australian Air Force

The RAAF would face a similar pressure to demobilise. Over 200,000 Australians had served in the RAAF during the war, operating over 70 squadrons of aircraft including bomber, fighter, reconnaissance and amphibian squadrons. Australians had also made a significant contribution to Britain's defence through the Empire Air Training Scheme, having been placed in RAAF and Royal Air Force (RAF) squadrons. Many of the Australians who signed up for the Empire Air Training Scheme ended up participating in the European and Mediterranean campaigns, including the Normandy invasion and the advance into Germany.[21]

The 1946 plan for the postwar RAAF proposed a force of 19,483 personnel with the overwhelming majority in the permanent force. They would operate a mobile task force, including three long-range/ground attack

---

18 Defence Committee Minutes 460/1946, 19 November and 19 December 1946, Appendix B, cited in Wright, *Australian carrier decisions*, 140; Maclean, 'The development of the Australian Army', 4.
19 'Army Post War Plan', March 1947, Australian War Memorial (AWM): AWM 123, Box 95/4.
20 David Chinn, 'Raising a regular infantry force' in *Duty first: A history of the Royal Australian Regiment*, ed. David Horner and Jean Bou, 2nd ed. (Crows Nest: Allen & Unwin, 2008), 1.
21 See John McCarthy, *A last call of empire: Australian aircrew, Britain and the Empire Air Training Scheme* (Canberra: Australian War Memorial, 1988); 'Empire Air Training Scheme', Australian War Memorial, at: www.awm.gov.au/articles/encyclopedia/raaf/eats (accessed 17 January 2019).

fighter, three heavy bomber and two transport squadrons, and static units including four interceptor squadrons and mixed heavy bomber/ground reconnaissance squadrons.[22]

The jet age had yet to reach the RAAF and the fleet of aircraft the nation retained at the end of the war remained exclusively propeller-driven. They would be employed in support of BCOF in Japan, with three fighter squadrons deploying there in 1946, although this force was gradually reduced to one (77) squadron by 1948.[23]

The decision was made in 1946 to acquire and then produce under licence the RAAF's first jet engine aircraft, the British De Havilland Vampire. The first three Vampires were built in the United Kingdom. Thereafter, 80 were built by the Commonwealth Aircraft Corporation (CAC) in Melbourne with the first one flying in June 1949. Additional Vampire training aircraft were also built. The Vampire-equipped RAAF 78 Wing, incorporating 75 and 76 Squadrons, would deploy to Malta in support of Britain's NATO commitments commencing in 1952.[24]

In the meantime, when the Soviet Union imposed a land blockade on Berlin, the RAAF contributed a dozen sets of aircrew to operate RAF Dakota transport aircraft in support of the relief efforts.[25] Interoperability with the British was a given. The relatively seamless integration of the Australian aircrew into British operations reflected the enduring legacy of the wartime Empire Air Training Scheme.

Meanwhile, demands for working alongside US counterparts would increase from mid-1950. RAAF 77 Squadron, still based at Iwakuni with its propeller-driven Mustang fighter aircraft, was conveniently placed to assist US-led efforts to counter the North Korean invasion of South Korea in mid-1950. Elements of RAAF 77 Squadron were promptly deployed, flying ground attack missions and bomber escort missions in support of US forces. The squadron soon relocated to Korea, supporting ground forces from a range of airfields. With the early introduction of Soviet-sourced MiG jet aircraft in support of the North Korean forces, the

---

22   Defence Committee Minutes 460/1946, 19 November and 19 December 1946, Appendix C, cited in Wright, *Australian carrier decisions*, 141.
23   *Royal Australian Air Force: A snapshot history 1921–2015* (Canberra: Air Power Development Centre, 2015), 124.
24   'A79 DHA Vampire', RAAF Museum Point Cook, at: www.airforce.gov.au/sites/default/files/minisite/static/7522/RAAFmuseum/research/aircraft/series2/A79.htm (accessed 30 September 2020).
25   *Royal Australian Air Force*, 131.

Mustangs proved obsolete. In time, the Mustang would be replaced by the Meteor – a British-sourced, twin-engine jet aircraft with considerably greater power but less manoeuvrability than the Soviet MiGs or American F86 Sabre aircraft used by the US Air Force. With Sabres in short supply and Meteors the only viable option, the RAAF subsequently had to adjust the spectrum of missions it could viably undertake. CAC-built Sabres would become the mainstay of the RAAF's fighter aircraft fleet once they became available after the Korean War.[26]

British precedents

As we have observed, despite having worked closely with the US armed forces since 1942, the Australian armed services still operated largely on British lines, following British-derived procedures and, principally, British-pattern military equipment. For both world wars, Britain had managed to secure the commitment of large dominion and Indian armies that could plan, fight, shoot, communicate and sustain themselves, in concert with the British Army and with each other, during the era of the two world wars.[27] While Britain's power was waning, the legacy of the investment in equipment, doctrine and procedures, and the shared experiences of the British and Australian military forces, combined to generate a lasting effect. The RAN, for instance, remained closely tied to British procedures, customs, traditions, uniforms and equipment, while becoming increasingly familiar with US Navy protocols. The Australian Army, similarly, remained closely modelled on British moderated patterns of organisation. With so much invested in terms of military hardware, there was little incentive to do other than retain British-pattern weapons, procedures, communications technology and uniforms.

In the latter stages of the war, plans were afoot to re-equip Australian forces with American kit in order to contribute to the planned Allied invasion of Japan. The Canadian Army, facing similar pressures to conform to American patterns in order to remain involved, had already begun converting forces from British patterns to American patterns. Canadian

---

26 See Richard Hallion, 'The air war in Korea: Coalition air power in the context of limited war', in *In from the cold: Reflections on Australia's Korean War*, ed. John Blaxland, Michael Kelly and Liam Brewin Higgins (Canberra: ANU Press, 2020), 121–42, doi.org/10.22459/iftc.2019.06.
27 See Douglas E Delaney, *The Imperial Army project: Britain and the land forces of the dominions and India, 1902–1945* (Oxford: Oxford University Press, 2018).

forces invaded Kiska Island in the Aleutians, for instance, alongside American troops in August 1943, employing American equipment and procedures.[28] But with the main invasion averted by the early surrender of Japan, the impetus for these changes in Australia dissipated.

Increasingly independent, Australia was a latecomer to the Statute of Westminster – an act of Britain's parliament in Westminster in 1931 that removed nearly all of Britain's authority to legislate for the dominions such as Canada, Australia and New Zealand. This had the effect of making them fully sovereign nations in their own right. Canada acted on it quickly, but it only came into effect in Australia following its passage through parliament in Canberra after the fall of Singapore in 1942. Despite this devolved authority, Australia remained eager to maintain and reinforce its ties with Britain. Reflecting this mindset, in mid-1943 the Curtin Government had decided that the key to Australia's postwar defence lay in participating in collective security arrangements.[29]

The Australian Army 'Post War Plan' of 1947 reflected the prevailing economic, strategic and military orientation of the nation towards Britain and empire.[30] This pattern of conformity with Britain applied particularly to the RAN and the Australian Army, and to a lesser extent to the RAAF, its inventory having become populated with some American aircraft. Indeed, with Britain's return in 1945 to Malaya and Singapore, Australia would look to continue coordinating its defence policy with the United Kingdom.

Without a strong incentive to change models, there remained compelling reasons for Australia to maintain, for instance, the British-derived wireless signals communications standards and equipment. This enabled Australia to maintain its links with Britain's global communications network but also helped ensure interoperability of its land, naval and air forces.[31] The efficiencies of scale, the economy of effort and the benefits of interoperability would endure for the better part of the following two decades.

---

28   Desmond Morton, *A military history of Canada: From Champlain to Kosovo*, 4th ed. (Toronto: McClelland & Stewart, 1999), 189.
29   'Post War Defence Policy', Minute, 7 February 1944, NAA: A816/1, 14/301/275, cited in Palazzo, *The Australian Army*, 193.
30   'Army Post War Plan', March 1947, AWM: AWM 123, Box 95/4, 1–4.
31   See John Blaxland, *Signals, swift and sure: A history of the Royal Australian Corps of Signals 1947–1972* (Melbourne: R.A. Signals Corps, 1998), 1–10.

In the absence of any particular appetite from the United States for formal ties with Australia beyond the war, Australia's arrangements centred around engagement with Britain. As the armed forces demobilised and began planning for the postwar period, endeavours to standardise the training and organisation of the Australian forces meant the links would continue. Such links included personnel exchanges and joint weapons and equipment research and development, not to mention the similarities in workaday mutual understandings.

This was the case with contributions Australia would make as part of BCOF in Japan from 1946 to 1950. Australia played a leading role in BCOF, but the very title of the organisation pointed to the enduring significance of the connections with Britain. This high degree of interoperability between the forces of the British Empire would also help facilitate a close coordination of effort by British Commonwealth forces at the outset of the Korean War in 1950.

Other legacies

Surprisingly enough, the wartime experience of the Australian armed forces did not lead to a great sense of shared purpose, organisationally. After all, to a large extent, the RAAF had operated as part of a British-led force in the Mediterranean and Europe, and as part of a US-led force in the Pacific campaigns. Similarly, Australia's land forces were more closely aligned with their British counterparts while operating in the Mediterranean and Middle East and then with their US counterparts when fighting in the Pacific. The RAN likewise had aligned itself with its British and American counterparts to contribute to a wartime strategy formulated mostly in London and Washington. Australia's experience in leading BCOF in Japan arguably could have helped develop a level of inter-service collaboration between the three armed services, but with the operational tempo rapidly diminished and the force largely withdrawn in a short time frame, there was little prospect of that level of inter-service interaction ensuing. As a result, what came to be known in the 1980s as the Australian Defence Force remained a disparate group of separate armed forces, with their own government departments and ministers for navy, army and air.

For the nation, the legacy of war was felt widely, far beyond the realm of the armed forces themselves. With hundreds of thousands of returned veterans, the Returned Sailors, Soldiers and Airmen Imperial League of Australia (what is now known as the Returned and Services League, or RSL) proved to be an influential body with considerable social and political clout. In the meantime, the Repatriation Department (the precursor to the modern-day Department of Veterans Affairs) oversaw the support provided for disabled military veterans, and widows of military personnel as well as their dependents. Arguably, however, considerable trauma lay unaddressed, beyond the reach of these organisations. What had been called 'shell shock' or 'combat neurosis' would reverberate for the Second World War generation as well. The extent of the damage on society is hard to measure, but is widely considered to have had a devastating knock-on effect on postwar society. Joan Beaumont's *Broken nation* addresses this tragedy with respect of the legacy of the First World War, but the issue recurs.[32]

Reflections

In conclusion, Australia's military went through a dramatic transformation after the Second World War. Having expanded rapidly, the three armed services quickly returned almost to their prewar state and size. Technology and experience drove some changes, notably the establishment of a postwar regular or permanent military land force.

The lingering legacy of British-derived technology and operating concepts developed and practised during the two world wars was profound and would have a lasting effect, not least because there was little spent on replacing wartime equipment in the immediate postwar years. While the Australian armed forces had operated closely with their US counterparts in wartime, there had been little imperative during the Pacific War to bolster interoperability by adopting US-derived procedures, practice and equipment. Even when based in Australia from early 1942, General MacArthur had operated his headquarters as an American organisation, not a particularly closely integrated one. Australian forces, with their considerable operational experience predating American entry into the war, retained the British-derived approach to warfare. That approach

---

32   Joan Beaumont, *Broken nation: Australians in the Great War* (Sydney: Allen & Unwin, 2013).

would linger after the war – a phenomenon reinforced by the evident US disinterest in providing any immediate security guarantees to Australia once the war ended.

While only a small residual force was available to be contributed to the Korean War in 1950, what was available drew on the legacy of the Second World War, with British-derived practices, procedures and equipment, albeit with an increasingly distinctive Australian flavour. As it happens, the postwar plans for the armed services came to reflect a pattern of organisation that would change incrementally over time. This would notably include a shift towards US-sourced and NATO-standard equipment and practices. But momentum for this reform was still several years away and would have to wait until after the eclipse of Britain's imperial ambitions following the Suez Crisis of 1956. That process would commence with the 1957 defence review and some interesting experimentation with US-derived pentagonal organisational structures.[33] Still, military practitioners in the early twenty-first century would recognise many of the hallmarks of their modern Australian Defence Force in the plans that were laid out in 1946 and 1947. Even through to the early twentieth century, UK ties and shared practices would permeate Australian practices, even as ties with the United States deepened.[34]

---

33   See John Blaxland, *Organising an Army: The Australian experience, 1957–1965* (Canberra: Strategic and Defence Studies Centre, 1989).
34   This issue is explored in John Blaxland, *The Australian Army from Whitlam to Howard* (Melbourne: Cambridge University Press, 2014).

3

The 'fourth arm' of Australia's defence: ASIO and the early Cold War

David Horner

The Cold War, as experienced by Australia in the late 1940s and the 1950s, saw the involvement of a new entity in Australian defence: the Australian Security Intelligence Organisation (ASIO).[1] Indeed the Australian prime minister, Robert Menzies, described ASIO as the 'fourth arm' of Australian defence, after the Navy, Army and Air Force. This was a remarkable statement about an organisation that only came into existence in 1949, but it indicated a major change to the concept of national security.

By contrast with the Australian armed forces that fought overseas in the South African War, the two world wars, the Korean War, the Malayan Emergency, Confrontation and the Vietnam War, in the Cold War ASIO fought its war at home against espionage, subversion and sabotage, and for the first time this theatre of conflict was seen as almost as important as those overseas. It is true that Australia had internal security concerns in the two world wars, but none of the security organisations in those conflicts saw themselves as involved in their own war in the way ASIO did in the early 1950s. It might seem extreme to describe ASIO as fighting a war,

---

1   This chapter is based on the author's book *The spy catchers: The official history of ASIO*, vol. 1, *1949–1963* (Sydney: Allen & Unwin, 2014). The author had privileged access to ASIO records, and where these are still held by ASIO they are identified simply as ASIO records. Further references to the events described in this chapter can be found in the book.

and certainly the 'war' did not involve weapons or physical casualties. But ASIO officers certainly felt they were in a conflict in which the security of Australia was at stake. This chapter seeks to explain why ASIO was formed, what role it played in the early Cold War, why its activities formed part of the Cold War, and whether it was effective in achieving its aims. But first we need a little background.

Internal security before the Cold War

From the beginning of the First World War, internal security formed a component of Australian defence. The initial concern was the threat of espionage and sabotage, particularly by enemy nationals living in Australia. As a result, foreign nationals, mainly Germans, were rounded up and placed in internment camps. Responsibility for dealing with espionage fell to the Army's Directorate of Intelligence, generally known as Military Intelligence. Navy Intelligence was focused more narrowly on preventing sabotage and the leakage of information about ship movements. In late 1915, at the request of Britain, Australia established a small civilian counterespionage bureau, later called the Special Intelligence Bureau (SIB).

The security agencies became increasingly involved in countering subversion, or what the historian Frank Cain has called 'political surveillance'.[2] Concerned about possible subversive organisations such as the Industrial Workers of the World (IWW), which was opposed to the war, in July 1917 the Federal Government made membership of the IWW illegal. As the largest security agency, Military Intelligence took the lead in watching the expanding number of bodies that seemed to have a connection with socialism or bolshevism. Prime Minister WM Hughes ruthlessly used the power of the *War Precautions Act 1914* (Cth) and the efforts of Military Intelligence to stifle any activity that seemed to threaten the war effort. The SIB also kept watch over other allegedly subversive bodies, such as trade unions and returned soldiers' organisations, hence Cain's claim about political surveillance.

In December 1917 the government established another body, the Commonwealth Police, to investigate matters concerning Commonwealth property and facilities, but after the war the Commonwealth Police was

---

2   See Frank Cain, *The origins of political surveillance* (Sydney: Angus & Robertson, 1983).

abolished and the SIB became the Commonwealth Investigation Branch (CIB), with responsibilities for investigating administrative offences against the Commonwealth, as well as espionage and subversion. The CIB was relatively small, and many counterespionage and countersubversion tasks were taken over by Military Intelligence.

On the outbreak of the Second World War, the requirements of the First World War – internment of aliens, censorship, protection against sabotage, and counterespionage – still remained, and again foreign nationals were rounded up and placed in internment camps. The most pressing internal security concern was the activities of the Communist Party of Australia (CPA). In August 1939 the Soviet Union had signed a non-aggression pact with Hitler's Germany, and the CPA told Australian communists to keep out of the Army and to boycott the export of war materials. On 15 June 1940 the government declared the CPA to be an illegal organisation.

The multiplying threats brought home the need to coordinate the work of the various security agencies. In February 1941 Australia established a small security service, but it was hampered by bureaucratic infighting. In March 1942, three months after the outbreak of war with Japan, the Labor Government established a new expanded security service named the Commonwealth Security Service, although the CIB still remained active.

By this time, General Douglas MacArthur had arrived in Australia to command the Southwest Pacific Area (SWPA). Within the SWPA there was a plethora of intelligence organisations. Each of the Australian and American services had their own security or counterintelligence staffs, responsible for their own internal security. While thousands of personnel were working in a score of different intelligence agencies, the crucial intelligence was provided by the interception and decryption of enemy radio traffic.

In December 1942 the government lifted the ban on the CPA and its membership grew, reaching a peak strength of about 23,000 by late 1944. According to its historian, Alastair Davidson, by 1945 the party controlled 275,000 out of 1.2 million trade unionists, and its supporters might have numbered 480,000, or 40 per cent of Australian trade unionists.[3] The CIB continued to issue fortnightly reports on communism, based

---

3   Alastair Davidson, *The Communist Party of Australia: A short history* (Stanford, California: Hoover Institution Press, 1969), 82–83.

on information provided by its agents.[4] Undoubtedly internal security was important, but the security services were fragmented. There was little enemy espionage and the internment of aliens reduced the possibility of fifth column activity.

Beginning of the Cold War

At the end of the war it seemed that the need for an internal security organisation had declined considerably. The Commonwealth Security Service was disbanded and its functions were taken over by a small section within the CIB. But it was soon clear that the postwar world posed new challenges to Australian internal security. The first was the threat of espionage.

On 5 September 1945, just three days after the Japanese formally surrendered, thus ending the Second World War, Igor Gouzenko, a 26-year-old cipher clerk in the Soviet embassy in Ottawa, defected to the West. Gouzenko revealed that the Soviets had set up a spy ring in Canada. Indeed, Dr Alan Nunn May, a British scientist working in Canada on atomic research, had passed information about the project to the Soviet Union. Further, Gouzenko revealed that the Soviets had inserted long-term undercover agents known as 'illegals' in Western countries.

At first the Australian Labor Government, led by Ben Chifley, was unconcerned by the Gouzenko revelations; but soon the opposition used them to question the government's handling of security. In response, in February 1947 the government formed a new body, the Commonwealth Investigation Service (CIS) out of the CIB, and provided 20 additional staff. But the government still did not take the threat of espionage seriously enough.

By 1947 Britain and Australia had established the Long Range Weapons Establishment at Salisbury, South Australia, and a rocket range at Woomera. In parliament on 7 March 1947 a Country Party member, Joe Abbott, spoke of the need to ensure 'that there shall be no leakage of information concerning these experiments', and urged the government to ascertain whether there was evidence of a spy ring operating in collaboration with

---

4   Communist Reports 18 and 19, National Archives of Australia (NAA): A9108, Roll 9, 11392043.

officials of the Soviet embassy. The Attorney-General, HV Evatt, agreed with the necessity to take 'adequate precautions against the leakage of secret information' and said the CIS would be given additional staff.[5]

Already the possibility of leakages of information was causing problems for Australia's relations with Britain and the United States. On 14 January 1947 Norman Makin, the Australian ambassador in Washington, advised that the United States was considering formal arrangements under which information could be released. Four months later a senior British official warned that the United States 'was worried about the possibility of leakage of secret information from Australia'.[6]

The second challenge to internal security came from the renamed Australian Communist Party (ACP). In September 1947, in response to the US-led Marshall Plan to provide large-scale economic aid to the countries of Western Europe, the Soviet Union formed the Communist Information Bureau (Cominform) to coordinate the actions of 10 European communist parties under Soviet direction. Although not a member of Cominform, the ACP chose to follow its direction, and in the first half of 1948 the ACP's Central Committee decided to go on the offensive, believing the time was right to seize control of the Labour movement. The government was coming to realise that it was in a fight with the Communist Party, but it was not yet willing to employ measures that might seem to infringe civil liberties.

Formation of ASIO

The formation of ASIO in March 1949 relates directly to the signals intelligence operation later known as Venona. Under the Venona program, American and British cryptanalysts had decrypted a small number of telegrams of the Soviet intelligence organisation, later known as the KGB, including communications between KGB headquarters in Moscow and the KGB resident in the Soviet embassy in Canberra. These intercepts, which began in 1943 and continued through to 1948, showed that about a dozen Australians, many identified only by cover names, had provided

---

5   Commonwealth, *Parliamentary Debates*, House of Representatives, 7 March 1947, 484–90.
6   Jacqueline Templeton, 'Australian Intelligence/Security Services', vol. 2, 298, 253. This report forms volume 1 of the *Seventh report of the Royal Commission on Intelligence and Security*, and is found in NAA: A8908, 7A.

information to the Soviet embassy. The Venona program was highly secret, because the Americans and British did not want to alert the Soviets to their success; the Australian Government was unaware of the program.

As the Venona program seemed to reveal the existence of Soviet spies in Australia, and as Australia was being given access to secret information about the joint British–Australian rocket project, the British Government was anxious to alert the Australians to the apparent lapses in their security. Hence, in February 1948 Sir Percy Sillitoe, director general of Britain's security service, MI5, visited Australia to warn Chifley, although he could not reveal the true source of his information. Sillitoe, and Roger Hollis, a senior MI5 officer accompanying him, tried, without success, to persuade Chifley to set up a new security organisation to replace the CIS, which was ineffective and lacked the skills to deal with this new threat.

Meanwhile, the United States cut off Australia's access to classified information. Realising he needed to do more to persuade Chifley, in June Sillitoe obtained approval to inform Chifley of the origin of the intelligence about the security breaches. Next month Chifley visited London to discuss economic matters. The British prime minister, Clement Attlee, then told Chifley that the source of information 'was intercepted telegrams from the Soviet Legation in Canberra … the authenticity of which has been fully verified beyond question'.[7] Chifley agreed that Hollis, and another MI5 officer, Robert Hemblys-Scales, could visit Australia to assist in the investigation of the leakages.

Hollis and Hemblys-Scales arrived in Australia in late July and began a round of meetings with key ministers and officials, although they could not tell the true source of their intelligence. The problem with the Venona decrypts was that they were often just incomplete telegrams, and the use of cover names meant that many individuals could not be identified. One who could be identified was Ian Milner, a former Department of External Affairs officer, then working for the United Nations in New York. The breakthrough came in August when the Venona decrypts revealed that Francis Bernie, who had worked as a secretary/typist in the office of the Attorney-General, Evatt, between 1944 and 1946, had given information to an ACP member, cover name KLOD, who had then passed it to the Soviet embassy.

---

7   Final brief for PM for his conversation with Mr Chifley, prepared by Sir Orme Sargent, 6 July 1948, UK National Archives (TNA): KV 4/451.

Persuaded by this evidence, on 20 September 1948 Chifley agreed to set up an Australian security organisation 'similar to MI5'.[8] But he delayed establishing the new organisation, partly because Evatt was overseas, and also because he wanted to make one final appeal to the Americans to release classified information. When the Americans rebuffed this effort, Chifley knew he had to proceed.

The foundations for the establishment of ASIO were laid at a secret meeting in Canberra on 7 February 1949 attended by Chifley, three key ministers and several officials, including three MI5 officers. They agreed that an Australian security intelligence service should be set up along the lines of MI5, that it should come under the Attorney-General, but the service's director-general should have the right of direct access to the prime minister.[9]

Justice Geoffrey Reed from the Supreme Court of South Australia accepted the appointment as the first head of the security service, which he later named the Australian Security Intelligence Organisation, for one year, while he was on leave from the court. Finally, on 2 March, Chifley informed parliament that 'a great increase in Australian security tasks and responsibilities has made it necessary to re-establish a separate security service' and that Justice Reed had been appointed to 'establish and organise an Australian Security Service'.[10] Reed's charter stated that the security service was part of the Attorney-General's Department, but it was also:

> part of the Defence Forces of the Commonwealth, and save as herein expressed has no concern with the enforcement of criminal law. Its task is the defence of the Commonwealth from external and internal dangers arising from attempts at espionage and sabotage, or from actions of persons and organisations, whether directed from within or without the country, which may be judged to be subversive of the security of the Commonwealth.[11]

---

8   Shedden, 'Notes of Discussions with Ministers in Canberra on 20th September 1938', 20 September 1948, NAA: A5954, 849/A.
9   Minute, 'Conclusions of meeting held on 8th February 1942 at Canberra', NAA: A5954, 849/A; and letter, Hollis to Sillitoe, 8 February 1949, TNA: KV 4/458. The Hollis letter and Shedden's appointment diary confirm the meeting was held on 7 February.
10 Public Statement Chifley, 2 March 1949, in *Digest of decisions and announcements and important speeches by the Prime Minister, the Right Hon. J. B. Chifley*, No. 142 (24 January 1949 to 6 March 1949).
11 'Prime Minister's memorandum to the Director-General of Security', 16 March 1949, NAA: A7452, A48.

ASIO: The first year

The new security service was formed as the Cold War was increasing in intensity. In January 1949, the Chinese People's Liberation Army captured Beijing and on 1 October the communist leader, Mao Zedong, proclaimed the People's Republic of China. The Berlin blockade continued in Germany until May, when the Soviet Union relented in the face of the successful Allied airlift. But for the West, this was only a tactical victory in what was shaping up to be a long conflict. In August the North Atlantic Treaty Organization (NATO) was established, and the Greek civil war ended, but also that month the Soviet Union successfully tested its first atomic bomb. In Malaya, the Communist Terrorists (as they were known) were stepping up their offensive. Everywhere, it seemed, the communists were on the march.

As the new Director-General of Security, Geoffrey Reed had three important tasks: to build his new organisation; to identify the spies as revealed in the Venona intercepts (known as 'the case'); and to deal with communist subversion. Although important to the story of ASIO, discussion of the first two tasks is beyond the scope of this chapter. In brief, Reed staffed ASIO by drawing on the CIS, state police special branches, and former and serving members of the armed forces. By 1 July 1949, ASIO had 94 officers; by June 1950, 141.[12] ASIO's counterespionage work focused on trying to solve 'the case', and in this respect ASIO had limited success. KLOD was identified as an ACP official, Walter Clayton. Another suspect, cover name TOURIST, was identified as an External Affairs officer, Jim Hill. The ASIO counterespionage effort reached its ultimate success with the defection of the KGB officer, Vladimir Petrov, in April 1954.

With regard to subversion, the Chifley Government was already taking action. In March 1949, at about the time he announced the formation of ASIO, Chifley directed the CIS to investigate whether a statement by the secretary of the ACP, Lance Sharkey, was treasonable or seditious. Sharkey allegedly had said that if Soviet forces entered Australia in pursuit of aggressors, Australian workers would welcome them.[13] In July 1949, Sharkey was sentenced to three years jail, later reduced to 18 months.

---

12 Letter, Reed to Menzies, 27 June 1950, NAA: A7452, A48.
13 'Sharkey statement to be examined', *Mercury*, 9 March 1949, 7.

Earlier, in January 1949, Cecil Sharpley, a leading ACP member in Victoria, had defected, and in a series of newspaper articles, and in a Royal Commission set up in Victoria in April, he exposed the ACP's apparent efforts to take over the trade unions.

Then, on 27 June 1949, communist-led unions began a seven-week strike in the Hunter Valley coalfields in NSW. In July the CIS, with police assistance, raided the ACP headquarters in Sydney, and other communist establishments, seizing documents. In a dramatic and unprecedented step, the Chifley Government moved troops into the open-cut coalfields to begin mining and distributing coal, and hence to break the strike.

The coal strike was taken as evidence by the government that the ACP was mounting a campaign against it. For its part, the ACP realised that the formation of ASIO presented it with a new and dangerous opponent. For example, on 11 March 1949, just nine days after Chifley announced the formation of ASIO, the *Guardian*, the communist newspaper in Victoria, branded the new organisation as a 'super-secret gestapo to spy on the Australian worker'. Further declarations followed a similar pattern, emphasising that ASIO was a 'danger' to trade unions, the 'peace' movement, people's 'democratic rights' and 'civil liberties'.[14]

As noted earlier, among his duties, Reed was directed to defend the Commonwealth against 'actions of persons and organisations, whether directed from within or without the country, which may be judged to be subversive of the security of the Commonwealth'.[15] He interpreted this to mean that he needed to gain a deep insight into the activities of the ACP, and this task involved developing sources within the ACP or communist-controlled unions.

The election of the Liberal-County Party Coalition, led by Robert Menzies, in December 1949 brought new emphasis to the countersubversion role. The government came to power with a different world view to its predecessor. It was more inclined to see the Cold War as a coordinated communist assault on the West, in which the ACP was playing its part. On 3 January 1950 Reed indoctrinated Menzies into the Venona program and told him about the source of the information on espionage.[16]

---

14   Bruce Campbell, 'History of ASIO', ASIO records, f 60.
15   'Prime Minister's memorandum to the Director-General of Security', 16 March 1948, NAA: A7452, A48.
16   Telegram, Young to Sillitoe, 9 January 1950, TNA: KV 4/452.

Throughout 1949, while in opposition, Menzies had made numerous speeches in which he had argued that the ACP needed to be banned. In one speech he asked rhetorically:

> Does anyone believe that if we are forced into war by the Soviet Union there will be no fifth column here and in every other Western democracy? I say that within 48 hours of war we would have an active fifth column of Communists in this country.[17]

Now he had concrete evidence that some communists had indeed been conducting espionage in Australia on behalf of the Soviet Union.

While the Australian Government understood the imperative to solve 'the case', its attention was focused more broadly on the problem of communism, and ASIO was to play a major role in the government's campaign. On 9 January 1950, ASIO circulated an 11-page secret report on the ACP, which covered membership, finances, trade union activity, the party's connections with overseas communist organisations, the role of the Australian Peace Council as a communist 'front' organisation, the organisations controlled by the ACP and its preparations for 'illegal work'.[18] Another report on the ACP claimed that:

> undercover … reliable sources indicated that: expenses incurred in fighting the Government's proposed ban on the ACP would be met by the Russian Embassy, [and] Communist union officials will organise continuous sectional strikes.[19]

A prime example of communist activity seemed to be a series of 'rolling strikes' on the Brisbane waterfront. On 23 March 1950, the government invoked the *Crimes Act 1941* (Cth), which meant that striking watersiders could be liable for jail for up to 12 months. When the waterside workers voted to take their claims to arbitration, however, the government did not follow through with its threat.

This was just an early shot in the war. In his speech when opening parliament on 22 February, Governor-General Sir William McKell foreshadowed that the government would be introducing legislation to ban the Communist Party. The government would be given the power to imprison 'declared' communists and to remove them from trade union offices and from the

---

17 Quoted in AW Martin, 'Mr Menzies' anticommunism', *Quadrant* 40, no. 65 (May 1996): 52.
18 Report, 'Australian Communist Party, Bulletin No 1, January 1950', 9 January 1950, National Library of Australia (NLA): MS 4936/20/436/3.
19 Report, 'Australian Communist Party: Review from 15 Jan to 15 Feb 50', ASIO records.

Commonwealth Public Service. ASIO was closely involved in drafting the preamble to the proposed Bill. When Menzies presented the Communist Party Dissolution Bill to the House of Representatives on 27 April he justified the decision, saying that earlier he had:

> resisted the idea of a Communist ban, on the ground that, in time of peace, doubts ought to be resolved in favour of free speech … But events have moved. We are not, except in a technical sense, at peace. The Soviet Union has perfected the technique of the 'cold war', has accompanied it by the organisation of peace demonstrations designed not to promote true peace, but to prevent or impair defence preparations in the democracies … The real and active Communists in Australia present us with our immediate problem. But our choice is clear. We can attack them frontally, or we can adopt inaction.[20]

The Melbourne *Argus* put the Bill in stark terms when it stated that Menzies had 'declared ruthless war on Australian Communists'.[21] Predictably, the trade unions were already mobilising to oppose the Bill, and ASIO was busy trying to keep tabs on the delegations that were arriving in Canberra. The Bill passed the House of Representatives on 23 May, but after it was delayed in the Senate, on 23 June Menzies had it put aside; he would reintroduce it later in the year.

The Cold War intensifies

ASIO's campaign against the communists during the early 1950s must be understood in the context of the Cold War. For ordinary Australian citizens, it was a time of uncertainty and concern. ASIO's officers, however, were not just concerned. They saw themselves as frontline warriors (even if they did not use that term) in a war against a twofold enemy – the Soviet Union and the ACP. Forty-five years later, Michael Thwaites, who had been ASIO's head of counterespionage, was quick to remind people that:

> there was a real fear which I don't think people understand today, that we were going to have a world clash … the Cold War was not an illusion. It had to be won.[22]

---

20 Commonwealth, *Parliamentary Debates*, House of Representatives, 27 April 1950, 1996–97.
21 'Reds "outlawed" in new bill', *The Argus* (Melbourne), 28 April 1950, 1.
22 Transcript, ABC TV program, 'Time Frame, War on Dissent', 27 March 1997, at: w.w.w.abc. net.au/time/episodes/ep8a.htm (accessed 5 July 2013, site now discontinued).

While internationally the Soviet Union, supported by its allies, was locked in a bitter contest with the West with actual conflict in areas such as Korea, Malaya and Vietnam, within Australia this threat was embodied in the Soviet embassy, which was seeking access to Australia's secret political, military and scientific information. ASIO therefore had a major counterespionage role. Further, ASIO expected the Soviet Union to seek the assistance of ACP members (as Venona had highlighted), so the government believed that they and the party's sympathisers needed to be kept out of positions where they might have access to secret information. ASIO thus had a role in vetting employees for such jobs.

ASIO's other target was the ACP itself. ASIO and the government believed that the ACP, on behalf of the Soviet Union, was engaged in a long-term campaign to undermine confidence in the Australian democratic system and ultimately to overthrow it. ASIO believed the ACP was pursuing its aims by infiltrating trade unions and by fostering 'front' organisations, which could draw support from idealistic but naïve Australian citizens who might not actually have supported the Soviet Union's aims.

Meanwhile, the government was responding to the Cold War in a direct fashion. In May and June 1950, RAAF aircraft were deployed to Malaya to assist the British in operations against the 'Communist Terrorists'. Soon after the outbreak of the Korean War in June, Australia sent a fighter squadron to South Korea. Early in July the government endorsed a three-year defence program and announced a national service training scheme for part-time service after an initial full-time training period. Then on 26 July the government committed an infantry battalion to the Korean War.

In the midst of these developments, on 17 July 1950 Colonel Charles Spry took over from Geoffrey Reed as Director-General of Security. Confident and capable, Spry, who had been director of Military Intelligence since 1946, was determined to reshape the organisation and to make it a professional security service. He established a proper headquarters in Melbourne, and restructured the organisation so that it could improve its efforts to penetrate the ACP. ASIO's staff continued to grow and by April 1951 numbered 181.[23]

---

23 Notes for DG, 'Statement of ASIO strength, as at 30/4/51', ASIO records. By 1963–64, ASIO staff had grown to 373 personnel. Horner, *The spy catchers*, 401.

Preparing for internment

ASIO was soon responding to the government's demands for information and support on subversion-related matters. The government began organising for a possible global war and it needed to update the *Commonwealth war book*. This book, first prepared before the Second World War, set out the actions to be taken by government departments both in the 'precautionary stage' before the outbreak of war, and during a war itself. The *War book* stipulated that in the precautionary stage the director-general of security was to provide the attorney-general with a list of persons for whom he recommended detention or restriction orders be made. Once war was declared, the director-general was to arrange for the persons to be detained. Similarly, the director-general was to provide lists of aliens (non-Australians or non-British subjects), and on the outbreak of war arrange for their internment.[24]

On 28 July 1950, just nine days after taking up his appointment, Spry directed that 'in view of the uncertain international situation' the measures were to 'be undertaken immediately'. To avoid any misconception 'the utmost discretion' was to be used and other government departments were to be advised that 'as a normal peacetime planning precaution we are accumulating certain information in case an emergency should arise'. By 14 August the ASIO regional offices were to provide lists of aliens who should be prevented from leaving the Commonwealth or should be interned in the event of war (as had occurred in both world wars), as well as a list of 'British subjects' to be interned. The latter group would include the leaders of the ACP and other communists in key positions.[25] One complication was the likelihood that the Communist Party Dissolution Bill would become law in the next sitting of parliament, due to begin on 27 September, and ASIO believed that the ACP was preparing to go underground, as it had done when it was declared illegal in 1940.

When parliament reassembled on 27 September, Menzies reintroduced the Communist Party Dissolution Bill and unexpectedly it was passed by the Labor-dominated Senate on 19 October. Immediately, 10 trade unions announced that they would be challenging the Act in the High Court, and they obtained an interim injunction to restrain the Commonwealth from putting it into operation.

---

24 *Commonwealth war book* (Melbourne: Department of Defence, 1956).
25 Memo, 'Measures to be taken in preparation for a possible emergency – Commonwealth War Book – policy statement No 1', 28 July 1950, NAA: A6122, 1285.

The High Court challenge prevented some activities, but ASIO remained busy gathering information to apply the provisions of the Act if it was found to be valid. On 23 October, three days after the Act was signed into law, officers of the CIS, assisted by the police and with ASIO officers present, raided ACP headquarters in Sydney, Melbourne, Perth, Hobart and Darwin. According to one account, in Melbourne the security officers seized 'more than half a ton of pamphlets, articles and other documents'.[26] On 6 December, Spry directed the regional offices to prepare new lists of aliens from communist countries to be interned. Approximate numbers were nearly 1,000 nationwide. Spry considered that 'the immediate detention of about 750 selected communists would render the party organisation innocuous for a period of time'.[27] With regard to non-enemy aliens, Spry directed that:

> those with an adverse pro-Communist security record should be listed automatically either for internment or restriction, depending on the degree of their subversive activities.[28]

In January 1951 Menzies attended the Commonwealth Prime Ministers' Conference in London, where he learned that Attlee had been working to persuade the Americans not to use an atomic bomb in Korea, and that the Western allies were likely to lose if a war developed with China.[29] He arrived home in mid-February to be confronted by a serious coal strike. About the same time, the US State Department's special negotiator, John Foster Dulles, arrived in Canberra for discussions with the Minister for External Affairs, Percy Spender, over a draft tripartite treaty between Australia, New Zealand and the United States (ANZUS). To Menzies's surprise and satisfaction, Spender and Dulles initialled the draft treaty that eventually became the ANZUS Treaty and a key element in Australian defence policy for the next 70 years.

As soon as Menzies returned to Canberra in February 1951 he began referring to the widespread belief that global war was inevitable. The government, he said, would, therefore, be aiming to place Australia on a 'semi-war footing'.[30] On 7 March he told parliament that the

---

26 'Swoop on Reds' offices', *Sydney Morning Herald*, 24 October 1950, 1.
27 Memo, Spry to regional offices, 'British Subjects (Natural born and naturalised)', 7 December 1950, ASIO records.
28 Memo, Spry to regional offices, 'Aliens Non-enemy', 7 December 1950, ASIO records.
29 Martin, 'Mr Menzies' anticommunism', 55.
30 'A semi-war footing', *Sydney Morning Herald*, 15 February 1951.

democracies had no more than three years to make defence preparations that alone could avert war. 'It is my solemn belief that we have not a minute more than three years at the best.'[31]

Then on 9 March the High Court ruled the *Communist Party Dissolution Act 1950* (Cth) invalid under the Constitution. A week later Menzies asked the governor-general to approve a double dissolution of both houses of parliament, on the grounds that Labor had stopped a banking bill, and a general election was called for 28 April. The Menzies Government won the election and secured control of the Senate.

The High Court's decision did not reduce ASIO's work. In the four and a half months since parliament had passed the Act, ASIO had prepared 'declarations' to be submitted to the relevant committee concerning key trade union officials and communist-dominated organisations. On 5 April, Spry wrote to his regional directors to thank them for this work and to assure them that it had not been a waste of effort. 'On the contrary', he said, 'the actual declarations will be very useful for research work now being undertaken by this headquarters.' He now urged:

> the utmost effort, diligence, and ingenuity in order that we may produce clear legal proof that the ACP as an organisation or its individual members are engaged in activity prejudicial to the safety of the Commonwealth.[32]

While ASIO no longer needed to produce lists of communists to be dealt with under the *Communist Party Dissolution Act*, it still needed to keep tabs on the ACP, even though it remained a legal party, because of its potential for subversion.

The referendum

On 5 July 1951, the Federal Government introduced in parliament a bill enabling it to hold a referendum, which, if successful, would give it the power to deal with the communists. In preparation, Spry ordered the regional directors to compile reports on the covert organisations that the ACP was preparing to use in the event of the party being dissolved.

---

31 'Three years – No more', *Sydney Morning Herald*, 8 March 1951.
32 Memo, Spry to Regional Directors, 5 April 1951, ASIO records.

The regional directors were also to prepare lists of premises to be searched and of trade union officials, public servants and communist 'front' organisations to be 'declared' under the *Communist Party Dissolution Act*.[33]

During the referendum campaign ASIO prepared a report on the ACP, in which it assessed the strength of the party at between a minimum of 6,845 and a maximum of 7,696 members, with almost half in NSW. According to ASIO's report, the Central Committee of the ACP did not believe that the situation in Australia allowed for 'the seizure of power in the foreseeable future'. Rather, it hoped to achieve a transitional 'People's Government' to be followed later by 'a Dictatorship of the Proletariat'. ASIO believed that the ACP's strategy was to split the Labor Party and 'collect around itself a coalition of left-wing elements which will fight for "People's Power"'. The ACP hoped to use the referendum campaign to establish a united front with the Labor Party, while at the same time conducting a separate campaign to publicise the work of the ACP itself. ASIO showed this summary to Menzies on 18 August.[34]

Spry took a keen interest in the conduct and outcome of the referendum campaign and directed his officers to keep a close watch on the ACP. Through its agent contacts and technical intercepts, ASIO was able to gain full coverage of the 16th National Congress of the ACP held in Sydney on 23–26 August 1951. ASIO learned that the party was 'most concerned' that as a result of the government's attack on them its strength had been reduced by 40 per cent. On 31 August, Spry told Menzies about this surveillance operation and suggested he include some of the information in his speeches to disconcert the ACP.[35] Clearly Spry did not believe that it was contrary to his charter to assist the government in its political campaign to win the referendum when he linked such assistance to achieving an advantage in his contest with the ACP. But while Spry's charter required him to watch the ACP and thwart any apparent attack on Australian society, it did not authorise him to assist the government in a purely political campaign.

By this time, Ben Chifley had died, and Bert Evatt had succeeded him as Leader of the Opposition. Evatt might have chosen to proceed cautiously, but he launched himself into one of his most vigorous barnstorming

---

33 Memo, Spry to Regional Directors, 30 August 1951, ASIO records.
34 Report, 'Summary of Current Information on the Australian Communist Party', n.d., but with note that it was shown to the prime minister on 18 August 1951, ASIO records.
35 Letter, Spry to Menzies, 31 August 1951, ASIO records.

campaigns, stumping the country for the 'No' vote, in defiance of public opinion polls that forecast majorities of between 70 and 80 per cent in favour of the proposal. Enough voters were persuaded to change their minds for the referendum to be defeated by a narrow margin on 22 September. Not everyone in ASIO supported the 'Yes' vote. Michael Thwaites recalled that within ASIO there was no 'great dismay among my colleagues at the result' of the 'No' vote. He claimed that he saw it as a 'victory for civil liberties', and that it made his job of watching the CPA easier. If the CPA had gone underground it would have been 'far harder for ASIO to get on with the task of building up accurate, detailed, systematic knowledge of the party'.[36]

Continuing efforts against the CPA

The 'No' vote did not alter ASIO's legitimate role of keeping watch on the ACP, which had now changed its name back to the Communist Party of Australia (CPA), and ASIO continued preparing lists of enemy aliens and others who would be interned in an emergency. Spry's problem was that while he could prepare lists of people for possible internment, it was the government's prerogative to decide who should be interned. Beginning in February 1951, Spry and his chief legal adviser, Bernard Tuck, had a series of meetings with Solicitor-General Kenneth Bailey and sometimes Attorney-General John Spicer, in which they attempted to refine the internment policy. In July 1951, ASIO estimated that in time of war it would need to consider the internment of about 3,100 persons, including 2,000 enemy aliens, 100 other aliens, and 1,000 British subjects and displaced persons. While ASIO had files on the 1,000 British subjects, it had files on only 300 aliens.[37] Discussion continued well into the following year as the policy was slowly developed. As a further complication, the situation in New Guinea was slightly different to that in the rest of Australia. For example, in January 1952 a total of about 270 persons were listed for internment. Of these, more than half were children, and most were described as 'Asiatics', which were mostly Chinese.[38]

---

36 Michael Thwaites, *Truth will out: ASIO and the Petrovs* (London: Collins, 1980), 40.
37 Memo, 'Internment Policy, Notes of discussion by Deputy Director-General (A&L) with Director-General on 26th July 1951', ASIO records.
38 Memo, L Sheedy, RD PNG, to Spry, 19 January 1952, ASIO records.

ASIO maintained the Australia-wide list for the rest of the decade, although it gradually reduced the number of people to be interned. Spry recognised the magnitude of the problem, observing in April 1955 that while members of the CPA were a 'security risk', the most dangerous were those holding office, particularly high office, in the party. The government would also need to detain CPA members in key positions in the Commonwealth and state public services, as well as in private industry, and 'approximately 982' 'British subjects' would need to be detained. There were also 500,000 Australian aliens in Australia and it might be necessary to detain 4,665 of them.[39] In January 1957, Spry advised that it had 'recently been decided to adopt a more liberal policy for the internment of aliens and to reduce the number of persons whom ASIO will recommend for internment in an emergency'.[40]

By this time the threat of global war had receded. In January 1953 the Cabinet endorsed the Defence Committee's 'strategic basis' paper, which concluded that while the Soviet Union's ultimate aim was a 'Moscow-controlled communist-dominated world', the development of NATO had forced the Soviet Union 'to direct its main cold war effort towards the Far East and South East Asia'. In addition, the Soviet Union was 'fostering subversive activities throughout the world'. Greater priority had to be given to Southeast Asia, and Defence preparations for a global war should therefore be reviewed, with the peacetime build-up for mobilisation being spread over a longer period.[41] Further, the armistice in Korea in July 1953 allowed the government to reduce its military commitment there and to consider providing forces for service in Malaya.[42] Despite this easing of the Cold War, ASIO did not let up in its campaign against the CPA, and in the 1960s the Vietnam War would see a vastly increased effort to keep tabs not only on communists, but on anyone actively opposing Australia's involvement in the war.[43]

---

39 Memo, 'Detention, restriction and control in wartime of persons whose activities may be prejudicial to the public safety', CCF Spry, 2 April 1955, ASIO records.
40 Memo, Spry to Regional Directors, 22 January 1957, ASIO records.
41 Report, Defence Committee, 'A strategic basis of Australian defence policy', 8 January 1953, in Stephan Frühling, *A history of Australian strategic policy since 1945* (Canberra: Defence Publishing Service, 2009), 175, 188.
42 Minute by Defence Committee, 13 August 1953, NAA: A5954, 1464/1.
43 See John Blaxland, *The protest years: The official history of ASIO, 1963–1975* (Canberra: Allen & Unwin, 2015).

The challenge of countersubversion

As illustrated by ASIO's activities in the early Cold War, the challenge for a security service charged with countering subversion is to differentiate between attempts to undermine the government and the democratic system, and the legitimate expression of free speech in a democracy. It is in this area where ASIO has come under most criticism. Over the years, critics have levelled numerous charges against ASIO, beginning with the general one of assisting the allegedly 'fascist' Menzies Government to suppress legitimate political dissent. ASIO also has been accused of planning to intern thousands of the government's political opponents, in preparation for which ASIO conducted a 'huge' surveillance operation and put together a 'massive' archive of dossiers on unsuspecting citizens. As we have seen, however, ASIO was acting at the direction of the government.

Nonetheless, not only ACP members, but indeed anyone vaguely connected with it were under suspicion, including trade unionists, members of front organisations, public servants, writers, artists and Labor politicians. It has been claimed that many Australians were persecuted, lost their jobs and generally had their lives 'wrecked' because ASIO had secretly asserted that they were a risk to national security. In pursuing its campaign of surveillance, ASIO officers allegedly acted illegally in tapping phones, conducting electronic bugging operations, opening private mail and breaking into ACP and front organisations' premises. An element of truth can be found in many of these claims, but ASIO would argue that faced by the threat of possible war, it was critical to national security to ensure that communist sympathisers were not employed in areas where they had access to classified information. If there were doubts about a person's reliability, the doubts needed to be resolved in the Commonwealth's favour. Further, the decisions about excluding individuals from Commonwealth employment were made by the heads of the relevant government departments, not ASIO. Unfortunately, a balanced understanding has been hampered by the partisan nature of much of the existing accounts and by ASIO's strong proclivity for secrecy.

Critics have also argued that ASIO exaggerated the ACP's threat to Australian security because the party's influence declined rapidly after the 1949 coal strike. With hindsight, we can question how dangerous the threat of subversion was, considering the decline in the ACP's membership and its small vote in federal elections. But the government knew that in the first two years of the Second World War, the Communist Party had sought to undermine Australia's war effort. Even after the Nazis attacked the Soviet Union in June 1941, bringing the Soviet Union into the war on the Allied side, Australia's war effort was repeatedly disrupted by striking unionists labelled as 'extremists' or 'Communists' by non-Labour leaders.[44] The government therefore believed that unless challenged, in the event of a general war the ACP had both the capacity and the inclination to undermine the nation.

The major consequence of the Cold War was that ASIO pursued its campaign against the communists with an almost religious fervour. ASIO, the relevant government ministers and indeed a large part of the Australian population believed that Australia was threatened by a monolithic worldwide communist campaign to undermine Western societies. With this view of the world, it was therefore considered legitimate to try to find out what the ACP and its members were doing. It was also considered legitimate to keep watch on citizens who, while not necessarily members of the ACP, were seen as possibly secret communists or at least communist sympathisers.

The reduction in the intensity of the Cold War after 1953 did not reduce ASIO's work. Counterespionage, countersubversion and the vetting of government employees remained important tasks. During the subsequent years ASIO might not have warranted Menzies' claim that it was the fourth arm of Australian defence. But circumstances change, and the rise of terrorist and cyber threats in the early twenty-first century again placed internal security high in the government's priorities. Perhaps the internal security agencies were once again the fourth arm of Australian defence.

---

44 Paul Hasluck, *The government and the people, 1939–1941* (Canberra: Australian War Memorial, 1952), 586–90, 600.

4

The Korean War

Thomas Richardson

The Korean War was the product of Korean politics colliding with those of the Cold War. The peninsula, a Japanese colony from 1910, was divided into separate zones of occupation along the 38th parallel by the Soviet Union and the United States after the Japanese surrender in August 1945. This was not intended to be a permanent measure, but efforts to create a national government in 1947–48 foundered on superpower caution and intra-Korean hostility. Instead, the split hardened and gave geographic expression to the divisions within Korean politics. By the end of 1948, the communist Democratic People's Republic of Korea (DPRK) had been established in the north, and the ultranationalist Republic of Korea (ROK) in the south.[1]

Despite this hardening, neither side accepted the division as permanent. The ROK president, Syngman Rhee, bombastically declared a desire to march north; his northern counterpart, Kim Il Sung, took more concrete measures. Beginning with an uprising on the island of Cheju-do in April 1948, the Communist Party in the south waged a bitter guerrilla war first to try and prevent the formation of the ROK and then to overthrow it.[2] In 1949 the conflict escalated, as units of the Korean People's Army (KPA) and Republic of Korea Army (ROKA) began clashing along the border. Even as this went on, Kim Il Sung was pressing his Soviet patrons

---

1 William Stueck, 'The Korean War', in *The Cambridge history of the Cold War*, vol. 1, *Origins*, ed. Melvyn P Leffler and Odd Arne Westad (Cambridge: Cambridge University Press, 2010), 266–73.
2 Allan R Millett, *The Korean War* (Washington DC: Potomac Books, 2007), 9–14.

to allow an outright invasion. Josef Stalin refused Kim's requests in March 1949 and again in September, but changed his mind in early 1950. Mao Zedong also signed off on the invasion, albeit reluctantly, in mid-May.[3]

The invasion itself began in the early hours of 25 June 1950. With significant advantages in firepower and mobility over the ROKA, the KPA advanced rapidly and captured Seoul on 28 June. The reaction from the United States was swift. President Truman and his Cabinet viewed the attack as part of a broader Soviet-directed conspiracy against the entire Western world, and believed a failure to make a stand in Korea would invite aggression elsewhere.[4] On the evening of 26 June in Washington (mid-morning on 27 June in Korea) Truman authorised US air and naval forces to attack North Korean military forces anywhere below the 38th parallel. Three days later, the President agreed to the deployment of a US Regimental Combat Team to the peninsula. The United States was now firmly committed to saving the ROK.[5]

This US commitment came in the context of a widening international condemnation of the invasion. On 25 June the United Nations Security Council (UNSC) had passed Resolution 82, calling for a cessation of the invasion, the withdrawal of the KPA to the 38th parallel, and for UN members to refrain from assisting the DPRK. Resolution 82 was made possible by the absence of the Soviet Union from the UNSC, as a result of an ongoing boycott at the refusal to seat the People's Republic of China rather than the Republic of China. When it became clear this resolution was being ignored, the Security Council adopted Resolution 83 on 27 June.[6] In recommending 'that the Members of the United Nations furnish such assistance to the Republic of Korea as may be necessary to repel the armed attack and to restore international peace and security in the area', Resolution 83 created the conditions necessary for an international military coalition to protect the ROK.[7]

---

[3] Stueck, 'The Korean War', 273–74.
[4] Millet, *The Korean War*, 20–21; John Lewis Gaddis, *Strategies of containment*, revised ed. (Oxford: Oxford University Press, 2005), 107–8.
[5] Robert F Futrell, *The United States Air Force in Korea 1950–1953* (Washington DC: Office of Air Force History, 1983), 34–37.
[6] Millet, *The Korean War*, 21.
[7] United Nations Security Council Resolution 83, 27 June 1950, S/1511, at: unscr.com/en/resolutions/83.

Even in this political climate, however, Australian participation in the Korean War was by no means guaranteed. Prime Minister Robert Menzies and much of his Cabinet shared the American view that the invasion of South Korea was part of a broader communist plan directed from Moscow, and they recognised the regional implications of a communist victory. But many of them believed the proper place for Australian forces in opposing communist expansion was in Southeast Asia and the Middle East, within the traditional security architecture of the British Commonwealth. At a meeting of Cabinet on 27 June, it was agreed that the invasion of Korea 'represented only one phase of Russian aggression and that Australia's primary [objective] in the matter of opposing Communism was located in Malaya'.[8] This was not idle discussion, and at the same meeting it was decided to agree to an outstanding British request for the commitment of a Royal Australian Air Force (RAAF) bomber squadron to Malaya.[9]

The notable exception to this view of Australia's strategic orientation was Percy Spender, the Minister for External Affairs. Spender believed Australia needed a security guarantee from the United States and since becoming minister in 1949 had pursued this objective, despite the scepticism of Menzies. The outbreak of the war in Korea seemed to present as a golden opportunity. A substantial commitment of Australian forces, independent of Britain, would build political goodwill in Washington and would help clear the way for an alliance with the United States. It was this belief, as much as a desire to halt communist aggression, that drove Australian involvement in the Korean War.[10]

Spender's tactics in achieving his aims have been discussed extensively elsewhere.[11] Although the Australian Government had made the decision to withdraw Australian forces from the British Commonwealth Occupation Force (BCOF), 3 Battalion Royal Australian Regiment (3RAR), No. 77 Squadron Royal Australian Air Force, and the frigate HMAS *Shoalhaven* were all still in Japan, while *Shoalhaven*'s replacement, HMAS *Bataan,* was in Hong Kong. Menzies had agreed on 29 June to commit the *Shoalhaven* and *Bataan* to combat operations after it became clear the British Government had offered ships of its own. The next

---

8   Cabinet Minute, 27 June 1950, quoted in Robert O'Neill, *Australia in the Korean War 1950–53*, vol. 1, *Strategy and diplomacy* (Canberra: Australian War Memorial and the Australian Government Publishing Service, 1981), 48.
9   O'Neill, *Australia in the Korean War*, vol. 1, 47–49.
10   Robert O'Neill, 'The Korean War and the origins of ANZUS', in *Munich to Vietnam*, ed. Carl Bridge (Carlton: Melbourne University Press, 1991), 99–106.
11   See O'Neill, 'The Korean War and the origins of ANZUS'.

day, Spender, well aware the US Air Force (USAF) was desperate for the F-51 Mustangs flown by No. 77 Squadron, convinced Menzies that it too should be offered to the United Nations.[12]

The Minister for External Affairs saved his most audacious effort to use Australian forces to cement a security guarantee. Menzies opposed the commitment of the Australian Army to Korea, believing its proper role in the event of a more general war lay elsewhere. Spender thought otherwise, and consistently argued that an Australian ground commitment to Korea independent of Britain would be immensely well received in Washington. He got his chance on 26 July, when the Australian Government learned that the British Government was going to announce the commitment of troops to Korea by 8 pm (Australian time) that day. Menzies was overseas, sailing from the United Kingdom to the United States onboard the liner *Queen Mary*. Believing Menzies to be out of contact, Spender seized the initiative. He convinced acting prime minister Arthur Fadden and Defence minister Philip McBride of the wisdom of his ideas in time to have a bulletin announcing the commitment of Australian soldiers to Korea to be read out on the ABC's 7 pm news bulletin. Menzies was unimpressed when he learned of what had taken place, but any unhappiness was lessened by the warmth of the reception he got in Washington.[13]

The result of Spender's manoeuvring was that the Australian forces committed to Korea represented what was available, rather than being the product of a coherent long-term plan. By the end of 1950, the Australian presence in Korea consisted of 3RAR, No. 77 Squadron and associated support units, and the destroyers HMAS *Bataan* and HMAS *Warramunga*.[14] This basic structure – an infantry battalion, a fighter squadron, two destroyers or frigates and support units – changed temporarily between September 1951 and January 1952, when the aircraft carrier HMAS *Sydney* raised the number of Royal Australian Navy (RAN) ships deployed to three, and then permanently after April 1952, when a second Australian infantry battalion arrived in theatre. The need for *Sydney* was driven partly by an operational concern; HMS *Glory* needed a refit, and the Royal Navy had no aircraft carriers available to replace her. Yet the decision to send *Sydney* to Korea came in the context of a

---

12 O'Neill, *Australia in the Korean War*, vol. 1, 50–53.
13 O'Neill, 'The Korean War and the origins of ANZUS', 103–5.
14 Jeffrey Grey, *A military history of Australia* (Cambridge: Cambridge University Press, 2008), 209–10.

formal US request in February 1951 for additional troops, one that the Defence Committee felt Australia unable to respond to.[15] The subsequent commitment of a second battalion in 1952 was a purely political decision; the Defence Committee again argued that any such deployment would badly hurt Australian mobilisation efforts in the event of a wider war, but they were overruled because of a perceived need to build up political capital in Washington.[16]

The Army

The fighting in the Korean War can be divided into four stages. The first was the opening North Korean invasion, which lasted from 25 June to early September 1950. In that time the KPA succeeded in pushing UN forces into the Pusan Perimeter in the south-east of the ROK, but was unable to obtain further success. The second phase opened on 15 September, when the US X Corps landed at Inchon, to the west of Seoul. The capture of Inchon marked the start of a UN counteroffensive that routed the KPA and drove them well into the north. By 19 October the Eighth Army had captured the North Korean capital Pyongyang, and one week later the ROKA 6 Division reached the Yalu River – the border between the DPRK and the People's Republic of China.[17]

It was this rapid advance that set the stage for the third phase of the war. Apprehensive about the presence of US forces on the Chinese border and under pressure from the Soviet Union, Mao Zedong ordered Chinese forces into the war.[18] Beginning in late October 1950, the Chinese launched a series of offensives that would drive the UN forces out of the north and prompt a major crisis within the UN Command. General Douglas MacArthur wanted to expand the war onto mainland China and use atomic weapons if necessary. President Harry Truman disagreed, and when MacArthur started agitating for his policies in public and in Congress Truman fired him on 11 April 1951.[19]

---

15   O'Neill, *Australia in the Korean War*, vol. 1, 212–13.
16   O'Neill, *Australia in the Korean War*, vol. 1, 251.
17   Robert O'Neill, *Australia in the Korean War 1950–53*, vol. 2, *Combat operations* (Canberra: Australian War Memorial and the Australian Government Publishing Service, 1985), 30–33.
18   Stueck, 'The Korean War', 278.
19   Stephen R Taaffe, *MacArthur's Korean War generals* (Lawrence: University Press of Kansas, 2016), 183–84.

MacArthur's relief and the defeat of the Chinese Fifth Phase Offensive in May marked the start of the fourth and final stage of the war. Neither side had the ability to win an outright military victory on the peninsula, nor had the desire to widen the war outside it. With the frontline now roughly astride the 38th parallel, negotiations between the two sides opened on 10 July in the town of Kaesong. It would take another two years for an agreement to be reached; in the interim, fighting continued.

It was during the second phase that 3RAR entered the war in Korea, landing at Pusan on 28 September 1950. In the two months between the government's commitment of the battalion and its arrival in Korea it had worked frantically to prepare for combat. A steady flow of reinforcements, weapons and equipment arrived in Japan during August and September, as the battalion was brought up from 550 officers and men to a wartime establishment of 960.[20] Entire sub-units had to be re-established, and an intensive training program begun. In the midst of this, Lieutenant Colonel FS Walsh's time as the battalion commander expired, and he was replaced by Lieutenant Colonel CH Green. In 1945 Green had earned the distinction of becoming the youngest Australian battalion commander of the Second World War; five years later, and still only 30, he faced an entirely new challenge.[21]

By the time Green arrived on 10 September the Australian Government had already made the decision that 3RAR would operate as part of the British 27 Brigade. Based in Hong Kong, Brigadier Basil Coad possessed only the understrength 1 Battalion, Argyll and Sutherland Highlanders and 1 Battalion, Middlesex Regiment. The brigade had gone into action in the Pusan Perimeter in late August and participated in the breakout that followed the Inchon landings. The addition of 3RAR gave Coad a third manoeuvre element, but the brigade lacked adequate transportation and remained dependent on the United States for supporting arms such as artillery and armour.[22]

On 5 October the brigade, redesignated 27 Commonwealth after the arrival of the Australians, was airlifted to Seoul and placed under the command of the US 1 Cavalry Division. For the next month 3RAR participated in the advance north, fighting a major action in an apple

---

20 3RAR War Diary, 11 September 1950, Australian War Memorial (AWM): AWM 85 4/20.
21 Wayne Klintworth, 'Formation of the Royal Australian Regiment', in *Duty first: A history of the Royal Australian Regiment*, ed. David Horner and Jean Bou (Crows Nest: Allen & Unwin, 2008), 52.
22 Jeffrey Grey, 'The regiment's first war', in Horner and Bou, *Duty first*, 57.

4. THE KOREAN WAR

orchard north of Yongyu on 22 October and helping the brigade clear and hold Chongju between 25 and 27 October. Despite its heavy losses over the previous months, the KPA continued to mount a determined defence, utilising armour and artillery alongside well-dug-in and camouflaged infantry.[23] Although Australian losses during this period were relatively light, among them was Lieutenant Colonel Green. On 30 October he was wounded by a shell fragment and died two days later. His replacement was Lieutenant Colonel Walsh.[24]

Green's death coincided with the Chinese entry into the war. The Australians' first encounter with this new enemy, on 5 November, left Coad dissatisfied with Walsh's performance and led to the Australian's immediate relief.[25] The battalion's third commander within a fortnight, Major IB Ferguson, would endure a difficult first month. The events of 5 November had been part of the Chinese First Phase Offensive, little more than spoiling attack to gain a sense of UN Command strength and intentions. The main effort, the Second Phase Offensive, opened on 26 November. Within days the ROK II Corps had given way, and the Eighth Army began to withdraw.[26]

The retreat itself was a bitter affair. From the start of the conflict certain US Army units had suffered from an absence of cohesion and leadership, and these problems became all too apparent during the desperate journey south.[27] The nadir occurred on 30 November when the brigade held open a corridor for the 2 US Infantry Division to retreat through. As the 3RAR war diary noted:

> as was obvious then and as later confirmed by official US Army reports, 2nd US Division … were completely disorganized and were not withdrawing in any sort of military fashion.

So poor was American discipline that units were firing randomly as they moved through the Commonwealth position, killing a soldier from the Middlesex.[28]

---

23   See for example 3RAR War Diary, 19 October 1950, AWM: AWM 85 4/21.
24   Grey, 'The regiment's first war', 74–76.
25   Grey, 'The regiment's first war', 76–77.
26   O'Neill, *Australia in the Korean War*, vol. 2, 68.
27   Grey, 'The regiment's first war', 65.
28   3RAR War Diary, 30 November 1950, AWM: AWM 85 4/22.

Brigadier Coad had already been critical in private of US performance during the UN counteroffensive – now he was scathing. This British dissatisfaction with US performance, coming as it did during a moment of wider diplomatic crisis brought on by the Chinese entry into the war, was taken seriously in Washington. It would have been a serious blow to the UN coalition if a senior partner had expressed public dismay at the fighting ability of US troops. Ultimately, the solution lay with a more general improvement in US performance, brought about by improved leadership within the Eighth Army and a greater flow of reinforcements to frontline formations. Yet is interesting to note that 3RAR's position as part of a larger Commonwealth formation rather than an independent Australian one appears to have insulated Australia from the worst of this intra-coalition disagreement.[29]

The worst of the retreat ended on 11 December, when the brigade went into IX Corps reserve. Even this was not a rest; on 13 December 6 Platoon B Company got into a firefight with one of the guerrilla groups that continued to lurk in the rear areas of the UN Command.[30] Ten days later, General Walker, the Eighth Army commander, was killed in a road accident. His successor, General Matthew B Ridgway, succeeded in stabilising the UN line and began a series of limited counteroffensives. 3RAR participated in Operation THUNDERBOLT (25 January) and KILLER (21 February), both of which saw an overall improvement in the performance of the Eighth Army. During this period, 27 Brigade was strengthened by the arrival of 16 Field Regiment Royal New Zealand Artillery in January and 2 Battalion, Princess Patricia's Canadian Light Infantry (2PPCLI) in March.[31]

The last sequence of the third phase of the war was the Chinese Fifth Phase Offensive, which commenced on 22 April and lasted until 20 May. The opening communist attack led to the collapse of 6 ROK Division. On the afternoon of the 23 April, 27 Brigade was warned to establish a defensive position north of the village of Kapyong, across a wide valley. As ROK soldiers began retreating down the valley, 3RAR occupied Hill 504 east of the river and 2PPCLI Hill 677 to the west. A fierce fight developed early on the morning of 24 April, in front of both 3RAR's

---

29   Jeffrey Grey, *The Commonwealth armies and the Korean War: An alliance study* (Manchester; New York: Manchester University Press, 1988), 78–80, 86–87.
30   3RAR War Diary, 13 December 1950, AWM: AWM 85 4/23.
31   Grey, 'The regiment's first war', 77–80.

company positions and around its HQ. By the time 3RAR was withdrawn on the afternoon of the 24th, 32 Australians were dead, 59 had been wounded and three captured. The cost to the Chinese was much higher, but more importantly they had been prevented from breaking through the UN position.[32]

From May to September 1951, 3RAR was engaged in halting the remainder of the Chinese Fifth Phase Offensive and conducting limited UN counterattacks to restore the line. During this period, several more important administrative changes occurred. Both British battalions and the headquarters of 27 Commonwealth Brigade were replaced by new units from the United Kingdom, and the brigade consequently renamed 28 Commonwealth Brigade. The brigade was then combined with 25 Canadian and 29 British brigades and an Indian field ambulance to form 1 Commonwealth Division. At the same time, 3RAR began to experience a high rate of personnel turnover, as those who had originally served with the battalion became eligible to return to Australia. Although the battalion remained at its wartime establishment, the loss of so many experienced personnel was less than ideal.[33]

The final large, mobile battle fought by an Australian unit in Korea was the seizure of Maryang-San in early October. Operation COMMANDO was conceived as an offensive by US I Corps to improve the UN position along what became known as the Jamestown line. As part of this, 1 Commonwealth Division was assigned to seize two key hills – Kowang-San (Hill 355) and Maryang-San (Hill 317). 3RAR's role was to support the initial assault on Hill 355 and then capture Hill 317. The division's attack began on 3 October, with 3RAR assaulting their main objective two days later. Although the initial assault was successful, the Australians continued to fight around the feature until the early morning of 8 October. In capturing Maryang-San, 3RAR had destroyed an estimated two Chinese battalions, at a cost of 20 killed in action and 89 wounded. The Official Historian, Robert O'Neill, argued that 'the victory at Maryang San is probably the greatest single feat of the Australian Army during the Korean war'.[34]

---

32   Grey, 'The regiment's first war', 81–84.
33   Grey, 'The regiment's first war', 85.
34   O'Neill, *Australia in the Korean War*, vol. 2, 200.

From the end of COMMANDO in October 1951 to the ceasefire in July 1953, the war in Korea was a static one. What this meant for the Australian battalions – for 3RAR was joined by 1RAR in April 1952 – was a war of digging, patrolling and camouflage.[35] 'Static' can be a misleading term; the failure to return a war of manoeuvre did not mean, as Jeffrey Grey has pointed out, 'that the fighting did not continue, or did so at a reduced and somehow less dangerous pace'.[36] Even in the absence of major action, the insistence from US I Corps leadership that units maintain an aggressive posture – and in particular mount raids to 'snatch' prisoners – caused considerable friction with 1 Commonwealth Division. The Chinese were skilled and aggressive fighters who possessed large numbers of automatic weapons; coming to grips with them at night was an extremely dangerous business. Commonwealth commanders remained unconvinced of the utility of 'snatch' raids, but could not ignore orders from higher headquarters. It was one of the few points of operational friction in the coalition relationship in the final two years of the war.[37]

The arrival of a second Australian battalion within 28 Brigade meant that Australian personnel were now in the majority, and so command of the brigade went to an Australian. The first such officer was Brigadier Thomas Daly, who took command in July 1952; his successor, Brigadier JGN Wilton, arrived in March 1953 and held the position until the ceasefire. Daly took the opportunity to put Australian officers into what was an entirely British headquarters, and exercise his own command style. Having a dominion officer in charge of British battalions was an unusual arrangement and one that was not entirely well received, but not to the extent that it impacted operational effectiveness.[38]

The Australian battalions rotated again in April 1953, with 2RAR replacing 1RAR.[39] Three months later, the ceasefire came into effect. The sudden transition from war to peace (albeit a fragile one) was startling. In the days leading up to the ceasefire, the Chinese fiercely bombarded Australian forward positions and mounted strong attacks on the neighbouring 1 US Marine Division, which were successfully repulsed. The ceasefire was signed at 10:00 am on 27 July 1953 and went into effect at 10:00 pm

---

35   Grey, 'The regiment's first war', 89.
36   Grey, 'The regiment's first war', 88.
37   Jeffrey Grey, *A soldier's soldier: A biography of Lieutenant General Sir Thomas Daly* (Cambridge; Port Melbourne: Cambridge University Press, 2013), 79–80.
38   Grey, *A soldier's soldier*, 76–78.
39   O'Neill, *Australia in the Korean War*, vol. 2, 216–19.

on the same day. Just over 12 hours later, 3RAR's intelligence officer, Lieutenant JM Mathers, toured one of the Marine positions. The ferocity of the Chinese bombardment was reflected in the fact most of the bunkers and trenches had been destroyed, and there were around 70 Chinese bodies scattered in front of the defences. Yet amid this carnage, Mathers noted the 'very young' Chinese stretcher-bearers recovering casualties 'were friendly towards us'.[40] It was an apt end for a limited war.

No. 77 Squadron at war

Even before it was formally committed to combat by the Australian Government on 30 June, No. 77 Squadron Royal Australian Air Force was in high demand. Unlike the jet-powered F-80C Shooting Star operated by USAF squadrons in Japan, the F-51 Mustang flown by the Australians had the range to loiter over Korea and the ability to operate from temporary strips on the peninsula.[41] As early as 26 June, the US Fifth Air Force was asking if Australian Mustangs were available to provide air cover for the evacuation of US citizens from Seoul. So intense was the desire for Mustangs that a week after the Australian Government agreed to commit No. 77 Squadron, the USAF decided to convert six jet squadrons in Japan back to the F-51.[42]

This need for Mustangs, and the worsening military situation, helps explain the intensive operations of No. 77 in the opening months of the war. The squadron flew its first sorties over Korea on 2 July and its first strike mission three days later.[43] A routine quickly emerged for No. 77 Squadron. Each day four flights of four Mustangs would take off from Iwakuni in Japan and land at Taegu, a makeshift strip within UN lines. From there they would fly anything up to six sorties in a single day, refuelling and rearming where necessary, before returning to Iwakuni in the evening.[44] It was an intense schedule for the Australians, with each day lasting from around 4:15 am to 6:30 pm, and flying taking place most days.[45] As the North Korean air force had largely been destroyed, the

---

40   3RAR War Diary, 28 July 1953, AWM: AWM85 4/55.
41   Futrell, *The United States Air Force in Korea 1950–1953*, 68.
42   Futrell, *The United States Air Force in Korea 1950–1953*, 70.
43   Alan Stephens, *Going solo: The Royal Australian Air Force, 1946–1971* (Canberra: Australian Government Publishing Service, 1995), 225–26.
44   Stephens, *Going solo,* 226.
45   Richard Cresswell, interview, 17 September 2003, Australians at War Film Archive, No. 582.

missions were focused on close air support of UN troops, and interdiction of communist supply lines. With their distinctive 'Dropkick' callsign, No. 77 became a familiar presence for the beleaguered soldiers of the Eighth Army.[46]

Even without a serious enemy air threat, or the vast amounts of light flak that would come to cover North Korea in the static phase of the war, the levels of danger were high for the Australian pilots. Ground attack missions required skilful flying, as pilots went into dives at low level to ensure accurate delivery of ordinance. Casualties were inevitable. On 7 July Squadron Leader Graham Strout, Spence's deputy, was killed during a raid on Samchok; Spence himself was killed when his Mustang failed to pull out of a dive on 9 September.[47]

Spence's death occurred as the UN forces began their long journey north, and No. 77 Squadron followed close behind. In mid-October the squadron moved, along with the USAF Mustang group, to Pohang, and again a month later to Hamhung in North Korea. The squadron's stay north of the 38th parallel was only brief, however; with the Chinese steadily driving UN forces back, the Australians relocated to Pusan East on 3 December. Throughout this period, and until the squadron was withdrawn to re-equip with the jet-powered Gloster Meteor in April 1951, a steady operational tempo was maintained.[48]

The emergence of the MiG-15 in Korean skies in November 1950 was the prompt for Australian authorities to seek a replacement for the Mustang. Flown by Soviet pilots, the MiGs had startled UN observers with performance levels that were superior to every UN fighter then in theatre.[49] It was quickly made clear to the RAAF that its first preference, the North American F-86 Sabre, would not be available until 1954. Instead it was able to secure 36 Meteor Mk VIIIs from Britain. Although it was powered by twin jet engines, the straight-winged Meteor had first debuted in combat in 1944 and was a clear generation behind the MiG-15 and the F-86. While aware of this, senior officers within the USAF and

---

46   Milton Cottee, interview, 19 September 2003, Australians at War Film Archive, No. 863.
47   Stephens, *Going solo*, 227.
48   Stephens, *Going solo*, 228–31.
49   Douglas C Dildy and Warren E Thompson, *F-86 Sabre vs MiG-15: Korea 1950–53* (Oxford: Osprey Publishing, 2013), 75–76.

RAF did not believe the gap between the Meteor and the MiG-15 was so great as to make the former unsuitable in an air-to-air role. It would be up to No. 77 Squadron to put this idea to the test.[50]

In the event, the gap would prove too great. A series of dogfights between 29 August and 5 September 1951 left one Meteor destroyed and two damaged, for no losses on the Soviet side. The commander of No. 77, Wing Commander Gordon Steege, requested that the Meteors be limited to operations south of the Chongchon River.[51] This prompted some disquiet amongst the upper echelons of the RAF and USAF, who were concerned by the political implications of limiting Meteor usage at a time when a swathe of NATO air forces were being equipped with the type. Senior British and American officers believed that Steege had thrown in the towel far too early and argued that, while acknowledging the limitations of the Meteor, deficiencies in Australian tactics and training were to blame for the poor results.[52] Steege, for his part, maintained that the gap in performance was simply too big for the Meteor to do anything but try and survive against a competently flown MiG.[53]

Any lingering doubts were settled on 1 December 1951, when three Meteors were destroyed in a dogfight by MiGs of 176 GvIAP (the *Gvardeyskiy Istrebitelniy Aviatsionniy Polk* – Guards Fighter Air Regiment), with no loss on the Soviet side.[54] In the aftermath the Australians were immediately relegated to air defence tasks. It was a bitter blow to professional pride made even more difficult by the fact that air defence duties were, in the words of a contemporary Australian report, 'a "soul destroying" task at the best of times'.[55] It also created a certain degree of tension within the coalition. Airfield space for jet units was at a premium in Korea, and No. 77 was one of just three squadrons based at Kimpo. The USAF began threatening to evict the squadron for a more useful unit. Finding an

---

50 Stephens, *Going solo*, 231–32.
51 Stephens, *Going solo*, 235.
52 Ministry of Defence, London to British Embassy Tokyo, Bouchier from Chiefs of Staff, 12 September 1951, UK National Archives (TNA): AIR 8/1709; Weyland to Johnson, 30 September 1951, TNA: AIR 8/1709; British Embassy Tokyo to Ministry of Defence, London, Chiefs of Staff from Bouchier, 19 September 1951, TNA: AIR 8/1709.
53 'No. 77 (I/F) Squadron Monthly Tactical Report No. 3/51', n.d., TNA: AIR 8/1709.
54 'No. 77 Squadron Tactical Report for the period 1 Nov 51 to 15 Dec 51', 16 January 1952, National Archives of Australia (NAA): A11250, 28/17/AIR; Igor Seidov, *Red devils over the Yalu: A chronicle of Soviet aerial operations in the Korean War 1950–53* (Solihull: Helion & Company, 2014), 273.
55 'No. 77 (I.F.) Squadron – Tactical Report for the period 15 Dec 51 to 15 Jan 52', 21 February 1952, NAA: A11250, 28/17/AIR.

expanded role for the Meteors now became not just a matter of restoring pride and unit morale, but also ensuring the squadron remained a valued part of the UN coalition.[56]

The answer came with Wing Commander RT Susans, who succeeded Steege as commander of the squadron at the end of December 1951. Susans pressed for the Meteors to be fitted with rails for unguided rockets and trialled in a ground attack role. An initial sortie on 8 January proved to be a success, and the remainder of the squadron quickly transitioned into the role. The ability to generate over 1,000 sorties a month, at a time when the USAF was conducting a series of massive campaigns designed to destroy communist logistics networks across the peninsula, was also welcome.[57]

The switch to a ground attack role did not mean the complete end of encounters with MiGs, however. When necessary, the Meteors continued to be tasked in escort or fighter roles that invited the potential for air combat. From the start of 1952 to the armistice in July 1953, No. 77 Squadron would claim three MiG-15s destroyed and a further two damaged, with only one Meteor damaged in return.[58] Yet overall air-to-air combat remained a rarity for Meteor pilots after December 1951, and the majority of an individual pilot's tour in Korea would be spent attacking ground targets.[59]

Some Australian pilots would argue after the war that the success against MiGs in 1952–53 showed that Steege's decision had been premature and that with better training and tactics the Meteor could have given a better account of itself – thus avoiding the entire unfortunate episode. Yet it is hard in retrospect to criticise Steege's actions. As he noted in early September 1951, the MiG's higher Mach number meant it could be controlled at higher speeds than the Meteor and thus – if competently flown – dictate the entire engagement. The aircraft shot down by the Australians in 1952–53 appear to have been piloted by inexperienced Chinese rather than Soviet flyers who were unaware of this key performance advantage.[60] Even Air Vice Marshal Cecil Bouchier, the senior RAF officer in Korea

---

56 Stephens, *Going solo*, 237.
57 Stephens, *Going solo*, 237–38.
58 David Wilson, 'Appendix 3: Aerial balance sheet', in *Lion over Korea: 77 Fighter Squadron RAAF 1950–53* (Belconnen: Banner Books, 1994).
59 Stephens, *Going solo*, 238.
60 Seidov, *Red devils over the 38th parallel*, 275–76.

and a strong critic of Steege, cautioned his superiors in London from drawing 'false conclusions' from the Meteor renaissance in May 1952: 'the MIG 15 can always dictate the fight and it has a superior performance which should make it impossible for a Meteor ever to shoot it down in equal combat'.[61]

Steege's decision not only reflected this basic technical reality but also an understanding that the RAAF simply could not sustain the level of attrition experienced by No. 77 Squadron in late 1951.[62] This in turn reflected a basic unpreparedness on the part of the RAAF for active participation in a high-intensity conflict.[63] Steege was left trying to balance Australia's strategic objective of garnering American approval with the operational reality that his squadron could not continue to do what was asked of it. While Susans ultimately crafted an acceptable solution by converting the Meteor to a ground attack role, the fact remained the government's goals had diverged from what was possible because of a failure of capability.

The Navy

Like the other two services, the initial commitment of the RAN to the Korean War was governed by what was available. The *Tribal*-class destroyer HMAS *Bataan* had left Sydney on 31 May to relieve the modified *River*-class frigate *Shoalhaven* on BCOF duties. When the Menzies Government authorised both ships to be put at UN disposal on 29 June, *Bataan* was en route to Kure from Hong Kong and *Shoalhaven* was in Kure. The latter was put to immediate use, escorting a US ammunition ship into Pusan on 1 July. When *Bataan* arrived on 6 July, she too was put to work escorting convoys to Pusan, and enforcing the UN blockade of the western coast.[64]

These tasks lacked obvious glamour but were crucial to the war in Korea. Although North Korea's navy amounted to a handful of ex-Kriegsmarine torpedo boats and ex-Soviet submarine chasers, an audacious attempt to capture Pusan from the sea on the first night of the invasion showed they

---

61 British Embassy Tokyo to Air Ministry London, 'For Chiefs of Air Staff from Bouchier', 10 May 1952, TNA: AIR 8/1709.
62 'No. 77 Squadron Tactical Report for the period 1 Nov 51 to 15 Dec 51', 16 January 1952, NAA: A11250 28/17/AIR; Weyland to Johnson, 30 September 1951, TNA: AIR 8/1709.
63 Stephens, *Going solo*, 244.
64 'HMAS Shoalhaven, Report of Proceedings, July 1950', 7 August 1950, AWM: AWM78 313/3; 'HMAS Bataan, Report of Proceedings, July 1950', 7 August 1950, AWM: AWM78 58/3.

appreciated the potential of sea power.⁶⁵ The entire UN effort in Korea rested on the ability to supply and reinforce the Eighth Army from the sea; securing these lines of communication was thus paramount. As it became clear the communist naval threat was minimal, the range of missions for UN naval forces rapidly expanded. Naval elements conducted amphibious landings, evacuations and raids. Gunfire support missions to interdict enemy supply lines or in direct support of UN troops were routine. US and British aircraft carriers conducted strikes up and down the peninsula, and screening them became an important task for other UN units.⁶⁶

It was into this environment that *Bataan* and *Warramunga*, which replaced *Shoalhaven* at the end of August, operated. *Bataan* had been part of the force that screened the landings of 1 Cavalry Division at Pohang Dong on 18 July, and both destroyers were part of the covering force for the Inchon landings in mid-September.⁶⁷ So rapid was the UN advance that by the start of November both destroyers found themselves, along with HMCS *Cayuga, Athabaskan* and *Sioux,* and USS *Forest B. Royal,* blockading the Yalu Gulf. Yet within days UN forces began to retreat, and both destroyers were part of the evacuation of Chinnampo on 5 December. By the end of the month, the Australians were back where they had started in September: off Inchon, where *Bataan* provided daily gunfire support to 25 Infantry Division.⁶⁸

As the frontline stabilised in early 1951, both Australian destroyers returned to what had become routine duties: screening larger British and American vessels, enforcing the blockade and providing gunfire support for troops ashore. *Bataan* was relieved by the frigate HMAS *Murchison* in May 1951, *Warramunga* by the new destroyer HMAS *Anzac* in August. In total, four RAN frigates and four RAN destroyers served in Korea, with all four destroyers completing two tours. The operations of HMAS *Tobruk* in the war's final month were as typical as any. She began the month escorting the light carrier HMS *Ocean,* spent several days replenishing in Saesbo, then conducted a war patrol on the east coast, where she enforced the blockade, conducted bombardments of communist installations and

---

65 Thomas J Cutler, 'Sea power and defense of the Pusan Pocket' in *The U.S. Navy in the Korean War,* ed. Edward J Marolda (Naval Institute Press, 2013), 16–17.
66 Cutler, 'Sea power and defense of the Pusan Pocket', 17–30.
67 Tom Frame, *No pleasure cruise: The story of the Royal Australian Navy* (Sydney: Allen & Unwin, 2004), 210–11.
68 'HMAS Bataan, Report of Proceedings, December 1950', 5 January 1951, AWM: AWM78 58/3.

4. THE KOREAN WAR

shore batteries, sank a junk suspected of minelaying, operated in support of guerrilla groups on offshore islands and searched for a downed USAF bomber crew.[69]

While these tasks became routine, they were far from safe or easy. *Bataan* fired the first shots of the Navy's war in Korea on 1 August 1950 when, while in company of the cruiser HMS *Belfast*, she was engaged by a shore battery near Haeju, northwest of Inchon.[70] Communist gunners proved more than willing to trade blows with UN ships, and while Australia's ships suffered only a few hits throughout the war many of their compatriots were not so lucky. Mines also represented a major threat, both inshore and at sea. HMAS *Bataan* recorded a typical event in April 1951:

> On another occasion whilst screening the carriers in bad visibility our 'next ahead' 'ATHABASKAN' reported cheerfully over T.B.S. [Talk Between Ships] that he had just sighted a floating mine directly ahead of 'BATAAN' (DD). The few moments that elapsed until the mine was sighted were anxious ones but, with this prior warning, the danger was easily avoided and the mine was sunk by gunfire a minute or two later.[71]

Beyond mines and shore batteries, the other great threat to Australian ships were local conditions. Korea's west coast was characterised by 'shallow waters, extensive sandbanks, rapid tidal currents and narrow channels'.[72] Combined with Korea's subarctic weather and the threat of hidden shore batteries and mines, patrols demanded a high level of seamanship from Australian crews at all times.

The most extreme example of the way in which enemy action and navigational hazards could combine to endanger Australian ships was HMAS *Murchison*'s time in the Han estuary. Conceived in July 1951, Operation HAN aimed to 'to probe forward as far as navigation would allow, into the HAN RIVER, to demonstrate Allied control of this area'.[73] The audience for this demonstration was the negotiators at Kaesong, with UN naval commanders hoping that sound of gunfire in the river

---

69 'HMAS Tobruk, Report of Proceedings, July 1953', 31 July 1953, AWM: AWM78 343/2.
70 Cutler, 'Sea power and defense of the Pusan Pocket', 20–21.
71 'HMAS Bataan, Report of Proceedings, April 1951', 5 May 1951, AWM: AWM78 58/3.
72 Anthony Cooper, *HMAS Bataan, 1952: An Australian warship in the Korean War* (Sydney: UNSW Press, 2010), 68–69.
73 'HMAS Murchison, Report of Proceedings, July 1951', 8 August 1951, AWM: AWM78 228/1.

would be able to be heard at the negotiating table.[74] Responsibility fell on Task Group 95.1 (TG 95.1), which consisted of a mixture of British, New Zealand, Australian and Korean frigates. Rear-Admiral Alan Scott-Moncrieff, of the UK Royal Navy, who commanded the Commonwealth Task Group, was sceptical of the value of the operation, but it went ahead anyway.[75]

From the outset the operation was demanding, with the frigates having to send out boats and survey parties in an effort to find channels through the mud flats to allow them to close with the enemy.[76] Initial enemy resistance was light, but on 28 September *Murchison* was ambushed as she completed her turn at anchor to return down the river. Fire came from anti-tank guns, heavy machine guns, bazookas and small arms in concealed position. So close was the distance that the Australians replied over open sights, with weapons under individual control. When a rain squall came in, *Murchison* was forced to anchor for fear of running aground; when the rain cleared a cable party had to raise the anchor while totally exposed, and then gunfire resumed.[77] Despite being hit numerous times *Murchison* suffered only a handful of light wounds and the loss of a Bofors gun. An even more intense ambush two days later resulted in one serious casualty, and Operation HAN ended shortly after. Despite the volume of enemy fire on both occasions, the captain of *Murchison*, Lieutenant Commander (later Commodore) Dollard, remained convinced the biggest threat of his ship had been the tides and mudflats.

The multinational command arrangements in Korea also caused some friction for the RAN, at least initially. Australian commanders found the orders from American commanders extremely detailed, so much so that they choked off initiative and were hard to comprehend or process in the time available. American signals and tactical procedure publications were so numerous that they presented problems of compliance and storage.[78] Although the issue of detailed orders had also been present in the Second

---

74 Alistair Cooper, 'The Korean War era', in *The Royal Australian Navy: A history*, ed. David Stevens (Melbourne: Oxford University Press, 2006), 175.
75 Cooper, 'The Korean War era', 175.
76 'HMAS Murchison, Report of Proceedings, July 1951', 8 August 1951, AWM: AWM78 228/1.
77 Commodore Allen Nelson Dollard DSC RAN (Rtd) interviewed by Lieutenant Commander Tony Hughes RANR, 22 November 2002, AWM: AWMS02803, 16.
78 O'Neill, *Australia in the Korean War*, vol. 2, 417–18.

4. THE KOREAN WAR

World War, the passage of five years was enough to erase operational experience of it, and commanders had to readjust.[79] By mid-1951 the captain of HMAS *Bataan* was reporting that

> during the past few months it has been apparent that the United Nations Navy in Korea has been operating more and more as a composite force using common doctrines and standardized procedures with complete success … the stage has now been reached when it is the rule and not the exception to operate ships drawn from the United States and British Commonwealth Navies together in units as small as Task Elements with the certain knowledge that they will work as an efficient and happy team.[80]

Even the presence of ships from non-English-speaking navies, such as HMNS *Piet Hein*, was handled smoothly.[81]

The one significant departure from the RAN pattern of destroyer and frigate operations was the deployment of the light carrier HMAS *Sydney*. Carrying an air group of 22 Sea Fury fighters and 12 Firefly attack aircraft, between 4 October 1951 and 25 January 1952 she conducted seven war patrols, primarily off the west coast.[82] Typical missions for the air group included combat air patrol, spotting for naval gunnery, search and rescue, and strike missions. It was the latter sorties that were the most dangerous. Like their RAAF counterparts, Navy pilots flew a mixture of close air support and interdiction missions against targets that were increasingly smothered in light flak. *Sydney* lost 10 aircraft to enemy action and another three to accidents, with three pilots killed.

The experience of the *Sydney* and her air group have come to dominate accounts of RAN participation in Korea. As the only Australian aircraft carrier to serve in combat operations in any war, she holds an obvious fascination for those interested in Australian naval affairs. Yet in retrospect the significance of her deployment lay in the circumstances in which it came about. It was yet another demonstration of the way in which the Australian Government was keenly aware of the political consequences of its decisions regarding force structure in Korea, and reacted accordingly.

---

79 O'Neill, *Australia in the Korean War*, vol. 2, 417–18; Frame, *No pleasure cruise*, 212–13.
80 'HMAS Bataan, Report of Proceedings, May 1951', 1 June 1951, AWM: AWM78 58/3.
81 'HMAS Condamine Report of Proceedings, December 1952', 1 January 1953, AWM: AWM78 88/3.
82 Cooper, 'The Korean War era', 177.

Conclusion

Australia entered the Korean War looking to fulfil two major objectives. The first was to use the commitment of Australian forces to clear the way towards a security pact with the United States. This was accomplished in September 1951, with the signing of the Australia, New Zealand and United States (ANZUS) agreement. The second was to preserve the independence of the Republic of Korea and to demonstrate the willingness of Western nations to resist what Canberra perceived to be monolithic communist aggression. In some senses this objective was largely achieved by mid-1951, when it became clear to all parties that there would be no outright military victory on the peninsula; but it was not consolidated until July 1953, with the signing of the armistice.

Crucially, there was no tension between these two objectives, and by actively participating in the fighting Australian commanders worked towards both. Alliance warfare delivered its share of irritations, but Australian forces were insulated from these to an extent by their participation in Commonwealth formations on land and at sea. The controversy around the role of No. 77 Squadron in the second half of 1951 did show that the commitment of Australian forces came with potential political downsides. Yet this issue was solved relatively quickly, and in retrospect while British and American commanders hinted at Australian underperformance, their primary concern was the reputation of the Gloster Meteor.

Australian success in Korea came at a significant human cost: 306 Australians were killed in action across all three services, a further 32 died in accidents or of illness, and 1,216 were wounded. Twenty-nine Australians ended up as prisoners of war, where they were subject to brutal treatment and attempted indoctrination; one prisoner was treated so badly they died. Although ultimately overshadowed by Vietnam in popular memory, it was a hefty price to pay for guarantees of Australian security.

Part 2. Planning for and fighting in Southeast Asia, 1955–65

5

Planning for war in Southeast Asia: The Far East Strategic Reserve, 1955–66

Tristan Moss[1]

During the early Cold War, Australia expected to fight any global war alongside the British. Somewhat ironically, while it was increasingly independent from Britain in foreign policy and security planning, unlike during previous wars, Australia planned to fight any future war with its units integrated into Commonwealth formations. The cooperation of Australian forces with the British and other Commonwealth countries in the Korean, Malayan and Borneo conflicts reflected the close strategic and operational integration that built on the experiences of the two world wars, and the strategic desire of both Britain and Australia to engage the other in the efficient pursuit of their own security. The integration of forces at the formation level also reflected the smaller scale of people and resources involved. From 1955, these efforts were centred on the Far East Strategic Reserve (FESR), a force that contained British, New Zealand and Australian troops, aircraft and ships and was based in Malaya and Singapore.[2] The FESR was Australia's first permanent peacetime overseas deployment, and ultimately stretched to decades. The FESR was both a symbol, in that it represented the Commonwealth's commitment to

---

1   The author would like to thank the Australian Army History Unit for the award of a grant that assisted in this research.
2   There seems to be no accepted name for the FESR, even in archival documents: some authors include a reference to the Commonwealth or British Commonwealth in the acronym.

defending the region, and a tangible contribution to Commonwealth Cold War aims, in its availability to fight wars in Malaya and Borneo and to ensure that the Commonwealth was 'at the table' with the United States and with the newly formed Southeast Asia Treaty Organization (SEATO). For thousands of Australian service personnel, it was a central and unique part of their service in the 10 years prior to Vietnam, shaping their experiences, and also the focus of the services of which they formed a part.

Creating the FESR

At the strategic level, postwar Commonwealth military cooperation was managed through coordination between the various Chiefs of Staff in each nation. The British Commonwealth Occupation Force, Japan was planned and overseen through senior military representatives from the United Kingdom, Australia, India and New Zealand. These meetings led directly to the creation of the ANZAM defence planning system in August 1949 (named after the Australia, New Zealand and Malayan area it was intended to safeguard). The organisation was limited in its early aims: to secure the maritime approaches to Australia and New Zealand.[3] ANZAM did not initially commit its members to particular troop numbers in the event of conflict, which was well enough for Australia, which had few permanent forces with which to make such a promise.[4] Australian strategic thinking also assumed that, in the event of war, a third Australian Imperial Force would be sent to the Middle East.[5] The result, to use historian Raffi Gregorian's phrase, was that ANZAM was 'a fairly moribund organization for the first years of its existence', as the Commonwealth's strategic direction in Asia was concentrated on the Korean War.[6]

---

3   Peter Edwards with Gregory Pemberton, *The official history of Australia's involvement in Southeast Asian conflicts 1948–1975*, vol. 1, *Crises and commitments: The politics and diplomacy of Australia's involvement in Southeast Asian conflicts 1948–1965* (North Sydney: Allen & Unwin in association with the Australian War Memorial, 1992), 61.
4   Hiroyuki Umetsu, 'The origins of the British Commonwealth Strategic Reserve: The UK proposal to revitalise ANZAM and the increased Australian defence commitment to Malaya', *Australian Journal of Politics & History* 50, no. 4 (December 1, 2004): 510, doi.org/10.1111/j.1467-8497.2004.00350.x.
5   DM Horner, *Strategic command: General Sir John Wilton and Australia's Asian wars* (Melbourne: Oxford University Press, 2005), 141.
6   Raffi Gregorian, *The British Army, the Gurkhas and Cold War strategy in the Far East, 1947–1954* (London: Palgrave Macmillan UK, 2002), 117, doi.org/10.1057/9780230287167.

Between August and October 1953, British, Australian and New Zealand military planners met in Melbourne as part of the ANZAM arrangements, and in particular to discuss the relationship's future. This meeting laid the foundation for Commonwealth cooperation in the region for the next decade and a half. Key among their agreements was the creation of a Commonwealth force that might respond quickly to threats in the region. This proposal reflected Britain's concerns about its own ability to provide troops to hotspots around the world, with the concurrent belief that the situation in Southeast Asia was deteriorating. In a letter to Menzies formally suggesting the reserve, the British Minister for Defence, Lord Alexander, wrote that 'the United Kingdom will be prepared to play its part. But, as you will understand … there are limits to what we can do'.[7]

The FESR was also an effort to draw Australia and New Zealand into Commonwealth (rather than US) defence agreements.[8] With all countries agreeing to the new arrangements, ANZAM became a permanent peacetime organisation, rather than one that would be staffed in the event of war. This decision also put an end to the concept of sending Australian troops to the Middle East in the event of global war.[9] A new, more closely integrated ANZAM Chiefs of Staff Committee assumed responsibility for all planning for the defence of the Malayan area, as well as the Australian and New Zealand maritime areas.[10] That this committee was based in Melbourne was further evidence of the British desire to draw the Australians deeper into the organisation, and to divest themselves of as much of the burden as possible.

For its part, the Australian Defence Committee saw ANZAM as an 'evolution in British Commonwealth Defence', given that now Australia would focus almost entirely on Southeast Asia in its strategic thinking.[11] The Defence Committee believed that the creation of a strategic reserve conformed with Australian government policy to, as the Defence Minister

---

7   Letter, Alexander to Menzies, 29 June 1953, National Archives of Australia (NAA): A5949, 1464/1.
8   Umetsu, 'The origins of the British Commonwealth Strategic Reserve', 517.
9   Edwards with Pemberton, *Crises and commitments*, 163; Robert O'Neill, *Australia in the Korean War 1950–53*, vol. 1, *Strategy and diplomacy* (Canberra: Australian War Memorial and the Australian Government Publishing Service, 1981), 347.
10 'Report on discussions between the Chief of the Imperial General Staff, the Australian Defence Committee and the New Zealand Chief of the General Staff', 21 October 1953, NAA: A5949, 1464/1; Umetsu, 'The origins of the British Commonwealth Strategic Reserve', 523.
11 'ANZAM as a regional arrangement: views of Australian Defence Committee', October 1953, NAA: A5949, 1464/1; letter, Alexander to Menzies, 12 October 1954, NAA: A5949, 1464/1.

stated to parliament in February 1952, check communist aggression while also ensuring that Australia made a tangible contribution in support of 'our powerful friends and to the Allied strategic starting point, should war occur'.[12] More broadly, the FESR, as tangible evidence of ANZAM's capabilities, was a means by which Britain, and the Commonwealth, could wield influence in US strategic planning. Having been kept out of the Australia, New Zealand and United States (ANZUS) Treaty, and conscious of the need for American support in any global war, the British sought to position ANZAM as the Commonwealth regional command structure that would fit within US direction should the Cold War turn hot; Commonwealth countries would work through ANZAM as a collective, rather than individually with the United States, thereby giving 'the ANZAM nations an effective voice at both political and strategic levels'.[13] Confirmed by the contributing nations in a 1955 London prime ministers meeting, the FESR was a force that was as much a tool of politics and diplomacy as it was a military and strategic one.[14]

The structures proposed in 1953 stayed largely stable throughout the FESR's existence. The force was based around a brigade of infantry, with supporting units. The experience of integrating Commonwealth battalions in the Korean War was fresh in the planners' minds, reflected in the decision to reraise the 28 Commonwealth Brigade that had served in last stages of Korea.[15] Australia provided a single battalion of the Royal Australian Regiment (RAR), with the remaining two battalions coming from the British Army. Australia also committed to maintaining another battalion at high readiness in Australia for use in Malaya should an emergency arise.[16] In 1957, New Zealand replaced one of the brigade's British battalions with their own, making it a truly Commonwealth force.[17] Other services were represented in the reserve. The Royal Australian Navy (RAN) provided two frigates permanently based in

---

12   Joint Planning Committee, 'Formation of a Far East Strategic Reserve', 13 August 1953, NAA: A5949, 1464/1. See also Umetsu, 'The origins of the British Commonwealth Strategic Reserve', 522.
13   'Report on discussions between the Chief of the Imperial General Staff, the Australian Defence Committee and the New Zealand Chief of the General Staff', 21 October 1953, NAA: A5949, 1464/1.
14   L MacLean, *ANZIM to ANZUK: An historical outline of ANZAM* (Canberra: Government Publishing Service, 1992), 16.
15   'Formation of a Far East Strategic Reserve in Malaya: Paper by the Australian Joint Planning Committee', 13 August 1953, NAA: A5949, 1464/1.
16   'Commonwealth Far East Strategic Reserve: Composition of Australian Contribution', no date, A5949, 1464/1, NAA.
17   Christopher Pugsley, *From Emergency to Confrontation: The New Zealand armed forces in Malaya and Borneo, 1949–1966* (Melbourne: Oxford University Press, 2003), 123.

Southeast Asia. An aircraft carrier was also allocated to the FESR, but given that Australian only had two, this ship rotated to Southeast Asia to exercise for a handful of months each year, and then returned to Australia for maintenance and training. Finally, the Royal Australian Air Force (RAAF) supplied three squadrons: two fighter squadrons of sixteen F-86 Sabres each, and a single bomber squadron of eight Canberras. These were based at Butterworth on the west coast of the Malay Peninsula, which needed to be substantially upgraded, necessitating the deployment of an airfield construction squadron alongside other maintenance and administrative staff.[18]

Australian forces in the FESR

While small numbers of Australian soldiers and airmen had been in Malaya since 1950, the first large contingents arrived to join the FESR in 1955.[19] The bulk of 2RAR and supporting units arrived in Penang in October, along with over 300 members of the RAAF who started work building Butterworth airfield. The destroyers HMAS *Arunta* and HMAS *Warramunga*, already in Malaya for ANZAM exercises, assumed their Strategic Reserve duties in June 1955.[20] While the British already had significant peacetime forces in Malaya, largely to fight the Emergency, such a force was a departure for Australia, which had only six years previously created the permanent Army. This was Australia's first permanent overseas deployment, and would amount to around 4,500 soldiers, sailors and airmen and would last until the 1970s.[21]

Australian forces came under the direction of the British Defence Coordinating Committee (Far East), the BDCC(FE). A civilian–military organisation, the BDCC(FE) was chaired by the British Commissioner-General for Southeast Asia and the three British service commanders in

---

18   Alan Stephens, *The Australian centenary history of defence*, vol. 2, *The Royal Australian Air Force* (Melbourne: Oxford University Press, 2002), 249.
19   Some units had been on loan to Far Eastern Land Forces (FARELF) , such as No 1 Detachment 101 Wireless Troop, and Lincoln bombers and Dakota transports had participated in the Emergency. Peter Dennis and Jeffrey Grey, *The official history of Australia's involvement in Southeast Asian conflicts 1948–1975*, vol. 5, *Emergency and Confrontation: Australian military operations in Malaya and Borneo 1950–1966* (St Leonards: Allen & Unwin in association with the Australian War Memorial, 1996), 77–78.
20   Jeffrey Grey, *The official history of Australia's involvement in Southeast Asian conflicts 1948–1975*, vol. 7, *Up top: The Royal Australian Navy and Southeast Asian conflicts, 1955–1972* (St Leonards: Allen & Unwin in association with the Australian War Memorial, 1998), 25.
21   Ibid.

the region. Australia and New Zealand were involved in decision-making only when the committee considered matters relating to the ANZAM area, through the High Commissioners in Malaya and the ANZAM Defence Committee in Australia. After much debate in Britain, the committee structure was disbanded in 1962, to be replaced with a single Commander-in-Chief for the Far East; the organisation they oversaw was known as Far East Command (FEC).[22]

28 Commonwealth Brigade itself fell under the purview of Far Eastern Land Forces (FARELF). From 1955, the use of Australian forces was subject to restrictions placed on it by the Australian Government: the Australian Cabinet, for instance, emphasised that the Australian component was not to be used in aid to the civil power and ensured that this was inserted into the directive to the British commander.[23] It was telling that the directive to the unified commander also instructed him 'to preserve our [Britain's] links with Australia and New Zealand, particularly in ANZAM, and to contribute to their forward defence'.[24]

The commitment of so much of Australia's combat power to the FESR allowed for excellent, and hitherto unparalleled, peacetime training not available in Australia. The opportunity to train was embraced by the RAN, for whom co-location with the Far East Fleet provided access to a far larger range of training activities not available in Australia, including anti-submarine warfare exercises; although the Department of the Navy was, at times, frustrated by what it saw as an overemphasis on training by Australian officers with the Strategic Reserve at the expense of other duties.[25] The Army also saw service in Southeast Asia as an opportunity to learn. In its assessment of the Strategic Reserve in 1953, the Joint Planning Committee believed that 'inclusion of Army units in the Reserve would enable them to gain experience in a new theatre and one in which the Army might be engaged in a global war'. The result would be the creation of a cohort of officers with knowledge of the region and the type of war that might be fought there.[26]

---

22   Ibid., 26–27.
23   'Minute by ANZAM Defence Committee meeting held on 28th July 1955', 28 July 1955, NAA: A5954, 1467/9.
24   'Directive for the Commander-in-Chief Far East', 1962, NAA: A1945, 287/2/13.
25   Grey, *Up top*, 30.
26   'Formation of a Far East Strategic Reserve in Malaya: Paper by the Australian Joint Planning Committee', 13 August 1953, NAA: A5949, 1464/1.

The 1961 SEATO exercise 'Pony Express' is illustrative of the benefits of service with the FESR. An Australian lieutenant colonel was sent as an observer to the exercise that simulated an amphibious landing in North Borneo. Composed of elements of the US Seventh Fleet, the British Far East Fleet, four Australian warships, the entire 3 Marine Division, 42 Commando Royal Marines and one company of 1RAR, the exercise was the perfect opportunity to compare the amphibious warfare doctrines of Australia's two partners, and ensure continued integration between them and Australia.[27] Secretary of the Army, Bruce White, believed that 'such an exercise, particularly on the scale on which it is to be conducted [means that] the lessons to be learnt will be of considerable value'.[28] For the Navy, the exercise saw HMAS *Melbourne* act as the flagship of the anti-submarine warfare group: participation in such a large fleet training was completely unachievable in Australia.[29]

Nonetheless, for the Army, operations took precedence over training for conventional war, at least in the FESR's early years. As the first battalion to be deployed, and with the Malayan Emergency still ongoing, 2RAR found little time for training for war as part of the Strategic Reserve, as opposed to the small unit and basic skill training of use in its ongoing operations in Malaya. For many troops on this deployment, the FESR 'was little more than a shadow compared with the reality of the foetid jungle'.[30] As the Emergency wound down, more time was found for training. 3RAR completed two months of training for conventional warfare during its tour, although much of this focused on company-level and below exercises; only two periods of a total of 299 were allocated to operations in an atomic battlefield, reflecting both the battalion's focus on low-intensity warfare, and the unreality of global war involving nuclear weapons to many.

By 2RAR's second tour from 1961 to 1963, most of its time was spent training with the Strategic Reserve; six months straight from October 1962.[31] While the time allocated to training changed, there was not necessarily an improvement in the Army's ability to meet its requirements in the event of war. During 2RAR's 1963 Exercise 'Bellbuster', significant

---

27 Report, P Falkland, 'SEATO Amphibious Exercise "Pony Express" Report by LT COL P Falkland', 24 May 1961, NAA: A6059, 65/441/125.
28 White to Secretary Prime Minister's Department, 29 March 1961, NAA: A6059, 65/441/125.
29 Press release, 27 April 1961, NAA: A6059, 65/441/125.
30 Dennis and Grey, *Emergency and Confrontation*, 132.
31 Ibid., 147, 156, 160–62.

deficiencies were identified by the commanding officer, Lieutenant Colonel AB Streeton, including inappropriate jungle equipment, lack of small arms readiness, the weight of signals equipment and lack of training with helicopters. Many of these issues were out of Streeton's control.[32] It is also worth noting that 28 Commonwealth Brigade was not necessarily ready to undertake its primary role of emergency force at a moment's notice: when Indonesian troops landed in Malaysia in 1964, for instance, only the New Zealand battalion was available, as 3RAR was on the Thai border, and the British battalion was in the process of being replaced.[33]

There was the more significant issue of the mismatch between the forces promised by each member of the Strategic Reserve in the event of war, and those actually available. If a limited war were to break out in Southeast Asia, the Strategic Reserve would be short destroyers and minesweepers. In 1959, when the RAN was requested to report on its readiness should the deteriorating war against communist-backed insurgents erupt into war in Laos, the two destroyers then with the reserve were ready but at reduced complements, and the troop transport HMAS *Sydney* and carrier HMAS *Melbourne* would take some weeks to be ready to be deployed.[34] For its part, the Army spent the period between 1955 and 1965 in flux. Faced with the possibility of a nuclear war in Southeast Asia, and responding to US experiments on the issue, the Army introduced the Pentropic divisional organisation in 1960.

Based around five combined-arms battlegroups of five companies each, the organisation was intended to pack more punch on the nuclear battlefield but was ultimately unwieldy in the field. The infantry battalion that was deployed to the Strategic Reserve was exempt from the Pentropic organisation, but a new battalion had to be raised to allow it to rotate back to Australia without having to reorganise on Pentropic lines. If war broke out, the Army planned to commit a Pentropic battlegroup as well, supporting American and Asian partners. This left the Army in the questionable position of maintaining two different structures in war. Pentropic organisation was discarded in early 1965, but not before causing a great deal of disruption as units were reorganised.[35] By 1964 the Army was also entering a long period of expansion, with the introduction of national service and the creation of additional units.

---

32   Ibid., 162.
33   Pugsley, *From Emergency to Confrontation*, 202.
34   Grey, *Up top*, 28.
35   JC Blaxland, *Organising an army: The Australian experience 1957–1965* (Canberra: Strategic and Defence Studies Centre, Research School of Pacific Studies, Australian National University, 1989), 53.

Commonwealth relations

The service of Australian units within a Commonwealth formation was a relatively new experience for Australia. During the Second World War, Australia vigorously resisted breaking up its divisions when fighting alongside the British. Australian troops served with British in the British Commonwealth Occupation Force (BCOF) in Japan, to which Australia contributed a brigade, three fighter squadrons and naval forces; about a third of the entire force.[36] One battalion – later two – served with 27 Commonwealth Brigade in Korea, part of 1 Commonwealth Division. This level of integration was continued and expanded on in the FESR, where Australians also served within integrated units, including provost, signals, field ambulance, service and engineering units.

The creation of integrated Commonwealth units created some teething problems as Australian and British service personnel learned to work together, particularly in the inclusion of an Australian platoon in a British Royal Army Service Corps company. An officer from 2RAR, Major LC Chambers, reported problems caused by differing experience levels between Australian regulars and the British national servicemen with whom they had to work, differing attitudes towards the proper relationship between officers, non-commissioned officers and other ranks, and the perception of unfair restrictions on 'the more mature Australian soldier', particularly curfews. Chambers believed that while individually the complaints were minor, 'even petty', taken together 'they could … add up to a general sense of disgruntlement if they were disregarded'.[37] The integration of a sub-unit within a company, Chambers felt, 'depends for its success too much on personalities and individual characteristics'. He recommended that from thereafter, Australian administrative units should be of company strength at least.[38]

Nonetheless, Australian sub-units were not withdrawn from integrated units: to do so, it was reasoned, would undermine the 'all arms' nature of the Australian commitment, and remove an important contribution to the

---

36 James Wood, *The Australian military contribution to the occupation of Japan, 1945–1952* (St Leonards: Allen & Unwin 1998), 11.
37 HQ 1 Federal Division District, 'Integration of Australian Components in Commonwealth Units', 22 August 1956, NAA: A6059, 41/441/32.
38 GOC Malaya Command, 'Integrated British/Australian Units', 30 August 1956, NAA: A6059, 41/441/32.

FESR at a time when British manpower was stretched. While there were always irritants, efforts by Australian and British commanders to ensure that integration ran smoothly seemed to keep a lid on any problems.[39]

One notable facet of the Australian deployment of troops to Malaya during peacetime was the presence of service families. Some had accompanied troops to BCOF but, alongside service families in Papua New Guinea, this was the first time that service families had travelled overseas in large numbers to permanent bases. While the Defence Minister at the time, Phillip McBride, promised that the deployment of 2RAR to Malaya would include provision for service families, shortages of appropriate housing caused problems. Almost 400 servicemen within the battalion were eligible for married quarters (although some did not take up the option); that the battalion was arriving in an area already occupied by British troops made for slim pickings either for married quarters on base or in the private market, contributing to low morale among Australian troops. Complaints to British commanders in the area went unheeded until the commanding officer of 2RAR, Lieutenant Colonel JG Ochiltree, himself made a statement by refusing the married quarter allocated him, in front of the entire officers' mess. While more housing was reallocated from British servicemen after this incident, inadequate housing dogged Australian forces for years.[40]

At a time when relatively few Australians travelled to Asia, life in Malaya was an eye-opening experience for hundreds of Australian service families.[41] Once housing issues were smoothed out in the 1960s, families lived in suburbs often more salubrious that those to which they were accustomed in Australia, with beautiful tropical gardens and access to base services such as a cinema, swimming pool and hospital – all only for the use of Commonwealth troops and their dependants. On and around bases in Penang, Butterworth and Singapore, Australians were exposed to a foreign culture to which they were the outsiders. All families were entitled to at least one domestic servant, an unheard-of luxury in Australia.[42] At the same time, there was shopping to be had in the towns near the base,

---

39 Dennis and Grey, *Emergency and Confrontation*, 86.
40 Ibid., 88–89.
41 For a detailed discussion of Australian life at Butterworth, see Mathew Radcliffe, *Kampong Australia: The RAAF at Butterworth* (Sydney: NewSouth Books, 2017).
42 Christina Twomey, 'Bring the family: Australian overseas military communities and regional engagement, 1945–1988', in *Beyond combat: Australian military activity away from the battlefield*, ed. Tristan Moss and Tom Richardson (Sydney: NewSouth Books, 2018), 13.

and excursions to the surrounding Malayan countryside. Australians were also exposed to the particular racial relations then prevalent in the former British colony and brought their own racial attitudes; this was the period of White Australia, after all. Throughout the 1950s and into the 1960s, the three Australian services actively discouraged their servicemen from marrying non-European women.[43] Defence policy was to emphasise the difficulties of marrying an 'alien' to soldiers hoping to marry.[44]

Planning for war

With the exception of the operations against Indonesian incursions into the Malaysian peninsula and in Borneo between 1963 and 1966, the FESR was never deployed on combat operations. Instead, its role was a 'force in being', prepared for whatever emergency might arise, from global war, regional conflict with China or counterinsurgency in Laos or Vietnam. Fundamental to this was an ongoing process of planning, with a series of operational plans produced, amended and discarded as the threats shifted during the Cold War.

British plans for war in Asia during the early 1950s centred on the defence of Malaya. While chastened by its disastrous experience in the opening months of the Pacific War, which ultimately saw the fall of Singapore, the British were beholden to the geographical reality that the easiest place to defend Malaya was the narrow Kra Isthmus, in particular where it narrowed north of the border, in Thailand. During the 1940s and early 1950s, they believed that the Thais would not be able – or willing – to defend their country from a concerted attack. The British therefore planned to move north into Thailand to occupy the so-called 'Songkhla position', around 70 kilometres from the border. The political sensitivities of both moving troops into Thailand, and the assumption that most of Thailand would fall to the enemy, placed the British in an awkward position, and made difficult the assessment of the right time to begin moving troops into the area.

---

43 Matthew Radcliffe, 'In defence of White Australia: Discouraging "Asian marriage" in post war South-East Asia', *Australian Historical Studies* 45, no. 2 (2014): 184–201, doi.org/10.1080/103146 1x.2014.911761.
44 Principal Administrative Officers' Committee (Personnel), 'Marriage between service personnel and aliens', 15 December 1966, NAA: A1946, 1967/3762.

The British planned to meet around 80,000 communists – with the same in reserve – at the Songkhla position. In 1951 they believed they required three divisions, with attached armour and artillery, in addition to internal security forces of around 22 battalions. With other commitments around the world, particularly in Europe, the British would struggle to provide these forces in a timely fashion, with the potential that they would have to rely on the mobilisation of a division from the Territorial Army.[45] Nonetheless, in the event of a global war, the British Chiefs of Staff revised its estimate upwards of the forces needed to defend the Songkhla position in 1954 to around five divisions, but admitted that it was 'improbable' that the United Kingdom could send forces additional to those already in country. Commonwealth contributions were therefore crucial.

Australia committed to sending a corps of three divisions to Malaya, the first of which would arrive three months after war being declared, and the other two at a rate of one per month thereafter. New Zealand agreed to send a single division.[46] This was a plan that followed the assumptions of the Second World War, in which there was time to mobilise forces to meet a threat. Increasingly, planners worried that this would not be possible. The mismatch of forces was not necessarily a grave issue: in November 1954, the ANZAM Defence Committee estimated that 'overt aggression in SE Asia is highly unlikely', but that the main threat facing the Commonwealth in Malaya was an 'intensification of the cold war and subversive action'.[47] Reflecting this, the force designated for the defence of the Kra Isthmus – by then called Plan Hermes – was downgraded in 1956 to two divisions, 65 naval vessels and 248 aircraft, but a new plan, Warrior, developed to meet a North Vietnamese and Chinese intervention in the region required four divisions, 600 aircraft and 200 warships.[48]

These plans were designed for the Commonwealth to defend its territory alone; the absence of the United States to these plans lent 'an air of unreality' to the process.[49] While the Commonwealth could, on paper and depending on the threat, potentially go it alone for a period of time, the

---

45 Gregorian, *The British Army, the Gurkhas and Cold War strategy in the Far East, 1947–1954*, 192.
46 'Visit of General Loewen and Admiral Lambe to Australia', 22 December 1954, UK National Archives: COS(54)393, DEFE 5/55.
47 ANZAM Defence Committee, 'Probably form and scale of attack against Malaya up to the end of 1956', November 1954, Australian War Memorial: AWM 121 408/A/1.
48 Damien Fenton, 'SEATO and the defence of Southeast Asia, 1955–1965' (PhD thesis, University of New South Wales, Canberra, 2006), 109–10.
49 Ibid., 110.

difficulties in procuring the troops called for in the plans – a minimum of two divisions for Hermes – made the prospect questionable. Manpower shortages in Britain, the reluctance of Commonwealth nations to commit troops during peacetime, and the time to deploy troops from Britain or elsewhere to Malaya were all factors. In the event of war both Australia and New Zealand, for instance, planned to raise divisions from reserves and volunteers, as they had during the Second World War; a process that would take at least six to nine months.[50] By 1957 Far East planners recognised that the Commonwealth would be hard pressed to provide adequate conventional forces, and instead sought to redress the balance by the deployment of nuclear weapons in wartime, although these plans similarly were more aspirational than concrete.[51]

Accepting that the United States would provide the bulk of troops in any future war (and therefore would direct strategy), the Commonwealth increasingly sought to gauge American intentions in the region and engage them in joint planning. The ANZAM plans were presented to the Chairman of the Joint Chiefs of Staff, Admiral Arthur Radford, for comment in early 1955. The Americans were highly critical of the gap between the plans and the actual ability of the Commonwealth to provide the troops to carry them out, and the plans' focus on defending Malaya and abandoning the rest of Southeast Asia. Refusing a request for four-power joint planning, the Americans insisted on working through SEATO, which had been created just a few months previously, in September 1954. In many ways, coordination with SEATO gave ANZAM's planning new life and the FESR a more concrete role.[52]

From 1956, SEATO planning began under the auspices of the Military Planning Office. The assembled staff officers from across the region focused their concern on the threat of Chinese and Vietnamese communist aggression against Southeast Asia. It was overt, rather than covert, communist action that was considered to be the principal threat: counterinsurgencies, after all, had been successfully waged in Malaya and the Philippines. The first priorities were therefore those states bordering China and North Vietnam: Laos, South Vietnam, Thailand and Cambodia.[53]

---

50 Ibid., 111.
51 David French, *Army, empire, and Cold War: The British Army and military policy, 1945–1971* (Oxford; New York: Oxford University Press, 2012), 245, doi.org/10.1093/acprof:oso/9780199548231.003.0001.
52 Gregorian, *The British Army, the Gurkhas and Cold War strategy in the Far East, 1947–1954*, 117.
53 Fenton, 'SEATO and the defence of Southeast Asia, 1955–1965', 134.

There were two types of potential operation: limited war, which would require part or all of the FESR; and large-scale conflict, which would see the Strategic Reserve deployed initially, with larger follow-on forces from ANZAM nations coming later.[54] Seven SEATO plans were developed. Plans 1 and 2 prepared for the defence of Southeast Asia, against the Viet Minh, and against North Vietnam and China, respectively. Plan 3 was concerned with the defence of South Vietnam from an attack from North Vietnam with Chinese assistance. Plan 4 was developed against the unlikely possibility of a Chinese attack across the whole of Southeast Asia, while Plan 5 focused on a communist insurgency in Laos. Plan 6 was a variant of other plans against North Vietnamese aggression in Southeast Asia, and Plan 7 prepared for an insurgency in South Vietnam.[55] While these plans were developed concurrently, those focusing on Laos, Thailand and Vietnam were considered more urgent.[56]

The escalating Laotian crisis, during which communist forces threatened the US-backed Laotian Government, was as close as the FESR came to being deployed in support of SEATO. Indeed, the large-scale training for air movements within 28 Commonwealth Brigade in preparation for such an operation were the first time that the various Australian, British and New Zealand battalions worked closely together.[57] One concept put forward by the ANZAM Defence Committee would have seen 28 Commonwealth Brigade seizing crossings on the Mekong River while a US airborne brigade took the nearby Laotian town and airfield of Seno.[58] As the likelihood of a deployment to Laos diminished, this plan (Buckram) morphed into the broader-focused Plan Taffy, which allowed for a deployment to either Laos or northern Thailand in support of Plan 5, and to the Mekong region in support of Plan 4.[59]

ANZAM planners recognised that these plans would meet some difficulty were they to be implemented, and there was ongoing discussion and refinement, with the constantly changing strategic situation adding a degree of uncertainty to the planning process. In the event of the conventional war envisaged in Plan 4, an Australian, New Zealand and UK (ANZUK)

---

54 MacLean, *ANZIM to ANZUK*, 23.
55 Horner, *Strategic command*, 182.
56 Ibid., 179.
57 Pugsley, *From Emergency to Confrontation*, 176.
58 ANZAM Defence Committee, 'Deployment of the Commonwealth Brigade and Supporting Forces in SEATO Plan 4 Operations', October 1963, NAA: A5799, 49/1963.
59 MacLean, *ANZIM to ANZUK*, 24–26.

Division was to be formed from the Strategic Reserve with an Australian battle group and the New Zealand Brigade. The divisional headquarters was to be Australian.[60] Ultimately, however, the inability of SEATO members to commit to action in Laos in 1961 also seriously undermined the organisation, and while planning continued, the possibility of deployment under the auspices of SEATO became less likely.[61]

The only SEATO-related deployment of Australian forces was the commitment of a squadron of Sabres to Ubon airfield in northern Thailand to protect Thailand's territorial integrity.[62] Around 220 airmen and officers made up the contingent, operating in basic facilities that amounted to the airstrip, tents and a lone US radar unit. The Sabres' role was to assist in the defence of Thai airspace and the aircraft were armed with Sidewinder missiles and cannon. Two armed Sabres were placed on alert during daylight hours. Ultimately, however, the Ubon-based Sabres never fired a shot in anger. The arrival of US Air Force Eight Tactical Fighter Wing from April 1965 relegated the Sabres, who were not permitted to join the US fight in Vietnam, to a secondary, local defence role.[63]

Confrontation

With the increase in antagonism between Indonesia and Malaysia that culminated in the period of Confrontation between 1963 and 1966, ANZAM came closest to war; it was also the last time that the Commonwealth planned to meet such an eventuality collectively.[64] The military strategy of FEC during Indonesian Confrontation was the product of uncertainty about Indonesian intentions, an unstable political situation in Malaysia, a British desire to decrease defence spending and

---

60 Ibid., 26.
61 Horner, *Strategic command*, 184.
62 Edwards with Pemberton, *Crises and commitments*, 242.
63 Stephens, *The Royal Australian Air Force*, 255–56.
64 Brian Farrell's detailed analysis of Far East Command's planning for Confrontation is by far the best study of that period, and the aims of the Commonwealth nations in developing their plans. Brian Farrell, 'Escalate to terminate: Far East Command and the need to end Confrontation', in *The 2005 Chief of the Army military history conference*, ed. Peter Dennis and Jeffrey Grey (Canberra: Australian Military History Publications, 2005), 125.

free up its stretched military, and the fact that the Commonwealth countries contributing to the defence of Southeast Asia did not always share the same goals.[65]

Australia, for its part, also sought to ensure its own security from its nearest neighbour.[66] Sharing a border with Indonesia in Papua New Guinea, and with Darwin only a short distance away, war with Indonesia was an occurrence that would quickly and directly affect Australia. While it could refrain from participating in Commonwealth actions against Indonesia or pull its troops out of the Strategic Reserve to bolster home defence, the automatic involvement of Australian interests in any war involving Indonesia meant that full participation in any offensive against Indonesia in an emergency probably offered the best chance of Australian goals being met.[67]

Throughout the conflict with Indonesia, a range of plans were maintained to allow for the ever-changing strategic situation and the uncertainty over Indonesian intentions, while also providing a suite of options for Commonwealth governments and FEC, ranging from open war to the redeployment of troops as in preparation for the possibility of future action or to send a political message to the Indonesians. These plans, at their heart, reflected the desire of Commonwealth planners to resolve the conflict through non-military means; there was no wish to occupy or destroy Indonesia.[68] The reaction of Commonwealth partners – and therefore their provision of forces to a conflict – had to be considered, as well as that of the world community who might provide support or opprobrium.[69] Finally, the political reactions of Indonesia were key to each and every plan, with the goal of convincing Indonesian leaders that war would be costly and contrary to their interests. The series of 'anti-confrontation plans', as they were termed, therefore, allowed for prompt and proportional Commonwealth reaction to Indonesian actions, rather than the opening blow of a wider conflict.

The Indonesian incursions into Malaya in August 1964 represented the high point of tension between Indonesia and the Commonwealth. The overt nature of these actions also fundamentally changed the nature

---

65 Ibid., 128–29.
66 See Dennis and Grey, *Emergency and Confrontation*, 197–204.
67 Farrell, 'Escalate to terminate', 136.
68 Ibid., 126.
69 Ibid., 142.

5. PLANNING FOR WAR IN SOUTHEAST ASIA

of the conflict. Nonetheless, the Indonesian landings were almost absurdly poorly planned and executed. Indeed, so woeful was the Indonesian planning that many of their forces landed near 28 Commonwealth Brigade, the battalions of which quickly and easily rounded up the Indonesian troops.[70] However minor, Indonesian actions galvanised the ANZAM partners, and caused them to commit more firmly to FEC and its plans. Equally as important, the British responded by sending additional forces to the region, including bombers, fighters, air defence units and infantry battalions. FEC now had firm plans for strikes against Indonesia, the forces with which to carry them out and the political will to do so.[71]

To meet the worst-case scenario, outright war with Indonesia, FEC planners developed a group of plans designed to destroy Indonesian offensive capability as quickly and as completely as possible. Initially named Cougar, the plan went through three more iterations: Hemley, Althorpe and Allvar.[72] Planners assumed four weeks' notice would be available, and the plan assumed that the United Kingdom would not be engaged in other operations in Southeast Asia at the same time (such that sufficient troops would be available), Indonesia would not receive outside support from countries such as China but nor would the United States intercede on the Commonwealth's behalf, and that nuclear weapons, then based at Singapore, would not be used in the conflict.[73]

While land forces took the brunt of limited conflicts, it was air forces that would take the lead if the conflict widened under Plan Cougar. Airpower was a key in plans to combat Indonesia; it was through air strikes that a decisive blow might be struck by either side.[74] Only Indonesia's air force represented a credible threat to Commonwealth forces in the region, and wiping out this capability in the first days of any conflict was seen as crucial. Having recently received 25 new Soviet TU-16 Badger bombers, Indonesia also had around 30 fighters, including MiG-17s, MiG-19s and 18 of the newest MiG-21s, as well as a number of piston-engine aircraft, including 16 P-51 Mustangs and 16 B-25 Mitchell bombers.

---

70 Dennis and Grey, *Emergency and Confrontation*, 225.
71 Farrell, 'Escalate to terminate', 146, 149–50.
72 ANZAM Defence Committee, 'State of Anti-Confrontation Plans', Agendum No. 9/65, 3 September 1965, Annex J to CINCFE 3182/2064/3, NAA: A7942, A227.
73 Commander in Chief Far East, 'Offensive Operations Against Indonesia: Reinforced Theatre Plan No. 7 (Draft) – Plan Cougar', 1964, NAA: A1945, 245/3/14.
74 Farrell, 'Escalate to terminate', 133.

The main threat to FEC was low-level attacks against the primary FEC bases in the region, at Singapore, Butterworth and in Borneo. Although this was considered unlikely, an airstrike launched by Indonesia with all the forces available to it could come with little warning, and cause a great deal of damage to aircraft caught on the ground and other vital defence installations such as radar and fuel storage areas.[75]

To meet an Indonesian air attack, FEC had a substantial force in theatre, but these initially fell short of what was required as many of the aircraft earmarked for the defence of Malaysia were to be deployed as and when the situation called for it. The plan included a total of 191 aircraft, including 24 medium bombers, 40 light bombers including Canberras, 52 all-weather fighters, 44 ground attack fighters (including RAAF Sabres) and reconnaissance aircraft. Of these, over 100 were already in theatre.[76] After the Indonesian escalation of the conflict in 1964, more aircraft were provided to FEC, including the powerful Vulcan bombers.[77] With these forces, FEC had close to the planned capability required to carry out Plan Cougar and could be confident in dealing a crippling blow against Indonesia if called to do so.[78]

More limited strikes were also planned for, should the situation have called for a tough response short of a comprehensive strike. Plan Florid, submitted in 1965, provided for more limited strikes on Indonesian targets in Kalimantan. Indeed, the target list was designed to be scalable, with the plan providing 'the option of ordering operations against any number of targets from one to eighteen according to the degree of severity required'.[79] Written shortly after the first Indonesian incursion on the Malaysian peninsula, Plan Mason provided for air and naval attacks against Indonesian bases from which paramilitary operations were launched. Plan Hedgehog expanded on Mason as the number of Indonesian bases increased, revising the target list and adding Indonesian military headquarters. Hedgehog was to be implemented 'when Indonesian preparations for attack or infiltration against Malaysia and Singapore were

---

75 Annex B to Appendix 1, 'Offensive Operations Against Indonesia: Reinforced Theatre Plan No. 7 (Draft) – Plan Cougar', 1964, NAA: A1945, 245/3/14.
76 Farrell, 'Escalate to terminate', 132.
77 Pugsley, *From Emergency to Confrontation*, 228.
78 Farrell, 'Escalate to terminate', 146.
79 ANZAM Defence Committee, 'State of Anti-Confrontation Plans', Agendum No. 9/65, 3 September 1965, Annex J to CINCFE 3182/2064/3, NAA: A7942, A227.

detected'.⁸⁰ Yet further plans provided for more limited scenarios, such as the reinforcement of certain areas; one plan, Salaam, was implemented to move troops to Borneo.⁸¹ The scalability of the plans available for the use of the FESR provide a variety of options for a range of contexts, but all nonetheless reflected FEC's desire to respond in such a way that an ongoing and ever-expanding war was avoided, and a political settlement might be reached through the precise application of force.

Conclusion

For a decade before the Vietnam War, Australia prepared to fight a conventional war in Southeast Asia. The FESR was ANZAM's contribution to SEATO and the force that allowed it a seat at the planning table. While at the strategic level Australia and the Commonwealth contributed to SEATO planning and alliance management, on the ground preparations for a regional war in Southeast Asia sometimes took second place to more pressing operational needs, such as the Malayan Emergency. Only after operations against communist guerrillas wound down did the FESR focus more energy on SEATO operations; by that time, political considerations made a deployment increasingly unlikely.

The plans developed by FEC to confront the Indonesian threat contrasted with its involvement in SEATO. First and foremost, the Commonwealth expected to fight Indonesia alone. Unlike British plans to defend the Kra Isthmus by itself, however, anti-confrontation plans were far more credible. The threat was clear, and it was immediate. Indeed, Indonesia had tipped its hand with incursions in Malaya. The plans themselves were closely aligned with political goals, which were most evident in their scalability. Importantly, the Commonwealth had the forces on hand to achieve its goals, particularly in terms of its air forces.

Confrontation was the FESR's zenith. At a time when the Australian armed forces were undergoing substantial change as they grappled with the postwar strategic landscape, the forces sent to the FESR were a well-balanced contribution that achieved their desired goals of deterrence

---

80   ANZAM Defence Committee, 'State of Anti-Confrontation Plans', Agendum No. 9/65, 3 September 1965, Annex J to CINCFE 3182/2064/3, NAA: A7942, A227.
81   Commander in Chief Far East, 'Offensive Operations Against Indonesia: Reinforced Theatre Plan No. 7 (Draft) – Plan Cougar', 1964, NAA: A1945, 245/3/14. These plans included Nightrider, Buxom, Haycock and Spillikin.

and alliance maintenance. However, the British 'East of Suez' policy, and the US and Australian focus on Vietnam saw the force decline even before Australia's decision to focus on the defence of the continent. Commonwealth involvement in the region continued briefly with the creation of the ANZUK force of around 7,000 from 1971, but this was disbanded in 1975. Australian forces remained in the region for some time longer: while Butterfield air base was handed to the Malaysian Government in 1971, RAAF squadrons were based there until 1988 and the Australian Army continues periodic rotations of a rifle company to Butterworth. These vestigial involvements reflect the continued importance of the peninsula to Australia's defence, and the origin of this involvement in the structures and relationships set in place during the 1950s and 1960s.

6

The Malayan Emergency

Thomas Richardson

The Australian commitment to the Malayan Emergency lasted from June 1950 to June 1962. The product of Australia's fear of a gradual communist takeover of Southeast Asia, this commitment never matched in size those made to the wars in Korea or Vietnam, and the intensity of the fighting was below that of Confrontation. Nevertheless, alongside the commitment to the Far East Strategic Reserve (FESR), the contribution to the Malayan Emergency was one of Australia's longest overseas deployments. The war itself was low-intensity. The Malayan Communist Party (MCP) and its armed wing, the Malayan Races Liberation Army (MRLA), were always deeply reluctant to engage British Commonwealth security forces – particularly by the time the major Australian commitment, an infantry battalion group, was deployed in 1955. The result was a war of intense frustration, as Australian soldiers and airmen searched for a comparatively small number of enemy who did not want to be found and had the advantage of hiding in the vast jungle wilderness of northern Malaya.

Yet the experience in Malaya exerted a strong influence on how the Australian Army thought about how it would, and ultimately did, fight across Southeast Asia. The Army entered Malaya with a large practical knowledge of jungle warfare gained in the Second World War, but unsure of how that knowledge would translate to a counterinsurgency. The Army was right to be sceptical; while this prior understanding of how to operate in a jungle environment proved valuable, the nature of the Emergency demanded a substantially different operational framework and tactics. Over the course of nearly seven years, Australian units had the opportunity to master these, benefitting in the process from a British system that had itself gone through a learning curve. The resulting understanding of tropical counterinsurgency would significantly influence Australian operations in Vietnam and beyond.

The Emergency

One of the most important factors in how the Malayan Emergency developed was the fact that the insurgents were almost as unprepared for the conflict as the government.[1] The MCP formed in the 1920s and had been banned by British authorities prior to the Second World War. Yet the Japanese invasion and occupation of Malaya in 1941–42 created a mutual enemy that saw the MCP and the British become allies of convenience. By the time of the Japanese surrender in August 1945, the MCP-controlled Malayan Peoples' Anti-Japanese Army (MPAJA) numbered around 3,500 men, armed with British weapons provided by the clandestine Force 136.[2] While never formally legalised, the credit accrued during the struggle against the Japanese helped allow the MCP to function as a quasi-legitimate political organisation in the immediate postwar period. The MPAJA disbanded and either surrendered its weapons or cached them, while considerable effort was poured into front organisations and the trade union movement.[3] This policy of moderation was championed by Lai Tek, Secretary General of the party, who had achieved an exalted status amongst his subordinates during the struggle against the Japanese.[4]

The prospects for political struggle initially seemed promising. Like much of Southeast Asia after the surrender of the Japanese, Malaya faced intense economic hardship and political uncertainty – conditions exacerbated by a botched series of British administrative decisions.[5]

---

1   John Coates, *Suppressing insurgency: An analysis of the Malayan Emergency, 1948–1954* (Boulder: Westview Press, 1992), 17–18.
2   The exact strength of the MPAJA appears to be disputed; this figure is taken from Karl Hack and CC Chin, 'The Malayan Emergency' in *Dialogues with Chin Peng: New light on the Malayan Communist Party*, ed. CC Chin and Karl Hack (Singapore: Singapore University Press, 2004), 5.
3   Cheah Boon Kheng, 'The Legal Period: 1945–8', in Chin and Hack, *Dialogues with Chin Peng*, 255–57.
4   Richard Stubbs, *Hearts and minds in guerrilla warfare: The Malayan Emergency 1948–1960* (Singapore: Oxford University Press, 1989), 54–56.
5   Peter Dennis and Jeffrey Grey, *The official history of Australia's involvement in Southeast Asian conflicts 1948–1975*, vol. 5, *Emergency and Confrontation: Australian military operations in Malaya and Borneo 1950–1966* (St Leonards: Allen & Unwin in association with the Australian War Memorial, 1996), 7–8.

Largest of these was the proposal put forward in January 1946 for the reorganisation and consolidation of the various British-controlled polities in Malaya into a single Malayan Union. The proposal included generous provisions for citizenship for Malaya's Chinese and Indian populations. This provoked an immediate backlash from Malayan leaders, one so strong that the British withdrew the union proposal. In its place came a proposal for a Federation of Malaya that, through its omission of the generous citizenship provisions, angered sections of the Chinese and Indian communities and seemingly provided the MCP with a significant political opportunity.[6]

Several factors conspired in early 1948 to shift the course of the MCP to armed struggle, however. The disappearance of Lai Tek in March 1947 and subsequent revelation he had been an agent of the British and Japanese left the MCP reeling and helped discredit the moderate policies he had championed.[7] Equally important, however, was the apparent failure of these policies by the start of the following year. Despite the success of the MCP in dominating the trade union movement and initiating repeated and widespread industrial action, no political concessions had been forthcoming from the British; Lai Tek's successor, Chin Peng, first discussed the possibility of a change in strategy over the sound of artillery salutes inaugurating the Federation of Malaya.[8] On top of this, new legislation promised to effectively gut MCP control of the trade union movement. 'The prominent factor that influenced us, when we decided to take up arms, was the British policy at the time,' Chin Peng later recalled. 'We felt we were being cornered, gradually, back to the corner. We had nowhere to move.'[9] As a result, at a meeting of the Central Committee between 17 and 21 March 1948, the party resolved to adopt a new strategy.

From March onwards, the MCP prepared for an open confrontation with the government – a confrontation its leadership expected to happen around September. Yet events outran it. Violence associated with ongoing strikes increased, and it was in this context that three European planters were murdered at Sungei Siput in the state of Perak by members of the MCP on 16 June.[10] A state of emergency was declared by the British

---

6 Dennis and Grey, *Emergency and Confrontation*, 8.
7 Anthony Short, *The communist insurrection in Malaya 1948–1960* (London: Frederick Muller, 1973), 41.
8 Chin and Hack, *Dialogues with Chin Peng*, 119.
9 Chin and Hack, *Dialogues with Chin Peng*, 117.
10 Coates, *Suppressing insurgency*, 18.

Administration in parts of Perak, and extended across the entirety of Malaya a few days later. A belated mass police operation on 18 June succeeded in arresting 1,100 party members or supporters, but the leadership and hardcore cadres of the old MPAJA had already escaped into the jungle.[11] Just over a year later in July 1949, in an attempt to expand the appeal of the struggle beyond the Chinese community, the military units of the party were renamed the National Liberation Army; the original Chinese phrase was poorly translated as the Malayan Races Liberation Army, and the acronym MRLA was commonly used afterwards. The British Commonwealth forces, for their part, described the enemy as 'Communist Terrorists' and the acronym 'CT' became commonplace.[12]

The initial MCP strategy reflected the influence of Mao and called for a three-phase struggle in which an initial wave of terrorism and guerrilla activity would then allow the creation of rural base areas to support larger guerrilla units; in the third and final phase, the base areas would begin to link up, and a general revolt would be initiated in urban areas.[13] It proved a failure, for several reasons. Rural base areas were simultaneously too remote from the civilian population and too vulnerable to attack by security forces thanks to Malaya's well-developed road and rail network. Only the base area in the Betong on the Thai border was established and lasted, and that was thanks largely to the ability of the CTs to hide within Thailand.[14] The party's disorganisation and decentralisation also meant that little damage was actually done to the government, security forces or economic infrastructure in the early days of the Emergency. Indeed, for the first two years of the Emergency rubber and tin production actually increased, despite the violence.[15]

Despite – or perhaps because of – the MCP being caught unprepared by the declaration of the Emergency, and the failure of its initial Maoist strategy, the British Government's response to the new insurgency was remarkably haphazard. The bombastic overconfidence evident in the July 1948 declaration by the General Officer Commanding (GOC) Malaya, Major General Boucher, that 'I can tell you this is by far the easiest problem I have ever tackled' appears to have been common but

---

11 Coates, *Suppressing insurgency*, 18.
12 Chin and Hack, *Dialogues with Chin Peng*, 149.
13 Coates, *Suppressing insurgency*, 51.
14 Coates, *Suppressing insurgency*, 51–52.
15 Coates, *Suppressing insurgency*, 51–52.

by no means universal within the British Administration in 1948–49.[16] Yet even those who appreciated the scale of the threat faced the problem of an emaciated police force, a non-existent intelligence system, an army untrained in jungle warfare or counterinsurgency and a government bureaucracy divided over what to do, how to do it and who it should be done by.[17]

The relative failure of the government response allowed the MCP to regroup and reformulate its thinking. While the MCP/MRLA never gave up its desire to create base or liberated areas, and indeed saw them as fundamental to victory, it did recognise from 1949 onwards that a change of tactics was required.[18] This was driven not only by the vulnerability of larger units to the Commonwealth security forces, but also the difficulty in supplying them. Instead, smaller units began operating in the fringe area of jungle next to cleared or cultivated land. From here they could mount attacks on isolated or vulnerable targets, and receive supplies from the MCP Masses Organisation (*Min Yuen*) that operated covertly within settlements. The MCP intended that a sustained period of such attacks would attrit security force strength and build up rural support for the party to such a degree that the establishment of base areas would become possible.[19]

While the MCP/MRLA shift in tactics still failed to bring about conditions favourable to the establishment of rural base or liberated areas, much less victory, they did dramatically increase the scope of the security crisis faced by the government. A total of 2,716 'incidents' were recorded across 1948–49; in 1950 the number jumped to 4,739 and continued to increase in 1951 to 6,082. As if to underline the seriousness of the situation, on 6 October 1951, High Commissioner Gurney and several members of his escort were killed when Gurney's car was ambushed by an MRLA platoon 60 miles outside of Kuala Lumpur. Sixteen days later, on 22 October, a British platoon was also ambushed, leaving 16 dead and 16 wounded.[20]

---

16 Stubbs, *Hearts and minds*, 72.
17 Coates, *Suppressing insurgency*, 23–41.
18 Coates, *Suppressing insurgency*, 59–61; Chin and Hack, *Dialogues with Chin Peng*, 151.
19 Dennis and Grey, *Emergency and Confrontation*, 11–12.
20 Dennis and Grey, *Emergency and Confrontation*, 18.

It should be noted at this point that despite the dramatic increase in MCP/MRLA activity and success in 1950–51, in retrospect there were significant structural barriers to any sort of communist victory in Malaya. The MCP lacked active support outside the Chinese community within Malaya, and even within it many had little interest in the party's political program. This lack of support helped explain the MRLA's military weakness; even at its largest it numbered no more than 8,000 men and women. Exacerbating this was the lack of external support available to the party. With the Thai Government hostile, and the sea and air approaches to Malaya dominated by the British, the MCP/MRLA was cut off from any kind of external help. This made it entirely reliant on supplies it could gain from the *Min Yuen* organisation in the villages, or later the Orang Asli tribes in the interior; and it also meant the MRLA was limited to the small arms it had cached after the Second World War and any weapons it could capture off the security forces. This further restricted the combat power of units, who only deployed small arms for the entire Emergency.[21]

These structural issues notwithstanding, the surge in communist violence in early 1950 finally pushed the British Administration into a stronger response. In March 1950 Gurney asked the British Government for a Director of Operations; that is, an official who could coordinate security forces operations against the MCP. The man eventually appointed was Lieutenant General Sir Harold Briggs, an officer with a long career in Asia that included command of a division in Burma and subsequent time as GOC Burma Command between 1946 and 1947.[22] Briggs produced an appreciation of the situation almost immediately, followed by a more detailed plan on 24 May 1950. As John Coates has argued, both documents make clear that Briggs understood that 'the Emergency was not a war in the classic sense, but a competition in government'.[23] The MRLA was able to exist and commit acts of violence because of the supplies, recruits and information that came from the Chinese population close to the jungle fringe. Those supplies did not magically appear in the jungle; instead they were extracted by the *Min Yuen*, whose very presence indicated to the population that the government could not protect them and that a political alternative to the Malay Administration existed.[24]

---

21 Coates, *Suppressing insurgency*, 49.
22 Dennis and Grey, *Emergency and Confrontation*, 13.
23 Coates, *Suppressing insurgency*, 82.
24 Appendix C, 'Appreciation of the Situation in Malaya, 10 April 1950, by Lieutenant General Sir Harold Biggs' in Coates, *Suppressing insurgency*, 203.

Briggs thus argued that in order to restore security, the government had to not simply defeat the MRLA but 'eliminate the Communist cells among the Chinese population to whom we must give security and whom we must win over'.[25] The second part of this formulation was key; the physical security of the population would not be sufficient, and indeed would not be possible, without winning their active support. This in turn would require both effective propaganda and certain political concessions. 'It must be realised that the Chinese are here for good', Briggs wrote, 'and such land as they occupy must carry promise of a permanent title subject to good behaviour'.[26] Moreover, active government administration had to be extended to all communities both as a measure of control and as a way of winning support through the provision of services. A combination of active support from the community, strong administrative control measures and a revitalised and rebuilt intelligence system and police force would allow the *Min Yuen* to be destroyed.[27] This in turn would force the MRLA, deprived of its supplies and already under intense pressure from army-led security operations, to 'attack us on our own ground' and thus be defeated.[28]

Briggs's ideas did not represent an instantaneous solution, and his own timelines proved wildly optimistic. Command arrangements continued to prove less than optimal and were subject to a major reshuffle in early 1951. Briggs had resigned in November 1951 due to poor health, and Colonial Secretary Oliver Lyttelton ended up combining the positions of Director of Operations and High Commissioner into one following Gurney's death.[29] The man appointed to this new post, General Sir Gerald Templer, benefited from Lyttelton's determination to centralise and streamline authority. Nor was the implementation of the Briggs Plan smooth. The basic issues that had dogged the authorities since the start of the Emergency, such as the lack of trained and capable manpower, money and coordination, were all still factors. The plan to resettle or relocate communities on the jungle fringe, primarily Chinese, was executed in haste and suffered accordingly.[30]

---

25 Appendix C, 'Appreciation of the Situation in Malaya, 10 April 1950, by Lieutenant General Sir Harold Biggs' in Coates, *Suppressing insurgency*, 203.
26 Appendix C, 'Appreciation of the Situation in Malaya, 10 April 1950, by Lieutenant General Sir Harold Biggs' in Coates, *Suppressing insurgency*, 204.
27 Dennis and Grey, *Emergency and Confrontation*, 15.
28 'Report on the Emergency in Malaya from April, 1950 to November 1951', UK Public Records Office (PRO): DEFE 11/47, pp. 3–5, quoted in Dennis and Grey, *Emergency and Confrontation*, 15.
29 Stubbs, *Hearts and minds*, 138–40.
30 David French, *The British way in counterinsurgency 1945–1967* (Oxford: Oxford University Press, 2011), 180.

Yet Briggs's basic plan, and his conception of the conflict as a struggle of governance, proved sound. During Templer's time in command between January 1952 and May 1954, the British hacked away at the MCP's political appeal by expanding citizenship throughout the community, empowering local leaders and ultimately granting Malaya independence. This independence settlement entrenched Malayan political power but still succeeded in undermining the central plank of the MCP's platform.[31] Resettlement continued and conditions inside the 'New Villages' improved, thanks in part to the provision of amenities such as electricity, running water, medical clinics and schools. The size and quality of the police force was upgraded, while the system for the collection and dissemination of intelligence through Special Branch was streamlined and improved. Templer also drove the creation of the *Anti-Terrorist Operations Malaya* pamphlet, which guided security force operations for the remainder of the Emergency. Increasingly eschewing the large-scale sweeps of the Emergency's first few years, security forces instead built a sophisticated concept of operations based around food denial that fulfilled Briggs's basic idea of disrupting the lines of communication between the *Min Yuen* and MRLA units in the jungle.[32]

By the time Templer left Malaya in May 1954, this raft of measures had broken the back of the insurgency. While the Emergency was far from over, both the number of incidents and estimated MCP/MRLA strength entered a steady decline that would not be reversed. The MCP, wracked by internal disagreements, began shifting to a policy of conservation as it looked to bring a negotiated end to the Emergency.[33] From a peak of around 8,000 armed guerrillas, by mid-1955 the MRLA was down to an estimated strength of between 3,100 and 3,800.[34] As its armed strength declined, the party also began to be overtaken by political events. The first federal elections were held in Malaya in July 1955, and full independence granted on 31 August 1957. Outflanked politically, the MCP concentrated on conserving its remaining strength in remote regions on the Thai/Malaya border in what it termed a policy of 'lowering the banners and muffling the drums'. While the party and what was left of its military

---

31 French, *The British way in counterinsurgency*, 194; Peter Edwards, *Australia and the Vietnam War* (Sydney: NewSouth Books, 2014), 57.
32 Stubbs, *Hearts and minds*, 168–80; Coates, *Suppressing insurgency*, 109–36.
33 Coates, *Suppressing insurgency*, 63, 69.
34 Hack and Chin, 'The Malayan Emergency', 20; Combined Intelligence Staff, 'An Estimate of Current Armed Terrorist Strength, 10th May 1955', n.d., Australian War Memorial (AWM): AWM347 208.

forces did not finally cease armed struggle until 1989, the threat they posed to Malaya had effectively been extinguished, and the Emergency was declared over on 12 July 1960.[35]

The Australian commitments, 1950 and 1955

It was in this context that the Australian Government made two distinct commitments of military forces to fight in Malaya. The first was the dispatch of a squadron of Lincoln heavy bombers of No. 1 (B) Squadron, and Dakota transports of No. 38 Squadron, in June 1950 after a request from the British Government in April.[36] While the Dakotas were withdrawn in 1952 due to demands imposed by the Korean War, the Lincolns remained until 1958. The second commitment was the deployment, announced by Prime Minister Menzies on 1 April 1955, of substantial military assets including ships of the Royal Australian Navy (RAN), additional Royal Australian Air Force (RAAF) squadrons, an infantry battalion, a field artillery battery and an engineering troop as part of Australia's larger commitment to the FESR.[37] While the destroyers and frigates of the RAN, and the Canberra and Sabre aircraft of No. 2, No. 3 and No. 77 Squadrons RAAF, largely focused on the 'primary role' of FESR, the Army units spent their time operating against CTs. Serving roughly two-year tours, in total four battalions would participate in operations against the MRLA – initially during the Emergency and then, in the case of 1RAR (1 Battalion, Royal Australian Regiment) and 2RAR during its second tour, after its formal cessation in 1960.[38]

The broader strategic logic of the Australian commitments is discussed elsewhere in this book, and so will only be briefly covered here. The Menzies Government deployed forces to Malaya because, as Peter Edwards put it, 'like the United Kingdom Government, it saw the conflict not as merely a local struggle but as part of the global conflict between communism and

---

35   CC Chin, 'In Search of the Revolution: A Brief Biography of Chin Peng' in Chin and Hack, *Dialogues with Chin Peng*, 365–70.
36   Dennis and Grey, *Emergency and Confrontation*, 22–24.
37   Peter Edwards with Gregory Pemberton, *The official history of Australia's involvement in Southeast Asian conflicts 1948–1975*, vol. 1, *Crises and commitments: The politics and diplomacy of Australia's involvement in Southeast Asian conflicts 1948–1965* (North Sydney: Allen & Unwin in association with the Australian War Memorial, 1992), 169.
38   Jeffrey Grey, *A military history of Australia* (Cambridge: Cambridge University Press, 2008), 222.

democracy'.[39] In addition, Australian deployments to Malaya achieved the wider objective of signalling its commitment to the defence of the region from communist threats and its willingness to pull its weight from a funding perspective. The utility of military force in Malaya in achieving Australian objectives was thus twofold: the Australian commitment contributed directly to the defeat of the MCP's insurgency, despite being a small part of the overall British Commonwealth force (which by 1954 numbered 24 British infantry battalions alone), while the commitment itself – regardless of operational results – helped achieve the goals of Australian alliance politics.[40]

This logic justified both the initial commitment of RAAF squadrons in 1950 and the subsequent FESR commitment in 1955, and meant that in both cases units became small cogs in the much larger British machine. There is, however, one notable wrinkle in the willingness of the Menzies Government to cede operational control of Australian units to the British command in Malaya. When the issue of deploying Australian troops first arose for the Menzies Government in 1950, at least one Cabinet minister expressed his disquiet at British tactics and wondered if they could not learn something from an Australian Army well versed in jungle warfare and open to adaptation.[41] These concerns led to Menzies proposing on 26 May 1950 to the British Government that a small mission of Australian officers be sent to Malaya in order to provide their expertise in jungle warfare to the British commanders and return information on British operations and tactics to the Australian Government.[42] The British quickly accepted and the Australian officers departed Sydney on 19 July.

Known as the Bridgeford mission after its commander, Quartermaster-General Major General W Bridgeford, the mission also included Lieutenant Commander AM Synnot (Director Staff and Training Requirements, Navy Office), Colonel JGN Wilton, Lieutenant Colonel FG Hassett (General Service Officer Level I, 2 Australian Division), Lieutenant Colonel GR Wharfe (Commanding Officer, 5 Infantry Battalion), Lieutenant Colonel GS Cox (Commanding Officer, 45 Infantry Battalion), Major SP Weir (General Service Officer Level II,

---

39   Edwards with Pemberton, *Crises and commitments*, 102.
40   Andrew Mumford, *The Counter-insurgency myth: The British experience of irregular warfare* (UK: Taylor & Francis, 2011), 33.
41   Edwards with Pemberton, *Crises and commitments*, 93–94; Dennis and Grey, *Emergency and Confrontation*, 45.
42   Edwards with Pemberton, *Crises and commitments*, 93–94.

Directorate of Military Intelligence) and Wing Commander G Steege (attached to RAAF headquarters).[43] The presence of officers from the RAN and RAAF was not initially anticipated by Menzies and stemmed from the Army's discomfort with the idea that Australian experiences in New Guinea had any particular relevance to the Emergency, in contrast to views of government ministers. In the event, Bridgeford's final report largely endorsed both the Briggs Plan and the tactical methods in use by the British Army, laying to rest the concerns of Cabinet and confirming the Army's initial impression of the situation.[44]

Moreover, in the four years between Bridgeford's report and the deployment of 2RAR in late 1955, there had been much improvement in British conduct of the Emergency. In 1949 the British Army had created the Far Eastern Land Forces Training Centre (FTC), located from 1950 in Kota Tinggi in Johore. Experience gradually drove a shift in tactics between 1950 and late 1951, from large-scale operations to smaller ones that emphasised patrolling, while the adoption of the Briggs Plan provided a new concept of operations. Briggs made clear that the role of the Army was to provide security for populated areas while government administration was restored and the *Min Yuen* attacked ('framework operations'), and that it was to interpose itself between the units of the MRLA and the populated areas they relied upon for support. These ideas, and the tactical lessons taught at FTC, were codified at Templer's insistence in late 1952 in a pamphlet entitled *The conduct of anti-terrorist operations in Malaya* (commonly abbreviated as *ATOM*).[45]

By 1953, therefore, the British had established and put into practice an effective system of counterinsurgency. This system relied fundamentally on separating the insurgents from the population in order to starve the MRLA of intelligence, recruits, supplies and, above all, food. This separation was achieved by the resettlement of population on the jungle fringes, an intensive program of physical control run primarily by police and auxiliary forces, and the use of Army units to dominate the area around settled areas. Templer left little doubt as to his view on the role of the Army, famously declaring in the introduction of *ATOM* that 'the job of the British Army out here is to kill or capture Communist terrorists in

---

43   Dennis and Grey, *Emergency and Confrontation*, 46–47.
44   Dennis and Grey, *Emergency and Confrontation*, 47–49; Edwards with Pemberton, *Crises and commitments*, 101.
45   Daniel Marston, 'Lost and found in the jungle' in *Big wars and small wars: The British Army and the lessons of war in the 20th century*, ed. Hew Strachan (UK: Routledge, 2009), 98–103.

Malaya'.⁴⁶ Yet where at the start of the conflict the British had emphasised large-scale sweep operations that had attempted to drive MCP/MRLA personnel within a certain area into pre-established blocking positions, *ATOM* counselled the used of many patrols and ambushes conducted from company or platoon 'bases' in the jungle to dominate an area.⁴⁷

The British system also emphasised not only the need to ground operations in accurate intelligence but also to shape them to maximise the quantity and quality of intelligence generated by the operation itself. Thus a typical priority operation was divided into three phases. The first was a preparatory phase in which Special Branch built a detailed picture of the insurgent network in the chosen area. The second was the start of the operation itself, with food control measures put in place and military operations shaped to exacerbate those measures – in particular through the ambush or patrolling of areas that likely saw the transfer of supplies between villagers, the *Min Yuen* and the MRLA. The third was the use of a growing body of intelligence – generated by surrendered or captured enemy personnel (at times through torture), information discovered in CT camps and general military operations – to further target operations, further increasing the pressure on the MCP/MRLA in the area and leading to further contacts, captures and surrenders.⁴⁸

Taken together, this meant that by the time 2RAR deployed in 1955, the dynamic anticipated by the Menzies Cabinet in 1950 had largely been reversed. It was the Australians who stood to learn, and would ultimately be absorbed into the British system.

Operations: 1955–63

The main body of 2RAR arrived in Malaya on 19 October 1955, and spent the remainder of the year training on Penang Island and in the state of Kedah. It began combat operations on 1 January 1956 with Operation Deuce in southern Kedah, and continued in that role into mid-April. At the end of April it shifted to Operation Shark North in the Kuala Kangsar – Sungei Siput area of Perak. With only a brief pause for training

---

46 General Sir Gerald Templer, 'Foreword to the First Edition', in *The conduct of anti-terrorist operations in Malaya* (Singapore: Directorate of Operations Malaya, 1954).
47 Chapter 7, 'Patrolling', in *The conduct of anti-terrorist operations in Malaya*.
48 Coates, *Suppressing insurgency*, 156–57.

in its 'main role' in December 1956, the battalion would continue Shark North until the end of July 1957, before spending another month training in the 'main role' and then returning to Australia. The service of 3RAR, which arrived in Malaya in October 1957, followed a similar course. Its first combat operation was the still-continuing Shark North in Perak, which the battalion entered on 1 December and continued until mid-January 1958. Shark North was then replaced by Operation Ginger, which commenced on 15 January 1958 and aimed 'to eliminate some 220 CTs in the area including 31 Independent Platoon and 13/15 Independent Platoon, the State Committee Secretariat and Press' through intensive food denial. 3RAR would continue Ginger through until its conclusion on 21 April 1959, and remain on operations in Perak until its eventual withdrawal on 12 September 1959.[49]

Both battalions thus spent the majority of their two-year tours conducting food- and contact-denial operations in central Perak, in particular the area in and around Sungei Siput. Although by the time 2RAR arrived in Malaya in late 1955 the Security Forces were in the ascendency, Perak remained a bastion of MCP strength. In May 1955, the Combined Intelligence Staff estimated that between 1,170 and 1,210 CTs were active in Perak or the adjoining Thai border areas; this was approximately a third of total estimated remaining CT strength within the Malayan Federation.[50] Moreover, the MCP was believed to enjoy widespread support within the state. Roughly half the non-indigenous population of the district were Chinese, and 'an alarmingly high proportion' were 'communist supporters or sympathisers, either by tradition, sympathy or fear'. The remaining half of the populace were believed to be split evenly between Indians and Malays; the former were 'dominated by Communism to a large extent' while the latter were considered 'on the whole unreliable', with 'a rather indifferent attitude towards the prosecution of the Emergency and its associated restrictive regulations'.[51] Even after nearly 18 months of intensive operations, Far Eastern Land Forces (FARELF) noted in

---

49 See 'Summary of Royal Australian Regiment War Diaries Malaya and Emergency', n.d., AWM: AWM269 B/12/16. For torture allegations see French, *The British way in counterinsurgency*, 157 and Leon Comber, *Malaya's secret police 1945–1960: The role of the Special Branch in the Malayan Emergency* (Singapore: Institute of Southeast Asian Studies, 2008), 82–84, doi.org/10.1355/9789812308306.
50 Combined Intelligence Staff, 'An Estimate of Current Armed Terrorist Strength, 10th May 1955', n.d., AWM: AWM347 208.
51 'Interim report: Operation "Shark North" 1 May – 3 Dec 1956', n.d., AWM: AWM125 27.

February 1957 that the Perak 'CT organisation is wealthy and has no difficult in acquiring … additional funds when required. It is supported by the Chinese population and the Masses Organisation is strong'.[52]

Yet if Perak remained 'the blackest of the black' by the standards of the Emergency, it was also true that the number of CTs remained small compared to the overall operational area.[53] Shark North aimed to destroy two Armed Work Forces, with a combined strength of around 20, and embraced an area of operations that covered 370 square miles – 80 per cent of which was primary jungle.[54] 2RAR had already learned during Operation Deuce just how difficult it could be to come to grips with the enemy. Four months of intensive patrolling produced just 18 contacts with the enemy and the discovery of 27 CT camps or food dumps – a rate of return reflecting the fact the 40 or so CTs targeted by the operation were spread out over an area of approximately 300 square miles.[55] As one Australian report from March 1956 noted:

> There is undoubtedly a feeling of frustration in 2RAR at the lack of positive results … Discussion with individual troops usually leads to a reference to 'looking for a needle in a haystack' and often to the disconcerting fact that the 'needle' moves about.[56]

Compounding such frustration was the inconclusive nature of many of the few encounters with CTs in the jungle that Australians did have. While this was broadly typical of combat in the Emergency, with the 28 Commonwealth Infantry Brigade Standing Orders noting that 'contacts with terrorists are comparatively rare and often fleeting', a feeling existed within 2RAR that they were not making the most of their opportunities.[57] Of the 18 contacts the battalion experienced during Operation Deuce, only four were believed to have resulted in enemy casualties, leaving one CT dead, an estimated five wounded, and one captured. In return one Australian was killed by enemy fire, and one killed and one wounded in separate friendly fire incidents.[58]

---

52   GHQ Far East Land Forces Sitrep No 462, 'FARELF Sitrep on the Malayan Emergency for Week Ending 0900 Hours 31 January 1957', 5 February 1957, AWM: AWM347 211.
53   Dennis and Grey, *Emergency and Confrontation*, 102.
54   'Interim report: Operation "Shark North" 1 May – 3 Dec 1956', n.d., AWM: AWM125 27.
55   'Incident Log "Op Deuce"', n.d., AWM: AWM125 27.
56   'Aust Army Force FARELF Monthly Report No. 2/56', 6 March 1956, AWM: AWM95 1/1/1.
57   'Aust Army Force FARELF Monthly Report No. 2/56', 6 March 1956, AWM: AWM95 1/1/1.
58   'Incident Log "Op Deuce"', n.d., AWM: AWM125 27.

Battalion commander Lieutenant Colonel JG Ochiltree attributed the failure to convert contacts into enemy casualties in part to the nature of the small arms training given to the battalion at the Jungle Training Centre (JTC) at Canungra. Based on the Australian experience in the Second World War, the battalion had been instructed to shoot from the hip during any contact.[59] This was in direct contradiction to the training given to British units in Malaya, which emphasised the value of taking the split second necessary to bring the weapon up to the shoulder and 'ensure an aimed shot, thereby increasing the certainty of elimination of the all too elusive communist terrorist (CT)'.[60]

This seemingly minor point reflected Ochiltree's broader concern that his battalion had not been adequately prepared for the situation it faced in Malaya.[61] The rush to get 2RAR ready for deployment meant the sophisticated training apparatus built by the British for the Emergency, and the lessons it was designed to impart, was bypassed by the Australians. Ochiltree did not see a copy of *Conduct of anti-terrorist operations in Malaya* before he landed in Malaya, and did not have time to do a pre-deployment reconnaissance. Nor did the battalion initially train at the British JTC at Kota Tinggi. Instead, it undertook a program at the Australian JTC at Canungra, based on Australian doctrine derived from the war in the Pacific between 1942 and 1945. 'In terms of preparing troops physically and mentally for the rigours of the jungle, Canungra excelled,' Peter Dennis later mused, 'but whether it fitted 2 RAR for the anti-CT role that it was subsequently called upon to perform is much more problematic.'[62]

2RAR also learned that while the enemy was elusive, they could also pose great danger. On 22 June 1956 a six-man patrol was ambushed along the water pipeline that led from the Sungei Bemban reservoir to Sungei Siput by a force of between 23 and 25 guerrillas from 13/15 Platoon. The initial ambush killed one Australian and mortally wounded another, and it was only the chance presence nearby of two other patrols that prevented the first being overrun. When the engagement concluded, two CTs had been killed, one wounded and one probably wounded, while 2RAR had three

---

59 Dennis and Grey, *Emergency and Confrontation*, 91.
60 Major JO Langtry, Memorandum 1/57, 'User comments: FN Rifle and Owen Machine Carbine', 9 August 1957, AWM: AWM B/7/15.
61 Dennis and Grey, *Emergency and Confrontation*, 91.
62 Dennis and Grey, *Emergency and Confrontation*, 91.

killed and three wounded.[63] The Australian patrol had committed the cardinal sin of returning to its patrol base via the same route it had used to go out, and blundered into a sophisticated ambush that was 100 yards long and studded with five improvised explosive devices.

3RAR was in some ways better prepared than its sister battalion; its time at Canungra emphasised fitness, constant action drills and acclimatising to the jungle, while a month-long stint at Kota Tinggi between 12 October and 18 November 1957 further refined its skills in anti-terrorist operations.[64] Nonetheless, it encountered many of the same frustrations as 2RAR. For both battalions, operations in Perak consisted of a relentless program of ambushing and patrolling. Platoons operated on a 14-day roster that was broken down to two days of leave, two days of preparation and 10 days of patrolling. Ambushing could require watching a track, CT food dump or camp for over a week at a time, with the only break coming when individual soldiers retired to a rear area to prepare food. In the meantime, soldiers had to lie still, exposed to all of the elements of the jungle. Platoon commander Claude Ducker recalled:

> You might sit on a track for a week or two at a time and it was very tedious of course, lying in mud, lots of leeches, and never knowing when the enemy was going to come along … It was a very difficult honed skill to be silent in an ambush for that long.[65]

In an effort to generate additional contacts, Commonwealth security forces and the Australians constantly innovated. 'Comds must always be searching for new ways by which to outwit the terrorists' noted the 28 Commonwealth Brigade Standing Orders. 'Ops must NOT be allowed to become stereotyped. Try anything that appears a good idea.'[66] Operation Rubber Legs (23 February – 7 March 1957) and Operation Captain Zip (21–30 July 1957) eschewed the usual method of trying to push CTs into established blocking positions and ambushes in favour of flooding the assigned operational area with patrols in the hope that CTs

---

63 Dennis and Grey, *Emergency and Confrontation*, 110–13.
64 'Summary of Royal Australian Regiment War Diaries Malaya and Emergency', n.d., AWM: AWM269 B/12/16.
65 Claude Ducker, interview, 16 May 2000, Australians at War Film Archive, No. 2562.
66 28 Commonwealth Independent Infantry Brigade GP, 'Operational Standing Orders for the Emergency', 29 December 1955, AWM: AWM347 209.

fleeing from one would bump into another. Both operations involved multiple battalions from 28 Commonwealth Brigade and both ultimately failed to deliver results commensurate with the effort expended.[67]

The other significant area of innovation was the intersection between the desire to make better use of Commonwealth firepower, particularly airpower, and the problems posed by MCP/MRLA operations in deep jungle areas. While, as already noted, bases in the deep jungle posed serious political and logistical challenges for the communists, the increasing success of the Briggs Plan and food denial operations in the early 1950s made them more attractive for the MCP. Moreover, the MCP had put significant work into building relationships with Malaya's indigenous peoples – the Orang Asli. These indigenous tribes functioned as an effective intelligence screen, alerting the communists to the approach of security force elements well in advance of their actual arrival.[68] As a No. 1 (B) Squadron's report later argued:

> What was required was a swift and accurate attack against the heart of the area to catch the C.T.'s off balance and to shatter their security screen and food supply organisation; then, as soon as possible after the attack, the aboriginals should be won over to the side of the Government.[69]

The use of airstrikes against communist camps thus offered the possibility of negating the MCP's intelligence advantage, while also justifying the deployment of valuable Royal Air Force (RAF) and RAAF aircraft in theatre at a time when questions were being asked in London and Canberra as to their suitability for use in the Emergency.[70]

No. 1 (B) Squadron RAAF was heavily involved in the first major operation to use these techniques, Operation TERMITE, in July 1954. The plan called for two flights of five Lincoln bombers each to execute simultaneous attacks on two suspected CT camps; three squadrons of 22 Special Air Service Regiment would then parachute into the area to clear the camps and establish blocking positions. Once this had been done, the main force, drawn from five infantry battalions and the police,

---

67 Dennis and Grey, *Emergency and Confrontation*, 120–22, 130–31; '2RAR Operations carried out in Malaya 1955–1957', n.d., AWM: AWM125 27 1, PART 1.
68 John D Leary, *Violence and the dream people: The Orang Asli in the Malayan Emergency, 1948–1960* (Ohio University, Athens: Center for International Studies, 1995), 102–05.
69 Air Headquarters, Malaya, 'Report on Operation "Termite"', July 1955, AWM: AWM269 B/13/12.
70 Dennis and Grey, *Emergency and Confrontation*, 38–39.

would move in while airstrikes by Lincolns and de Haviland Hornet fighters continued. While the operation went largely to plan, it resulted in the confirmed death of just 15 CTs, a seemingly low return for the level of investment.[71] Between May and July 1956, Support Company 2RAR conducted Operation Eagle Swoop, which aimed to use MCP defector Tow Sen to guide a patrol to the camp of District Committee Secretary Wai Shan on the Thai–Malaya border and then to destroy it with airstrikes.[72] While Wai Shan's camp was never located, on 24 June a 4-man patrol contacted a large CT camp. Two of the Australians were killed in the initial contact, while a nearby patrol killed one of the CT and wounded another as they attempted to break contact. Elements of B and C Company were deployed in pursuit, and both airstrikes and artillery were also used liberally in the hope of hurting the fleeing enemy. Such hopes, however, appear to have been in vain.[73]

One other operation illustrated both the possibilities but also the severe limitations of airpower in the context of the Malayan Emergency. In March 1958 the pilot of an Auster spotter aircraft observed five CTs walking through the jungle. The pilot was able to divert five Lincolns from No. 1 (B) Squadron who had had to abort on their primary target to attack this moving target, and then a subsequent strike by RAF Venoms. While this displayed an impressive degree of flexibility, the fact that the CTs escaped the initial deluge of 70 500-pound bombs from the Lincolns – necessitating the subsequent strike by Venoms – and that a follow-up police patrol found no evidence that any CTs had been killed did seem to suggest that if CTs were the proverbial needle, airstrikes were the equivalent of throwing darts into the haystack and hoping for a hit.[74]

Although the Emergency officially ended in July 1960, Australian units would continue intermittent operations against the remaining CTs until August 1962: 1RAR from 1959 to 1961, and 2RAR from 1961 to 1963. Of the 609 CTs that Special Branch estimated in April 1960 to still be active, just 107 were believed to be within Malaya.[75] The remainder lived on the Thai side of the Thai–Malaya border, although incursions back into Malaya were frequent. Ensconced in the deep jungle, the surviving MCP

---

71   Dennis and Grey, *Emergency and Confrontation*, 84.
72   '2RAR Op Instr 3/57 – Op EAGLE SWOOP', 19 May 1957, AWM: AWM125 27, PART 1.
73   Dennis and Grey, *Emergency and Confrontation*, 126–29.
74   GHQ Far East Land Forces Sitrep No 546, 'FARELF Sitrep on the Malayan Emergency for Week Ending 0900 Hours 4 Sep 1958', 6 September 1958, AWM: AWM347 211.
75   Dennis and Grey, *Emergency and Confrontation*, 150.

and MRLA communicated via courier routes and relied on the Orang Asli for intelligence, supplies and even recruits. Despite the complications introduced by the border, the security force concept of operations against the MCP/MRLA remained basically the same. The first operation undertaken by 1RAR, Operation Bamboo (24 November 1959 – mid-April 1960), aimed to disrupt the flow of food and supplies to the MCP/MRLA by destroying the 12 Regiment Asal Organisation, which served as a conduit between the Orang Asli and the communists.[76] Subsequent operations by the battalion (Operation Bamboo Bar, August 1960 – June 1961) and its successor 2RAR (Operation Magnus, 1 August 1962 – 6 October 1962, 1 May 1963 – late June 1963) had a similar focus.[77]

Operations during this period posed unique challenges for the Australian battalions. Even more so than in previous years, MCP/MRLA personnel were determined to avoid contact with the security forces. The standing orders of 1RAR noted that:

> at this stage of the Emergency it appears that CTs are loath to risk contact with S[ecurity] F[orces], and will normally retreat with speed on contact, or suspicion of the presence of SF.[78]

In the event, the battalion did not have a single contact with a CT during its time in Malaya, although it found clear evidence of the presence of the enemy during operations. Despite conducting operations for a much shorter period of time 2RAR had two contacts – a successful ambush on 4 August 1962 that left one CT wounded, and a contact on 3 May 1963 in which the enemy escaped unharmed. So rare were contacts by mid-1962 that the battalion executed an entire operation, Hot Trail, in an effort to locate the man wounded on 4 August. The man was never found, emphasising just how elusive the enemy had become.[79] In the absence of CTs, the jungle remained the major threat to the Australians. Standing orders emphasised the need for patrols to carry sufficient supplies in case they became lost, kits to deal with snakebite, and the dangers posed by scrub typhus and leptospirosis.[80]

---

76 1RAR OO No 1, 'Brief: "Op Bamboo" to 3 Nov 59 – final verbal briefing by IO prior to move into FWD bases', 10 November 1959, AWM: AWM95 7/1/1.
77 Dennis and Grey, *Emergency and Confrontation*, 150–63.
78 '1RAR SO's for Anti-CT Ops', 14 November 1959, AWM: AWM95 7/1/1.
79 Dennis and Grey, *Emergency and Confrontation*, 157–63.
80 '1RAR SO's for Anti-CT Ops', 14 November 1959, AWM: AWM95 7/1/1.

Legacy

Just over a month after 2RAR began withdrawing from operations on the Thai–Malaya border in June 1962, members of the Australian Army Training Team Vietnam (AATTV) touched down in Saigon, Republic of Vietnam (RVN).[81] The arrival of the AATTV marked the start of just over a decade of active Australian involvement in the defence of the RVN, a commitment that ultimately dwarfed that made to Malaya during the Emergency. Thirteen Australian soldiers and two airmen were killed on operations in Malaya between 1950 and 1963, with a further 36 dying from non-operational causes.[82] Over 400 Australians would be killed in action in Vietnam, with thousands more becoming casualties.[83] This disparity in numbers reflected not only differences in the size of the Australian commitment, but also the nature of combat. In Malaya, Australian battalions faced an enemy who was never encountered in groups larger than a reinforced platoon, whose heaviest weapons were small arms, and who invariably wanted to avoid contact. In Vietnam, Australian units faced enemies who were known to operate in battalion- or regimental-sized groups, possessed larger numbers of modern automatic and infantry support weapons, and were often prepared to offer sustained resistance. Unsurprisingly in light of this, combat in Vietnam was not only more frequent than in Malaya but could also be considerably more intense.

Yet despite these differences, the experience of the Malayan Emergency exerted a strong influence on the Australian Army during its years in Vietnam. Australian doctrine, codified in 1965 in *The division in battle* series, was heavily informed by what had occurred in Malaya and by *ATOM*.[84] The ideas encapsulated in *The division in battle* and *ATOM* in turn influenced the vision of Australian commanders in Vietnam as to how they should fight. In a postwar interview, Major General SC Graham, the second commander of 1 Australian Task Force, explained his concept of operations (itself an extension of that of his predecessor) as a focus on 'the breaking of the links between the main and local forces'. Graham

---

81 Ian McNeill, *The team: Australian Army advisers in Vietnam* (Canberra: Australian War Memorial, 1984), 15.
82 'Casualties in Operational Areas', May 1966, AWM: AWM269 B/7/17.
83 Grey, *A military history of Australia,* 249.
84 RN Bushby, *Educating an army: Australian Army doctrinal development and the operational experience in South Vietnam, 1965–72* (Canberra: Strategic and Defence Studies Centre, The Australian National University, 1998), 16–22.

went on to argue that 'if we could be successful in this we would deprive the main forces of their supplies; their information; their recruits; their contact with the people and their prestige'.[85] The parallels with the British system in Malaya are unmistakable, as is the contrast with an American approach that emphasised targeting not the linkages but the main forces themselves.[86] Equally, the Australian concept of close ambushing – in which access to the villages of Phuoc Tuy province was denied to the enemy through an intensive program of ambushing at night – was explicitly based on experiences in Malaya. Highly successful, it formed the basis of Australian operations from early 1970 through until mid-1971.[87]

---

85   Major General Graham, interview, 29 March 1971, transcript at AWM: AWM107 2, 8–9.
86   Thomas Richardson, *Destroy and build: Pacification in Phuoc Tuy, 1966–72* (Melbourne: Cambridge University Press, 2017), 69–72, doi.org/10.1017/9781316995648.
87   Richardson, *Destroy and build*, 150–54.

7

Australia's Confrontation with Indonesia and military commitment to Borneo, 1964–66

Lachlan Grant and Michael Kelly

In response to the newly formed Federation of Malaysia, in 1963 the government of Indonesia, led by President Sukarno, adopted a policy of '*Konfrontasi*' (Confrontation) with the new state. As a result of this new and dangerous situation, following continual requests by the Malaysian Government, in 1965 Australia deployed troops to the Malaysian states of Sabah and Sarawak in North Borneo to help protect the borders from incursions by Kalimantan (Indonesian Borneo) insurgents. The events surrounding the Indonesian Confrontation of the Federation of Malaysia occurred against the backdrop of the escalating war in Vietnam, which has cast a long shadow over Australian experiences and memory of Confrontation.

The Vietnam War, lasting from 1955 to 1975 was the defining conflict of the Cold War in Southeast Asia. Australia had sent military advisers to Vietnam in 1962, and then on 29 April 1965 Sir Robert Menzies's Liberal Government announced the commitment of Australian troops. In June 1965, 1 Battalion, the Royal Australian Regiment (1RAR) and supporting units arrived in Vietnam; by 1975 some 60,000 Australians had served in the conflict, and over 500 were killed.¹ Yet at the time of Australia's escalation of commitment to the Vietnam conflict and the dispatch of 1RAR, Australia was most concerned about Confrontation and the possibility of open conflict with Indonesia. In unison, Australia was committed to curbing the expansion of communism in the region, supporting the new nation state of Malaysia and keeping good terms with its closest allies. In doing so, Australia trod a fine diplomatic path to avoid war with its neighbour and the largest state in Southeast Asia. Where Vietnam escalated and demanded a significant Australian commitment, Confrontation would evolve into a small conflict that petered out in August 1966, costing the lives of 22 Australian servicemen.² However, the engagement in Borneo provided important experience for the Australian Army in patrolling and fighting guerrilla forces and counterinsurgency in Southeast Asia ahead of significant deployments to Vietnam.

Creation of Malaysia and Indonesian retaliation

In 1961 a proposal was put forward by the Malayan prime minister, Tunku Abdul Rahman, to create a new nation state, the Federation of Malaysia. This would combine the current states of Malaya, Singapore and the British territories of North Borneo (to be renamed Sabah), Sarawak and the Sultanate of Brunei. Britain came to support the proposal. Brunei would later withdraw from discussions, the benefits for the oil-rich territory being less appealing than for its neighbours, and subsequently did not become part of Malaysia. The proposal was opposed by Indonesia, who shared a border with Sabah and Sarawak in Borneo. Sukarno declared the Malaysia proposal neo-colonialism, painting Tunku as a puppet of the British.³ An unsuccessful revolt in Brunei by the 'North Borneo National Army', with clandestine Indonesian support, in December 1962 increased tensions. The instigators of the rebellion were cadres who had received both military training and political indoctrination in Indonesia, and their

---

1   Ashley Ekins with Ian McNeill, *Fighting to the finish: The Australian Army and the Vietnam War 1968–1975* (Sydney: Allen & Unwin, 2012), 828, 834.
2   Figures from the Australian War Memorial's Roll of Honour, www.awm.gov.au/advanced-search/people?roll=Roll%20of%20Honour&facet_related_conflict_sort=16%3AIndonesian%20Confrontation%2C%201962-1966 (accessed 27 June 2018).
3   Peter Edwards, *Australia and the Vietnam War* (Sydney: NewSouth Books, 2014), 81–82.

aim was not to overthrow the sultan but to protest Malaysia's federation. The revolt was short-lived and put down by British forces, some of whom were ferried from Singapore by a C-130 Hercules transport aircraft of the Royal Australian Air Force (RAAF).[4]

A diplomatic feud ensued, and resulted in Indonesia declaring a policy of Confrontation. This was formally announced by the Indonesian foreign minister Dr Subandrio on 20 January 1963.[5] What was specifically meant by the term 'confrontation' was not defined, but the intention by the Indonesians was probably to use bluff, both diplomatic and militarily, as it had to wrest West New Guinea from the Dutch. But unlike the Netherlands, Malaysia had strong diplomatic and military support from its allies: Britain, Australia and New Zealand.[6]

Australia's response

Diplomatically, Australia was placed in a difficult position. It wanted to support the new state of Malaysia but avoid war with Indonesia. A concerted approach in partnership with its major allies, Britain and the United States, proved difficult as both had fundamentally different policies.[7] The Anglo–Malayan Defence Agreement between Britain and Malaya, entered into following Malaya's independence in 1957, ensured Britain's commitment to the defence of Malaysia. Australia came under pressure from Britain to commit to the defence of Malaysia, but had its own regional concerns. It was important to Australian forward defence strategy to encourage Britain and the United States to remain committed to security in Southeast Asia.

---

4   Peter Dennis and Jeffrey Grey, *The official history of Australia's involvement in Southeast Asian conflicts 1948–1975*, vol. 5, *Emergency and Confrontation: Australian military operations in Malaya and Borneo 1950–1966* (St Leonards: Allen & Unwin in association with the Australian War Memorial, 1996), 175–76; Peter Edwards with Gregory Pemberton, *The official history of Australia's involvement in Southeast Asian conflicts 1948–1975*, vol. 1, *Crises and commitments: The politics and diplomacy of Australia's involvement in Southeast Asian conflicts 1948–1965* (North Sydney: Allen & Unwin and the Australian War Memorial, 1992), 257.
5   Edwards with Pemberton, *Crises and commitments*, 258.
6   Dennis and Grey, *Emergency and Confrontation*, 171–73.
7   David Lee and Moreen Dee, 'Southeast Asian conflicts', in *Facing north: A century of Australian engagement with Asia*, vol. 1, *1901 to the 1970s*, ed. David Goldsworthy (Melbourne: Melbourne University Press, 2001) 270.

However, where Prime Minister Menzies was keen to support Britain, the Minister for External Affairs, Sir Garfield Barwick, and his departmental officials wanted to proceed cautiously. They were fundamentally aware that Britain and the United States could abandon the region, and since Australia and Indonesia would always be neighbours, Barwick proceeded on a path to try and avoid risking hostility with Indonesia. The resulting Cabinet decision on 5 February 1963 was to support Malaysia, and make clear to Indonesia Australia's disproval of its campaign. While pursuing this path of avoiding conflict while expressing disapproval for Confrontation, it was also desirable to improve relations with Indonesia.[8] Thus, Australia kept its relationship with Indonesia steady and meetings between officials continued – such as cooperating on the demarcation of the border between Papua New Guinea and West Irian – and Indonesian students were still welcome under Australian training programs, and development aid continued to be provided under the Colombo Plan. Notably, during Confrontation a small number of Indonesian army officers remained enrolled at the Australian Army's Staff College.[9]

It was quite a balancing act, which occupied the Australian Government for over 12 months from early 1963 until 1964, in which time Malaysia had officially come into being on 16 September 1963. Barwick, his department and ambassadors in Kuala Lumpur and Jakarta worked tirelessly throughout the year, urging restraint on both sides.[10] During this period, Barwick was accused of 'appeasement' by sections of the press and opposition, a word that derived negative connotations associated with British Prime Minister Neville Chamberlain's handling of Adolf Hitler's Nazi Germany prior to the outbreak of the Second World War.[11] Regardless of these accusations in Australia, Sukarno recognised that Australian policy was distinct from those of Britain and the United States. On 16 September 1963, mobs in Jakarta protesting the creation of Malaysia attacked the British and Malaysian embassies: the British embassy was burnt down, but the Australian embassy was left alone.[12]

In contrast to Britain, the United States was concerned by military intervention against Indonesia over the defence of Malaysia. The United States wished to develop long-term ties with Indonesia, and did not want

---

8 Edwards with Pemberton, *Crises and commitments*, 258–59.
9 Lee and Dee, 'Southeast Asian conflicts', 273.
10 Edwards with Pemberton, *Crises and commitments*, 262–63.
11 'Barwick accused on appeasement', *The Canberra Times*, 17 May 1963, 10.
12 Edwards with Pemberton, *Crises and commitments*, 262–63.

them falling into the communist bloc, knowing that the Communist Party of Indonesia was a pillar of support to the Sukarno presidency (and may become more influential) and that the Indonesian military build-up had been enabled by extensive loans from the Soviet Union.[13]

There was a widespread concern in Australia, amid both government and the general public, as to the extent to which the United States might support Australia militarily under the Australia, New Zealand and United States (ANZUS) Treaty if war broke out with Indonesia. The messages from the United States were mixed. When asked by Prime Minister Menzies in a meeting on 7 June 1963 about the application of the ANZUS Treaty should Australian troops defending Malaya come under attack, United States Under-Secretary of State for Political Affairs Averell Harriman was positive that 'the ANZUS Treaty would, according to the advice given to the United States Administration by its lawyers, come into operation'.[14] United States President John F Kennedy was concerned when he learned of Harriman's statement, and the matter was discussed with Menzies who sought further clarification when he met with President Kennedy during a visit to Washington on 8 July. The ultimate outcome of these discussions in June and July, as the Australian Government concluded, was that the American reassurances meant Malaysia was now considered part of the Pacific under the terms of the ANZUS Treaty.[15]

Regardless, US support was lukewarm and included qualifications that the United States would act if there were an 'armed attack by Indonesian armed forces, on the armed forces, public vessels or aircraft of Australia in Malaysia', but only if the attack was 'overt' rather than 'subversion, guerrilla warfare or indirect aggression'. Further, the involvement of American troops was excluded; limiting support to 'air and sea forces and to provide logistics' and any action needed to be 'subject to the constitutional processes of the United States'.[16]

---

13 Lee and Dee, 'Southeast Asian conflicts', 271; Edwards with Pemberton, *Crises and commitments*, 258.
14 Report of meeting with Mr Averell Harriman, United States Under Secretary of State for Political Affairs, in the Cabinet Room, Parliament House, Canberra, 'Malaysia – Application of ANZUS Treaty', 7 June 1963, National Archives of Australia (NAA): A1209, 1963/6587.
15 Edwards with Pemberton, *Crises and commitments*, 265–67.
16 Washington memorandum, 'ANZUS – Interpretation – Malaysia', 17 October 1963, NAA: A1838, 270/1/1, Part 1.

Although Australia did not commit troops to Borneo in the face of continued requests by Britain and Malaysia during the second half of 1963, it did hold discussions with the British to plan such a scenario.[17] In December 1963, the British and Malaysians asked Australia to send an infantry battalion and a squadron of the Special Air Service (SAS) to Borneo. At this point, Australia agreed that 3 Battalion, the Royal Australian Regiment (3RAR), recently arrived on the Malaysian peninsula as part of the Far East Strategic Reserve (FESR), be posted on the Thai–Malaysian border for anti-terrorist operations, so as to free up a Malaysian battalion for service in Borneo. Following a second request in April 1964 along similar lines, Australia committed a squadron of army engineers to Sabah, and two Royal Australian Navy (RAN) minesweepers for patrol duties in Borneo waters.[18] British and Malaysian units in Borneo at this point numbered 10 battalions, and 187 contacts with insurgents had been reported in the 12 months since April 1963.[19]

At this time, the Australian Government decided against sending the requested infantry battalion and SAS squadron, as it risked involving direct contact with Indonesian forces. It recognised the possibility of their need in future but felt the British and Malaysian forces present were equipped to deal with the current threat. In May 1964 Prime Minister Menzies wrote to his British counterpart, Sir Alec Douglas-Home, outlining Australia's position. While being 'sensitive to the burden you are carrying in Malaysia', wrote Menzies, 'we face an unhappy choice'. He felt there was 'no pressing military requirement to commit Australian combat forces to action in Borneo at this stage of covert aggression'.[20] The following week, the government reaffirmed Australia's position to assist the defence of Malaysia gradually while not giving up on the prospect of 'persuading Indonesia by political means to call off confrontation'.[21]

Throughout 1963 and 1964, Australian foreign and defence policies were dominated by discussion of Confrontation. The situations in both Borneo and Vietnam were monitored closely, but by the end of 1964,

---

17 Edwards, *Australia and the Vietnam War*, 87.
18 Department of External Affairs outward cablegram, 'The military situation in Borneo', 22 May 1964, NAA: A1209 1964/6040, PART 1.
19 Attachment to Defence Committee Minute No. 26/1964, NAA: A1209 1964/6040, PART 1.
20 Message, Sir Robert Menzies to Sir Alec Douglas-Home, 15 May 1964, NAA: A1209 1964/6040, PART 1.
21 Department of External Affairs outward cablegram, 'The military situation in Borneo', 22 May 1964, NAA: A1209 1964/6040, PART 1.

Confrontation was still considered the 'only direct threat to Australia and its territories'.[22] Nevertheless, Paul Hasluck, who in April 1964 replaced Garfield Barwick as Minister for External Affairs, was more aligned to the view of the United States that the situation in Vietnam was a more significant threat than Confrontation. Events in the second half of 1964 and early 1965 changed Australia's position leading to the deployment of troops to Borneo.

In August, the Gulf of Tonkin incident in Vietnam led to the escalation of American involvement in South Vietnam, which was to be supported by an increased Australian commitment. The same month, Indonesian paratroopers landed on the Malaysian peninsula. They were quickly rounded up, with assistance from 3RAR. These two separate events had increased regional tensions and Australian commitments to both conflicts.[23]

A response to these developments was the introduction of conscription in November 1964 to increase the size of the Australian Army. This saw the passing of the *National Service Act 1964* (Cth) by parliament. By the final month of 1964, Australia and Britain were planning military responses to further unprovoked attacks by Indonesia. These plans included an agreement for the Royal Air Force to use Darwin as a 'strike base' in northern Australia for reprisal attacks on targets in Indonesia.[24] On 1 January 1965, Sukarno announced that Indonesia was withdrawing from the United Nations, in a direct protest of Malaysia gaining a non-permanent seat on the Security Council. Sukarno also became more extreme in his pronouncements, and relations between Indonesia and China had firmed, with talk of a 'Beijing–Jakarta axis' or 'Beijing–Jakarta–Hanoi–Phnom Penh–Pyongyang' alliance.[25] Such talk linked the conflicts in Vietnam and Borneo, raising US concerns about the influence, or possible takeover, of the communist party in Indonesia. As historian Peter Edwards has stated, 'the Australian government faced its most acute crisis in foreign policy since 1945'.[26]

---

22   Edwards, *Australia's Vietnam War*, 99.
23   Edwards, *Australia's Vietnam War*, 98–103.
24   Message, Sir Robert Menzies to Mr Harold Wilson, 'Chronological exchanges of information with UK government on Malaysian confrontation', 8 December 1964, NAA: A1939, TS687/9/3, PART 1.
25   Edwards with Pemberton, *Crises and commitments*, 340.
26   Edwards, *Australia's Vietnam War*, 104.

During this time, Indonesia had been moving more troops to Borneo and positioning them near the borders of Sabah and Sarawak.[27] In December 1964, British intelligence sources estimated that the Indonesians had placed 10,000 combat troops in Kalimantan. They were being reinforced by the equivalent of another six more brigades and it was expected that they would be ready for operations by late January or early February 1965.[28] To meet the growing threat to Malaysia and the Indonesian military build-up in Kalimantan, Australia agreed in January 1965 (announced publicly in February) to send 3RAR and an SAS squadron to Borneo.

3RAR arrives

When Confrontation began in December 1962, there was barely a full British brigade in Borneo, but by March 1965, there were some 17,000 Commonwealth troops deployed across four infantry brigades: the West Brigade consisted of five battalions and had responsibility for 290 kilometres of the Kalimantan border; the Mid-West Brigade had two battalions and covered 707 kilometres; the Central Brigade had two battalions and covered 427 kilometres; and the East Brigade, which covered the eastern extremity of Sarawak and all of Sabah, had three battalions covering 130 kilometres. All four brigades were controlled by the Director of Borneo Operations (DOBOPs) from his headquarters on Labuan.[29]

3RAR was warned to prepare for deployment to Borneo on 13 February where the battalion would relive 1/7 Gurkha Rifles in West Brigade, located in Sarawak.[30] In the lead-up to the deployment, 3RAR had received lessons on conducting operations in Borneo as well as weapons training.[31] During February and early March, 3RAR's commanding officer Lieutenant Colonel Bruce McDonald, and other officers of the battalion, visited Sarawak to

---

27 Message, Mr Harold Wilson to the Rt Hon John McEwan, 15 January 1965, NAA: A1939, TS687/9/3 PART 1.
28 Joint Intelligence Committee report on the military situation in Malaysia, 'Borneo territories – Sarawak, Sabah and Brunei – Confrontation', 13 January 1965, NAA: A1838, TS696/14/1.
29 David Horner and Jean Bou, ed., *Duty first: The Royal Australian Regiment in war and peace* (North Sydney: Allen & Unwin, 1990), 160.
30 '3 Battalion Royal Australian Regiment, narrative, annexes [1–28 Feb 1965]', Australian War Memorial (AWM): AWM 95 7/3/45, 6.
31 '3 Battalion Royal Australian Regiment, narrative, duty officer's log, annexes [1–31 Mar 1965]', 6–7, AWM: AWM 95 7/3/46; Ian Kuring, *Redcoats to Cams: A history of Australian infantry 1788–2001* (Loftus: Australian Military History Publications in association with the Australian Army History Unit, 2004), 309.

gain an appreciation of the area that the battalion would be operating in. At the same time, other battalion officers were being sent to South Vietnam to gain an appreciation of the situation there as well.[32]

The main body of 3RAR arrived off Kuching in mid-March, having sailed from Terendak aboard the Royal Marine Commando fast troop transport, the converted Royal Navy aircraft carrier, HMS *Albion*.[33] The Australian companies were flown directly from the flight deck to their forward bases with the Gurkhas being brought out on the return journey. 3RAR was seconded to West Brigade, which was commanded by Brigadier William Cheyne.[34] West Brigade was under the most direct threat from Indonesian forces as the capital Kuching was less than 50 kilometres from the border. By December 1964, Indonesia had moved eight regular companies of up to 200 men and 11 irregular companies to the area, which presented a clear and immediate danger to the capital of Sarawak.

3RAR was given the most direct line of advance to Kuching as its area of operations. The battalion was responsible for a zone around 48 kilometres long and 48 kilometres in depth along the border. Three of the rifle companies occupied company bases along the border; the fourth rifle company and battalion headquarters were located south of Kuching.[35] 3RAR was considered by the British to be a 'veteran' battalion, with many of its members having served during the Second World War, the Malayan Emergency and the more recent operations hunting Communist Terrorists along the Malay–Thai border and rounding up Indonesian infiltrators in mainland Malaysia. Unlike British battalions, who had to serve one operational tour in either Sarawak or Sabah before being able to conduct Claret operations – top-secret, cross-border incursions by Commonwealth forces – the Australians would take part in these operations after only a month of acclimatisation in North Borneo.[36]

A Company, which had arrived in Sarawak the week prior, had been sent to Stass, where patrols began immediately. B Company was deployed to Bukit Knuckle and C Company to Serrikin. Battalion headquarters and D Company were flown to Bau. The handover was completed at 11:00 am

---

32 '3 Battalion Royal Australian Regiment, narrative, duty officer's log, annexes [1–31 Mar 1965]', AWM: AWM 95 7/3/46, 5–10.
33 Kuring, *Redcoats*, 303.
34 Dennis and Grey, *Emergency and Confrontation*, 246.
35 Kuring, *Redcoats*, 303.
36 Dennis and Grey, *Emergency and Confrontation*, 246.

on 23 March.[37] The seriousness of their task was brought home sharply to the men of 3RAR that afternoon when members of a patrol from 3 Platoon, A Company triggered a mine near the Sarawak–Kalimantan border. Sergeant Reg Weiland was killed instantly and a local Iban tracker, Mudah anak Jali, died of his wounds some 15 minutes later while being carried out of the jungle. Another three men were wounded.[38] The same platoon suffered a second fatal mine incident on 17 May when Private Larry Downes triggered a mine and was killed along with Sergeant Vince Vella, who had replaced Reg Weiland as acting platoon sergeant.[39]

The company bases that the Australians occupied were a key feature of the operations against Indonesia. They were not static defensive positions, rather bases from which patrols could deploy on local tasks and cross-border operations. A full rifle company could be housed there, as well as the supporting artillery or mortars. Corporal Bob Wyssenbach of B Company, 3RAR, recalled that after arriving at Bukit Knuckle:

> one platoon had to move out immediately for four days, the other two platoons had to double up at the fort for two days, then one move out … thus setting the pattern … four days out on patrol and two days in [Company] base.[40]

The same pattern was followed in the other company bases. The bases also gave the remote border people a sense of security, knowing that any incursion by Indonesian soldiers would be swiftly dealt with. The forward company bases were resupplied by helicopter, as no roads stretched that far south.[41]

Following the first mine incident, 3RAR maintained border patrols, including 'hearts and minds' operations. Much like the Malayan Emergency, 'hearts and minds' operations were key to keeping the local populace on side, especially as many of them had relatives in Kalimantan. The Australians were also faced with having to deal with the sizeable Clandestine Communist Organisation (CCO), based mainly around the Bau area. Though the CCO was meant to be handled by Malaysian security forces, the Australians remained aware of the threat they posed.

---

37 '3 Battalion Royal Australian Regiment, narrative, duty officer's log, annexes [1–31 Mar 1965]', AWM: AWM 95 7/3/46, 15.
38 Dennis and Grey, *Emergency and Confrontation*, 266.
39 Bob Wyssenbach, 'Bukit Knuckle (Borneo Campaign 1962–1966)', in *We were there in the R.A.R.*, ed. Bill Parry (Baguio City, Philippines: Immaculate Heart Printhall, 2005), 50.
40 Wyssenbach, 'Bukit Knuckle', 57.
41 Kuring, *Redcoats*, 305.

Australian patrols moved slowly and took care not to use worn tracks. Tracks, it was thought, could be mined or ambushed by the Indonesians. With the border area being mountainous and covered in thick jungle, contact was usually initiated by those in static positions. When patrol contacts did occur, Australian and other Commonwealth forces fired first 70 per cent of the time and inflicted greater casualties at a rate of 1 to 12.7 Indonesians.[42] But it was the Claret operations that succeeded beyond all expectations by destabilising Indonesian efforts, causing heavy casualties and pushing the enemy back from the border with Sarawak.

Claret operations: Patrolling the border

Operation Claret came about in response to Indonesia's increasingly hostile cross-border incursions into Sarawak, Sabah and mainland Malaysia during 1964. Britain's parliament authorised the cross-border operations in July, following Malaysia's concern that Indonesia's continued attempts to land troops by air and sea on its mainland, as well as the increasing incursions into Sarawak and Sabah, would lead to an escalation of the conflict.[43]

Major General Walter Walker, as DOBOPs, pushed for permission to cross the border into Kalimantan with the aim of throwing Indonesian forces off balance, thereby gaining the initiative. He understood the application of low-intensity operations, having been one of the key architects of the successful counterinsurgency during the Malayan Emergency.[44] To maintain operational security and minimise the risk of any escalation of the fighting, Walker drew up a strict set of regulations with which Claret operations would be prosecuted. Known as the 'golden rules', these were:

1. Every operation will be authorised by DOBOPs.
2. Only trained and tested troops would be used.
3. Depth of penetration must be limited and the attacks must only be made to thwart offensive action by the enemy.

---

42 Bob Hall, Andrew Ross, and Derrill de Heer, *Comparative study: Combat operations in North Borneo (Indonesian Confrontation) and 1ATF in Vietnam* (Sydney: University of New South Wales, 2012), 57.
43 Will Fowler, *Britain's secret war: The Indonesian Confrontation 1962–66* (Oxford: Osprey Publishing, 2006), 24.
44 John A Nagl, *Learning to eat soup with a knife: Counterinsurgency lessons from Malaya and Vietnam* (Chicago: University of Chicago Press, 2005), 97–98.

4. No air support will be given to any operation across the border, except in the most extreme of emergencies.
5. Every operation must be planned with the aid of a sand table and thoroughly rehearsed for at least two weeks.
6. Each operation will be planned and executed with maximum security. Every man taking part must be sworn to secrecy, full cover plans must be made and the operations to be given code-names and never discussed in detail on telephone or radio. Identity discs must be left behind before departure and no traces – such as cartridge cases, paper, ration packs, etc. – must be left in Kalimantan.
7. On no account must any soldier taking part be captured by the enemy – alive or dead.[45]

The border crossings were authorised by the British Government with an initial depth of 5,000 yards (about 4,500 metres). This was to keep troops within support range of artillery and mortars, but this distance was increased to 10,000 yards by the end of 1964.[46] Some operations conducted by the SAS went up to and beyond 20,000 yards. The golden rules, including the incursion depths, were adapted as the campaign went on, but the security and planning elements were strictly adhered to, and Walker later credited to them the minimising of Commonwealth casualties.[47] As 3RAR made ready to deploy to Sarawak, Walker handed over as DOBOPs to Major General George Lea, who was the polar opposite to Walker in demeanour. However, the quiet and considered Lea continued to use the golden rules when planning operations.[48]

During its time in Sarawak, 3RAR carried out 32 Claret operations, which resulted in four major contacts with Indonesian regular forces, all of which were Australian-initiated ambushes. The last of these, known as Operation Blockbuster, conducted by 2 Platoon, A Company and an attached forward observation officer (FOO) party, was the most successful. The total strength of the ambush party was two officers and 32 other ranks.[49] The operation was authorised after Second Lieutenant

---

45   Fowler, *Britain's secret war*, 24; Raffi Gregorian, 'CLARET operations and Confrontation, 1964–1966', *Conflict Quarterly: Journal of the Centre for Conflict Studies* 11, no. 1 (1991): 54.
46   Horner, *Duty first*, 165.
47   Gregorian, 'CLARET operations and Confrontation', 54.
48   David Horner, *SAS: Phantoms of war, a history of the Australian Special Air Service* (Crows Nest: Allen & Unwin, 2002), 78.
49   'Operation Blockbuster' After Action Report (AAR), 16 June 1965, document held in private collection.

Douglas Byers's platoon located an east–west track in Kalimantan that had shown signs of recent use. The ambush party spent three days in position before hearing the approach of their quarry. The Indonesians apparently believed they were safe as they moved openly along the trail and were talking loudly, had their weapons slung and were tightly bunched up.

When about 25 men had entered the killing zone, Byers initiated the ambush by standing up and opening fire with his Owen Machine Carbine at a range of no more than 6 yards. The resulting fusillade resulted in heavy casualties to the Indonesians with at least 12 men killed outright. Three men at the head of the group attempted to escape along the track, but were killed instantly when a cut-off group fired two Claymore mines. The Indonesians responded with small arms, machine gun and mortar fire. The FOO, Lieutenant Stephen Overton, Royal Artillery, called in fire support in the form of artillery and mortars, which silenced the Indonesian mortar and was believed to have inflicted further heavy casualties on the Indonesians. Overton continued to call in fire as Byers called for the withdrawal of the ambush patrol; by the following morning they reached their company base at Stass.

The operation had been entirely successful with 25 Indonesians confirmed killed, but the final tally was thought to be up to 50 killed, due to the accurate artillery fire brought down by Overton. The Australians had suffered two men wounded: one by small arms the other by mortar fire.[50] Byers was awarded a Military Cross for his actions during the operation. Brigadier Willian Cheyne later stated that 'the perfect ambush only happens once in a while but this is one of those occasions'.[51] After four and half months, 3RAR was replaced by 2/10 Gurkhas. In September they were relieved at Terendak by 4RAR. By the end of its operational tour in Borneo, 3RAR had suffered three men killed, all by mines, and five wounded.[52]

After several months of training, 4RAR deployed to Sarawak in April 1966; this was the first time that national servicemen were deployed on operations with the Australian Army. 4RAR joined West Brigade and was sent to the Bau area, where the battalion occupied similar positions to those of 3RAR the year before. As the battalion had a high number of

---

50   'Operation Blockbuster' AAR, 16 June 1965.
51   Dennis and Grey, *Emergency and Confrontation*, 277.
52   Kuring, *Redcoats*, 304.

officers and non-commissioned officers with previous active service, and a number of men from 3RAR who had already served in Borneo in 1965, Brigadier Cheyne considered the battalion to be 'tried and tested'.[53] Patrols on the Malaysian side of the border were constant, and 4RAR began Claret operations in early May. At least a dozen Claret reconnaissance operations had been completed by the time cross-border operations were suspended later in the month due to the start of peace talks between Malaysia and Indonesia.

The suspension of Claret operations led to an increase in the rate of Indonesian incursions into Sarawak. In June, Major General Lea authorised Claret operations to recommence to once again push the Indonesians back from the border of Sarawak and keep their attempted operations off balance. 4RAR fought its most significant action on 15 June 1966, when C Company was involved in a series of rolling firefights with a 10-man Indonesian patrol on the Sarawak side of the border. The initial contact was made by 8 Platoon, commanded by Lieutenant Doug Byers MC, who had transferred to 4RAR at the end of 3RAR's deployment. During the first contact, the Indonesians broke into two groups of five and began to withdraw, with one of the groups evading the Australians and escaping back into Kalimantan. 8 Platoon pursued the other group and pushed it into an ambush, which was initiated by 9 Platoon. Four Indonesians were subsequently killed and 4RAR's only combat loss occurred during the action when Private Vic Richards was shot in the stomach and mortally wounded. He died from his wounds several days later.[54] 4RAR's operational tour came to an end on 11 August 1966 when the peace treaty between Malaysia and Indonesia was signed. The battalion left Borneo soon after and was back at Terendak at the end of the month.[55]

Australian SAS operations

The Australian SAS saw active service for the first time during Confrontation with both 1 and 2 SAS squadrons being deployed. Led by Major Alf Garland, 1 SAS Squadron arrived in Brunei in mid-February

---

53 Brian Avery, *Our secret war: The 4th Battalion, the Royal Australian Regiment: defending Malaysia against Indonesian confrontation, 1965–1967* (Melbourne: Slouch Hat Publications, 2002), 126.
54 AWM 152 Roll of Honour cards: Sabah/Sarawak, 311512 Private Victor Herbert Richards, 4th Battalion, Royal Australian Regiment; Dennis and Grey, *Emergency and Confrontation*, 293.
55 Kuring, *Redcoats*, 305.

1965 and served in the border regions of Sabah and Sarawak. 2 SAS Squadron, commanded by Major Jim Hughes, arrived at Kuching in January 1966 and operated in the western side of Sarawak. For their respective deployments, both squadrons were attached to the British 22 Special Air Service Regiment, which came under the direct control of DOBOPs. The SAS's primary role was reconnaissance. Both SAS squadrons adopted the British four-man patrol set-up, which gave them the ability to deploy more patrols and cover more ground. It was thought that smaller patrols would be less easy to detect, and if enemy contact did occur, the 'shoot and scoot' method would be applied, which meant delivering a large amount of initial firepower, followed by rapid fire and movement away from the contact point.[56]

With 1 SAS Squadron based in Brunei Town and 2 SAS Squadron in Kuching, the only way the patrols could be effectively deployed was by helicopter. Patrols would be dropped off at cleared landing sites near the Kalimantan border, after which they would patrol on foot across into Kalimantan. Soon after arriving, both squadrons deployed on lengthy patrols, primarily to familiarise themselves with their operational areas and conduct 'hearts and minds' operations among the border tribes, providing medical aid and gathering intelligence with which to assist planning of future operations. During their deployment both 1 and 2 SAS squadrons conducted numerous deep reconnaissance operations into Kalimantan, which yielded valuable intelligence and identified numerous Indonesian bases, and on several occasions the SAS also conducted ambushes against Indonesian troops. On 21 July 1965 a 10-man patrol by 1 SAS Squadron ambushed a boat with six Indonesian soldiers, all armed and carrying kit bags. All six Indonesians were killed, after which the SAS patrol withdrew. Indonesian soldiers in the area opened fire in all directions in a clumsy effort to locate the Australians, who made it to their exfiltration point unharmed.[57]

The cancellation of Claret operations in late May 1966 proved frustrating for 2 SAS Squadron. Recently arrived in Borneo, they had conducted a number of familiarisation patrols and were preparing to deploy across the border. The squadron did complete a number of Claret operations when Claret was reactivated in June in response to an Indonesian incursion,

---

56 Kuring, *Redcoats*, 308.
57 Dennis and Grey, *Emergency and Confrontation*, 305.

and though these were predominantly reconnaissance patrols, there were a number of contacts with Indonesian troops. 2 SAS Squadron's tour ended on 21 July, after which it left Borneo and returned to Perth.[58]

The Australian SAS suffered three men killed over the course of two deployments. In early June 1965 a four-man reconnaissance patrol met with disaster when it disturbed a wild elephant in the jungle. The elephant, which had a broken tusk, charged the patrol, goring Lance Corporal Paul Denehey under his ribcage. The limited size of the patrol and the nature of the terrain meant that extracting Denehey, who was a tall man, by stretcher was extremely difficult. With the patrol radio damaged and only able to send signals, the patrol members were unaware if their calls for assistance had been heard. With no helicopters able to enter Indonesian airspace, the patrol commander and another man were forced to walk to the extraction point to find assistance. Along the way they were stalked by the elephant and were forced to evade the animal. The third trooper, after running low on medical supplies, also left Denehey to look for assistance. Sadly, by the time help did arrive, Denehey had died a lonely and agonising death.[59]

Further misfortune occurred during 2 Squadron's deployment. On 21 March 1966 two members of a patrol, Lieutenant Ken 'Rock' Hudson and Private Bob Moncrieff, were swept away and drowned while attempting to cross the flooded Sekayan River in darkness and driving rain. The remaining two troopers survived and made their way out of the jungle. Despite an 11-day search by another patrol, their remains were unable to be located and both men were declared dead on 1 April.[60] Local villagers had recovered and buried Hudson's and Moncrieff's remains, which were located and positively identified in 2010 by the Australian Army's Unrecovered War Casualties team, with support from the Indonesian Armed Forces.[61]

---

58 Dennis and Grey, *Emergency and Confrontation*, 308.
59 Horner, *SAS*, 110–21.
60 Horner, *SAS*, 158–60.
61 Mark Dodd, 'Remains of SAS diggers lost in Borneo recovered', *The Australian*, 17 March 2010, at: www.theaustralian.com.au/news/nation/remains-of-sas-diggers-lost-in-borneo-recovered/news-story /13732e3c6ff470ee3ddc088ba983a517.

Australian artillery, engineers and signallers in Borneo

Australian artillerymen, engineers and signallers played vital roles during Confrontation. The regular units of the Royal Australian Artillery had replaced their 25-pounder guns with the Italian-made L5 105 mm Pack Howitzer, which was light and easy to break down, making it ideal for transport by helicopter to remote company bases. Australian artillerymen served at company bases in Sarawak and Sabah, and provided vital gunfire support and FOO parties to Commonwealth troops on local and Claret operations.[62] Prior to deploying to Borneo, gunners from 102 Battery had served as infantry with 3RAR, hunting Communist Terrorists along the Malay–Thai border, and had also assisted in rounding up Indonesian infiltrators who had been landed south of Terendak in October 1964.[63] In the context of Confrontation, Australia also contributed assets to defend installations on the Malaysian peninsula against possible Indonesian attacks, and 111 Light Anti-Aircraft Battery was sent to the Royal Australian Air Force (RAAF) Base Butterworth to provide air defence. The battery did not have to fire a shot in anger, and after 26 months of service the unit returned to Australia.[64]

Royal Australian Engineer Field and Construction Squadrons were also deployed to Borneo from 1964 and were employed on a variety of tasks, which included road and airfield construction and maintenance. Many engineers became friendly with the local people and conducted 'hearts and minds' operations, building infrastructure such as schoolhouses and wells. Some of these projects were done during off-duty hours. Engineers also carried out surveying operations, the results of which were used to provide more accurate maps to the infantry and SAS.[65] Australian signallers served with British signals units at Labuan and Singapore during Confrontation. The nature of their work collecting signals intelligence remains largely shrouded in secrecy, but signals intercepts were used to gain an accurate picture of the Indonesian order of battle in Kalimantan and to plan Claret operations.[66]

---

62   Alan H Smith, *Gunners in Borneo: Artillery during Confrontation 1962–1966* (Manly: Royal Australian Artillery Historical Company, 2008), 31–102.
63   Kuring, *Redcoats*, 302.
64   Dennis and Grey, *Emergency and Confrontation*, 309.
65   Dennis and Grey, *Emergency and Confrontation*, 311–14.
66   Dennis and Grey, *Emergency and Confrontation*, 248–50.

The RAN and RAAF contributions

Australia's naval commitment to an independent Malaysia had begun during the Malayan Emergency following the formation of the British Commonwealth Far East Strategic Reserve (FESR). When the Indonesian Confrontation began in earnest in 1964, the Australian Government increased the RAN's presence in Malaysian waters by sending HMAS *Sydney* (III), which by this time had been converted from an aircraft carrier to a fast troop transport, and the destroyers HMA Ships *Vampire*, *Vendetta* and *Duchess*. In addition, 16 Minesweeping Squadron, which consisted of six Ton-class coastal minesweepers, was also committed.[67] The minesweepers were sent to patrol the coastal waters of Borneo and were involved in many stop and search operations, which led to the arrest of a number of Indonesians, including military personnel.

A notable incident took place during the night of 13 December 1964 when HMAS *Teal* detected two unlit Indonesian vessels travelling together. The vessels separated immediately and made for Indonesian waters. *Teal* gave chase and illuminated one of the vessels with a searchlight. The Indonesian vessel responded with a burst of automatic fire, but did no damage. The Australians returned fire, killing three of the seven Indonesians on board. The remaining four men surrendered and their vessel was boarded. One of the men was later found to be an Indonesian Marine officer. A search of the vessel located and seized explosives, weapons and other equipment.[68] *Teal*'s commanding officer Lieutenant Keith Murray was awarded a Distinguished Service Cross, 'for his coolness and judgement during this, and a previous interception'.[69] It was the only gallantry award made to a member of the RAN during Confrontation.

RAN vessels were also involved in shore bombardments against Indonesian forces. On 28 July 1965 Indonesian troops crossed the border onto the eastern side of Sebatik Island. In response to a call for assistance most likely by Malaysian troops, HMAS *Yarra* conducted three runs and fired

---

67 Jeffrey Grey, *The official history of Australia's involvement in Southeast Asian conflicts 1948–1975*, vol. 7, *Up top: The Royal Australian Navy and Southeast Asian conflicts, 1955–1972* (St Leonards: Allen & Unwin in association with the Australian War Memorial, 1998), 8, 60.
68 'Reports of proceedings, HMA Ships and establishments, Class 339 – HMAS *Teal*', June 1964 – December 1965, AWM: AWM78 339/1, Part 2, 81; 'Incursion into Indonesian Waters by HMAS *Teal*', NAA: A1813 1623/202/28, 54–55.
69 Grey, *Up top*, 61; Honours and awards – Gallantry awards (operational) – Award: Distinguished Service Cross; Recipient(s): RAN Lieutenant Keith Murray, NAA: A2880, 5/5/7, 3.

70 rounds to harass the Indonesians as they withdrew. In early July *Yarra* was twice called on to fire at Indonesian targets, which on both occasions were in Sabah.[70] At the end of Confrontation, the RAN maintained its presence in the region as part of FESR as well as its commitment to the escalating war in Vietnam.

Though the RAAF was not involved in Claret operations, No. 36 Squadron, flying C-130 Hercules transport aircraft, ferried troops and supplies between Malaysia and Borneo. During the same period of time, the squadron supported Australia's commitment to Vietnam. The RAAF also flew in support of operations along the Malaysia–Thailand border. One unit that made a particularly interesting contribution was No. 5 Squadron, Detachment C, flying the UH-1 Iroquois. This is noteworthy as it is the first RAAF deployment using helicopters. This squadron flew operations in support of 28 Commonwealth Infantry Brigade Group, including ferrying soldiers to the Malaysia–Thailand border where they would search for Communist Terrorists, hold-outs from the Malayan Emergency. The unit was disbanded in 1966 and its personnel redeployed to Vietnam.[71]

The end of Confrontation

Indonesia's efforts to destabilise the Malaysian Union ultimately failed. Much like the Malayan Communist Party's efforts failed to win over the populace by acts of brutality during the Malayan Emergency, so too did Indonesia's efforts to win over the border tribes between Kalimantan, Sarawak and Sabah, for much the same reasons. Indonesian operations in Kalimantan were further negatively impacted in October 1965 when members of the military attempted to depose Suharto. The failed coup led to a purge of communist sympathisers in the government and military, paving the way for a change in leadership. With the ascension of General Sukarno to the Presidency of Indonesia in March 1966, there was still no immediate guarantee of an end to Confrontation. However, the goal of destabilising Malaysia was now unattainable and it was thanks in the

---

70 Grey, *Up top*, 70.
71 Chris Coulthard-Clark, *The RAAF in Vietnam: Australian air involvement in the Vietnam War* (St Leonards: Allen & Unwin, 1995), 8; John Moremon, 'No 5 Squadron', *Wings: The official publication of the RAAF Association* 69, no. 1 (Autumn 2017): 25; 'No. 5 Squadron (RAAF)', Australian War Memorial, at: www.awm.gov.au/collection/U60467 (accessed 10 March 2019).

main to the Claret operations conducted by British and Commonwealth troops that Malaysian sovereignty was defended. Facing the prospect of a drawn-out conflict, as the nearby war in Vietnam was clearly becoming, Sukarno's government began peace negotiations with Malaysia in May 1966. Much like the Korean War, negotiations between the parties dragged on and the fighting in Borneo continued. On 11 August 1966 a peace treaty between Malaysia and Indonesia was signed in Bangkok, bringing hostilities to an end. The following day an order was sent to all British and Commonwealth units to cease operations in Borneo.[72]

Conclusion

The Malaysia–Indonesia Confrontation was a challenge for Australia, as it maintained diplomatic relations with the Indonesian Government while conducting a low-intensity conflict against its military. Australia risked and avoided outright war with its much larger neighbour. In courting the United States to shore up regional security and help stop the spread of communism, Australia also became increasingly committed to the war in Vietnam. As that war escalated in the second half of the decade and into the 1970s, it would become Australia's largest Cold War conflict, rapidly overshadowing Australia's commitment to Malaysia. But at the time of Confrontation, it was events in Borneo and the risk of war with Indonesia that caused most concern for the Australian Government.

The British and Commonwealth response to Indonesia on both political and military fronts, especially Operation Claret, remains a model of conducting a successful low-intensity conflict while maintaining diplomatic relations with the opposing nation. Australia's armed forces, particularly the Royal Australian Regiment and Australian Special Air Service, learned many valuable lessons in the jungles of Borneo, which were then applied for future service in Vietnam. Despite their skilful application of low-intensity warfare, the success of Borneo did not necessarily directly translate to Indochina, where different local circumstances in Vietnam led to a different outcome.

---

72 Dennis and Grey, *Emergency and Confrontation*, 298.

8

Defending Australia's land border: The Australian military in Papua New Guinea

Tristan Moss

Although no war was fought there after the defeat of the Japanese in 1945, Papua New Guinea (PNG) occupied an important place in Australia's strategic thinking during the early Cold War. Not only was the island seen as a barrier to Australia's enemies, it was also a potential base from which to strike the Australian mainland should it fall. During the 1950s it continued its position as a barrier to invasion against the threat of communist aggression from the north. However, with the Indonesian takeover of West Papua in 1962, Australia, for the first time, shared a land border with a potentially hostile nation, and when Indonesia embarked on its policy of Confrontation with Malaysia the following year, PNG was never far from Australian planners' minds.[1] As a result, throughout this tumultuous period PNG was closely integrated into Australian strategic thinking and wider planning in the event of a conflict with Indonesia, with Australian forces also drawing on experiences in Borneo against Indonesia to inform their preparations in PNG. At the same time, the Australian Army's units in PNG had a clear peacetime role, helping to

---

1 Bruce Hunt, *Australia's northern shield? Papua New Guinea and the defence of Australia since 1880* (Clayton, Victoria: Monash University Publishing, 2017), xxii.

patrol the border, gathering topographical and human intelligence, and building relationships with the people on whom they would rely during any war or conflict.

By the 1950s, PNG's geographic importance had long been a significant part of Australian strategic thinking. It was concern about the defence of the Australian mainland that led to the 1888 annexation of Papua, the south-eastern portion of the island of New Guinea. In late 1914, Australia annexed German New Guinea in the country's first military operation of the First World War and demanded that the territory be administered by Australia at the end of that conflict. In Australian defence thinking thereafter, the two separately administered territories of Papua and New Guinea together formed a land barrier to Australia's north and would add depth to Australia's defence. Australian defence of New Guinea would also deny its use by hostile powers, as Germany had threatened. The island, former prime minister Billy Hughes informed the Defence Committee in 1939, would be a 'dagger aimed at the heart of Australia' should it be occupied by a hostile power.[2] The physical barrier of the PNG landmass, with its rugged terrain and impenetrable jungle, combined with the power of the British (and Royal Australian) Navy, was considered by Australian planners to be a suitable foundation of the nation's defence.[3]

The Second World War undermined the assumption that PNG would be a sufficient barrier without significant defence investment, while at the same time the desperate battles across the Owen-Stanley Range and the campaigns to isolate the Japanese naval base at Rabaul served to reinforce the strategic importance of the island to Australia. The campaigns in the jungle between 1942 and 1945 also forced Australia, like its allies, to come to grips with operating in a tropical environment. While technically and operationally Australia learned that there was 'no black magic' in jungle fighting, this appreciation took time. Adjusting equipment and structures, training troops and learning the quirks of the jungle were all key to this process.[4] Alongside these efforts, Australia recruited Papua New Guineans to act in a scout and reconnaissance role, thereby lending their indigenous knowledge of the environment to the Allied war effort. The Papuan Infantry Battalion was raised in 1940 and, after serving

2   Cited in ibid., 37.
3   Ibid., 25–46.
4   See John Moremon, 'No "black magic": Doctrine and training for jungle warfare', in *The foundations of victory: The Pacific War 1943–44*, ed. Peter Dennis and Jeffrey Grey (Canberra: Army History Unit, 2004), 76–85.

in the Kokoda campaign, were joined by four New Guinea Infantry Battalions by war's end, grouped under the Pacific Islands Regiment (PIR). These battalions saw action in all Australia's campaigns, save that at Milne Bay, and were disbanded at the end of the war. The general demobilisation of the Australian armed forces was the main reason for this. However, Australian civilians and the colonial government (termed 'the Administration' and run by the Department of External Territories in Canberra) were also wary of the threat an armed body of Papua New Guineans might pose to colonial rule.

The Cold War

It did not take long for the security of PNG, so assured after the unequivocal victory of the Second World War, to be brought into question again. The potential threats of a hostile and newly communist China, a global conflict with the Soviet Union and the spectre of communist-inspired insurgencies soon came to shape Australian defence policy.[5] PNG remained an Australian responsibility after the Second World War and remained on Australia's strategic doorstep. The Defence Committee, as the body responsible for advising the government on strategic policy, emphasised the role of PNG in safeguarding sea and air communications, and as a final strategic barrier, when formulating its strategic vision for Australia. In this, PNG was considered alongside Australia's north, and in particular the Darwin region.[6] The regular Australian Army was created in 1947; that year also saw the last company of the PIR disbanded, leaving no combat forces in PNG. The Royal Australian Navy (RAN) maintained a supply base on the strategically positioned Manus Island, inherited from the United States, and the need for additional manpower saw the creation

---

5   Robert O'Neill, *Australia in the Korean War 1950–53*, vol. 1, *Strategy and diplomacy* (Canberra: Australian War Memorial and the Australian Government Publishing Service, 1981), 21–34. For a detailed discussion of Australian defence policy during the late 1940s, see DM Horner, *Defence supremo: Sir Frederick Shedden and the making of Australian defence policy* (St Leonards, NSW: Allen & Unwin, 2000), 236–315.
6   See the Defence Committee's 'Strategic basis of Australia's defence policy' for 1953 and 1956, in Stephan Frühling, *A history of Australian strategic policy since 1945* (Canberra: Defence Publishing Service, 2009), 167–246.

in 1948 of the first Papua New Guinean peacetime unit, the RAN PNG Division. It was not, however, a fighting force, and was instead intended to assist in maintaining the naval base.[7]

By 1950, the absence of combat forces defending PNG worried Australian politicians, expatriates in PNG and the press. One Labor politician, FM Daly, criticised the Menzies Government for leaving the 'practically defenceless' New Guinea 'wide open to infiltration'. Daly pointed particularly to the possibility of Indonesia making good on its claim to neighbouring Dutch New Guinea, reflecting a similar concern in the Defence Committee.[8] The Australian Administrator, JK Murray, voiced similar concerns, referring to reports that foreign submarines had been spotted in the area.[9] Murray called for the power to raise emergency units from expatriates in the territory; this was not granted, not least because Murray, as a member of the Department of External Territories, did not have vice-regal powers, as in other colonies.

Both the Army and the Menzies Government agreed that a volunteer force drawn from Europeans in PNG would best serve its interests and approved a Citizen's Military Force battalion in January 1950. Drawing on the lineage of the New Guinea Volunteer Rifles, the Papua New Guinea Volunteer Rifles was to be the first line of defence for the territory. The decision to raise an all-European force also reflected the racialised nature of colonial rule at the time, in which Australians were suspicious of the loyalty of Papua New Guinean soldiers and doubted their capability of serving in a modern army as a result of their supposed inherent racial characteristics. However, while Australians in PNG had clamoured for improved defences, they were less enthusiastic when it came to surrendering their own time to serve in part-time military, and recruitment rates were disappointing. While better than having no force there at all, the unit's effectiveness was hampered by its small size, and the fact that it would be scattered around PNG in small depots, unable to fight as a coherent whole.

---

7   For an overview of the RAN PNG Division see James Sinclair, *To find a path: The Papua New Guinea Defence Force and the Australians to independence*, vol. 2, *Keeping the peace, 1950–1975* (Gold Coast: Crawford House Press, 1990), 179–80.
8   'New Guinea defenceless', *Townsville Daily Bulletin*, 16 August 1950. See also '"Defence lack in N. Guinea"', *The Courier-Mail*, 16 August 1950. See also 'New Guinea defence: Infiltration reports', *The West Australian*, 5 August 1950; 'New Guinea defence: Liberal M's HR critical', *The West Australian*, 17 August 1950; 'Measures to stop Reds in N.G.', *The Advertiser*, 20 March 1951.
9   Taylor to Morgan, 30 May 1949, National Archives of Australia (NAA): MP729/8 37/431/114; JK Murray to Secretary External Territories, 16 July 1950, NAA: A5954 2331/9.

Almost immediately, the Defence Committee recognised that a regular force was also needed. The dispatch of an Australian infantry battalion to Port Moresby was out of the question. The outbreak of the Korean War in June 1950, the need to maintain a reserve on mainland Australia and the cost of sending Australian troops and their families to PNG in peacetime all mitigated against such a move. Equally, in late 1950 only three infantry battalions existed. Papua New Guinean troops, however, represented an inexpensive means by which to defend Australia's north, as they could be paid and equipped at a lower rate compared to Australia-based units.

The postwar PIR was raised in mid-1951 around a cadre of Papua New Guineans who would later form many of the non-commissioned officers for the battalion. The first commanding officer, Lieutenant Colonel Herbert Sabin, arrived on 2 October 1951, and the PIR achieved its full establishment of around 600 Papua New Guineans in November 1952. The unit made use of the wealth of infrastructure remaining from the Second World War in PNG, establishing itself on the site of a former hospital at Taurama, about 8 kilometres from Port Moresby.[10] Newer materials were scarce, however, and soldiers were housed in tents while huts were built.

The reraised battalion had its role shaped by the Second World War. In the event of war in the 1950s, the PIR was to fight as a reconnaissance and raiding force that was auxiliary to Australian-manned Army units. The battalion would form the initial tripwire should an enemy invade PNG, fighting to delay the enemy and trading space for time in PNG's difficult geography. Once troops were deployed from the mainland, Papua New Guinean soldiers would act as a reconnaissance force for the rest of the Australian Army, with subunits attached to Australian battalions. Small groups from the PIR were also to conduct long-range fighting patrols.[11] The PIR was structured as a battalion, with four companies of infantry, and the equivalent of two companies of administration troops. However, with these roles, it was not intended to fight as a complete unit. Indeed, the battalion never trained as a whole during the 1950s. Moreover, the PIR was established on a 'light scale', lacking the heavier infantry weapons allocated to the battalions of the Royal Australian Regiment, such as medium machine guns, mortars and anti-tank weapons.[12] This unique

---

10   Seacombe to AHQ, 'Construction of a Permanent Barracks – Pacific Islands Regiment – Moresby', 9 March 1951, NAA: MT1131/1 A259/47/3.
11   Jeffrey Grey, *The Australian Army* (Melbourne: Oxford University Press, 2001), 194.
12   Northern Command, 'Proposal for a New Lower Establishment to Supersede II/23C/2 (LE)', 27 July 1956, NAA: A6059 21/441/15.

structure reflected the rugged nature of the Papua New Guinean terrain, in which heavy weapons were difficult to move and supply. But it also stemmed from an Australian perception, rooted in racism, that Papua New Guineans were unsuited to managing these more technical weapons, and other equipment, such as radios.[13]

While the PIR was reraised to defend Australia's north, its existence cannot be divorced from the colonial context. In creating the PIR, the Australian Army reflected and sometimes reinforced the colonial structures of PNG – themselves based in radicalised conceptions of Papua New Guineans. In addition to different rates of pay, Papua New Guineans were not permitted to rise above the rank of sergeant during the 1950s. Their conditions were also substantially different to those allocated Australian troops in the territory: their rations consisted of only seven items, and they were not regularly issued with shoes until 1962.[14] Nonetheless, the PIR represented a popular occupation in PNG, and many young Papua New Guineans joined what they considered to be an elite group. This elitism was at the heart of two euphemistically termed 'disturbances' during the unit's first decade, which saw some of the unit march out of barracks in 1957 to clash with other Papua New Guineans over supposed insults to the regiment, and again in 1961 over the difference in pay between the Army and their traditional rivals in PNG, the police. Despite some hysterical reactions on the part of the colonial authorities, neither of these incidents was directed at Australian rule.[15]

Confrontation

By the 1960s, the Indonesian assumption of control of West Papua from the Dutch, long feared by Australia, meant that, for the first time, Australia shared a land border 'with a country whose long term friendship cannot be assumed'.[16] With Indonesia already having embarked upon

---

13   Tristan Moss, *Guarding the periphery: The Australian Army in Papua New Guinea, 1951–75* (Melbourne: Cambridge University Press, 2017), 33, doi.org/10.1017/9781108182638.
14   Ibid., 92–93.
15   For a detailed discussion of these incidents, see ibid., 42–63.
16   Defence Committee 'Minute No. 4/1963: The Strategic Importance to Australia of New Guinea', 7 February 1963, NAA: A452 1972/4342. See also 'Defence Implications of changes in West New Guinea', October 1962, NAA: A452 1962/7075. Peter Edwards with Gregory Pemberton, *The official history of Australia's involvement in Southeast Asian conflicts 1948–1975*, vol. 1, *Crises and commitments: The politics and diplomacy of Australia's involvement in Southeast Asian conflicts 1948–1965* (North Sydney: Allen & Unwin in association with the Australian War Memorial, 1992), 200–7, 230–32.

a policy of Confrontation with Malaysia, and by extension the British Commonwealth, the Defence Committee feared that Indonesia might turn its attention towards PNG. The series of Indonesian raids in Brunei in December 1962, and increased activity along the border in Borneo, raised the possibility of similar incursions into Australian territory. Although the distance from Indonesian bases and the difficult terrain made such action less likely – and unlikely at the same scale – as against Malaysia, the Defence Committee nonetheless worried about Australia's ability to respond. This was partly related to the overall size of the Australian armed forces at the time, and in 1963, the committee believed the Australian armed forces were too small to 'make an effective and sustained contribution to South-East Asia and at the same time deter Indonesia from possible activities inimical to our strategic interest'.[17]

The Menzies Government was acutely aware of the changed strategic situation, and the growing demands placed on the armed forces, which had already deployed troops to the Far East Strategic Reserve and trainers to Vietnam. The armed forces, and in particular the Army, had little flexibility to meet any crises that, as in PNG, now looked more likely.[18] In May 1963 the Menzies Government announced an increase in defence spending, including the purchase of additional Mirage fighters and transport aircraft for the Royal Australian Air Force (RAAF), ships and an extension of the fixed-wing capability for the RAN, and an increase of the regular Army to 28,000 soldiers.[19] In PNG, the Menzies Government's expansion focused on creating layers of defence against Indonesia and other hostile forces. Australia's ability to detect threats was improved through the establishment of an intelligence capability in the territory, which would 'provide warning of infiltration or subversion'.[20] Coastal security was to be provided on a permanent basis with the creation of a Papua New Guinean patrol boat squadron, which would be based at the naval base at Manus Island under the RAN. With PNG's long coastline, this capability was essential in detecting Indonesian incursions and helping to move patrols around the country. Australia's strike capability in the territory was to be improved through the upgrading of Boram airfield

---

17   Defence Committee Minute, 4 February 1963, NAA: A1945/40 832/8, cited in DM Horner, *Strategic command: General Sir John Wilton and Australia's Asian wars* (Melbourne: Oxford University Press, 2005), 203.
18   Ibid.
19   Ibid., 203–5.
20   Defence Committee, 'Minute No. 5/1963: Territory of Papua/New Guinea – Immediate Defence Measures', 7 February 1963, NAA: A452 1972/4342.

at Wewak to help make the area a suitable base on the northern coast from which the defence forces could operate, or stage further afield.[21] Previously, aircraft operating out of Jackson Field at Port Moresby had a limited loiter time over the border; now, they would be far closer.

The most significant expansion of Australia's military capability in PNG was found in the PIR. Following the recommendations of Defence, Cabinet authorised the expansion of the PIR from its peacetime establishment to a full battalion, supported by an increase in pioneers, signals and supply troops. A larger training depot was also to be created to support this expansion, which would make the PIR a far more well-rounded and capable force. The Defence Committee saw this as but the first of a series of steps that it, and the Army, had long advocated. The second step included raising another battalion and additional support units. To support these two battalions, an expanded headquarters formation was to be created and a building program to be instituted to house new personnel and their dependants. In the third and final phase, a third battalion would be raised and existing support units expanded.[22]

The PIR did not have to wait long to advance to the second phase of its expansion. In 1964, in response to Indonesian attacks in Borneo, the Menzies Government authorised the use of Australian units along the Thai–Malaysian border, and in August Australian troops helped round up Indonesian infiltrators on the Malay Peninsula. Vietnam also became of increasing concern to the government. In response, the Menzies Government again announced an expansion of the armed forces, part of which was the introduction of national service to help meet its varied commitments.[23] As part of these preparations, the government authorised the PIR to proceed to expand to three full battalions. The Army's units in PNG were to achieve their full complement of around 3,500 troops by 1968, necessitating a sizeable increase in recruiting and training.[24] The airfield at Nadzab, outside Lae, was also to be improved to take Mirage fighters.[25]

---

21   Cabinet Submission No. 603, 23 March 1963, NAA: A5619 C174; Cabinet Decision No. 791, 8 May 1963, NAA: A5619 C174.
22   Defence Committee, 'Minute No. 5/1963: Territory of Papua/New Guinea – Immediate Defence Measures', 7 February 1963, NAA: A452 1972/4342.
23   Edwards with Pemberton, *Crises and commitments*, 303.
24   'List of past, current and proposed strengths of PIR -1965', n.d., NAA: A452 1966/4989.
25   'Prime Minister's Statement on Defence: Full re-assessment of the needs', *The Canberra Times*, 11 November 1964.

The PIR's expansion occurred more quickly than the Army had planned or hoped for. By 1964, the PIR grew from 660 to 810 Papua New Guineans, along with over 100 Australian troops. The following year, another 700 Papua New Guineans had been recruited and were in various stages of training.[26] In 1965, PNG Command was created, which reflected the growing strategic importance of PNG to Australia. Where the previous PNG Military District had been subordinated to Northern Command, based in Brisbane, the Army elevated PNG to equal footing with other regional commands. The creation of the PNG Command also expanded Army capabilities in PNG, particularly in the raising of an engineer component, vital in undeveloped PNG. Reflecting its new size and importance, a brigadier, AL McDonald, was appointed PNG Command's first commander.

The second battalion of the PIR (2PIR) was formed in 1965 by splitting the first battalion in half. While this diluted the skill base of the PIR, it was a step towards greatly expanding the Army's capability in PNG. Given the pace of expansion, and the continuing threat from Indonesia, the Army operated under the assumption that the third battalion would be raised and planned accordingly. 2PIR was based at Wewak on the PNG north coast, next to the airfield at Boram, providing a northern base of operations. With third base planned for PNG's second largest city, Lae, on the country's east coast near the proposed fighter-capable airport at Nadzab, the Army could cover the breadth of PNG. The size and location of the PIR was not the only change made: rather than be an auxiliary force to Australian units, during the early 1960s, the PIR was expected to be able to fight alongside Australian-manned forces, at least in the PNG context. This was as much a product of changes in the status accorded Papua New Guineans under Australian rule as it was one of Australia's defence needs. This shift was swift, mirroring and building on shifts occurring in race relations in PNG.

In its combat role, the PIR continued its earlier focus on reconnaissance and patrolling forces, but began to be equipped and trained to take on additional roles. The three PIR battalions were to be based on a more lightly equipped 'tropical' version of standard Australian infantry battalions. In contrast to the 1950s, this reflected the terrain and likely roles of the battalions, rather than the supposed capabilities of the

---

26   Prime Minister's Department Minute, 20 August 1968, NAA: A5619 C174.

Papua New Guineans within them. The battalions consisted of four rifle companies, but with increased support company capabilities, particularly the mortars and machine guns, and also larger signals and administration subunits.[27] Heavy equipment, such as anti-tank weapons and trucks were omitted from the PIR's establishment; operating in the jungle, the PIR would fight with what it could carry.

Peacetime operations

Patrolling made Papua New Guinean units unique within the Australian Army, in that they had an ongoing operational peacetime responsibility alongside their wartime roles. Aside from training for an actual outbreak of conflict, during the early 1960s the PIR's peacetime role was border surveillance, in order to deter and detect Indonesian incursions. It did so by mounting patrols from outstations. On the north coast, this was the permanent Vanimo outstation, while in the south, PNG Command made use of temporary bases as required. Vanimo usually accommodated an infantry company and supporting troops, and saw its airfield and barracks expanded throughout the early 1960s. It was not fortified, in contrast to the entrenched bases used by Australian forces in Borneo during Confrontation. Rather, during peacetime it provided a jumping-off point for patrols of the northern border region; indeed, at any one time, a significant portion of the infantry company based there would be in the jungle.

The patrols mounted from Vanimo and other bases were the bread and butter of PNG Command. These had three goals: training for war, laying the groundwork for any conflict, and detecting and deterring Indonesian incursions. Patrolling was a substantial commitment of resources, and PNG Command planned each year's training and other activities around them.[28] Tensions with Indonesia caused a threefold increase in patrolling man-days, from around 9,000 in 1964 to over 30,000 in 1965, a sign of the importance of this activity.[29] This equated to between 20 and 50 patrols

---

27 Sinclair, *Keeping the peace*, 98.
28 Sio Maiasa, interview with Tristan Moss, 3 August 2013.
29 Northern Command, 'Administrative Appreciation for the Expansion of the Army in Papua New Guinea', 11 January 1965, NAA: J2818, 22/1/7.

per year in most of PNG's provinces.[30] The burden of patrolling mainly fell on the two battalions of the PIR, although other subunits also headed off into the jungle. Patrolling was usually based on individual platoons; while whole companies would often patrol, in practice companies would also break into their constituent platoons, operating from a forward base, only concentrating when needed.

While the Defence Committee assumed that Indonesian incursions across the border would be unlikely, the tense situation coupled with the difficulty in actually finding a border in a region with poor maps and Dutch, Indonesian and Australian markers in different locations meant that clashes with Indonesian troops were an ever-present risk. In this sense, Australian patrols not only had the role of detecting and deterring Indonesian forays into PNG but might also spark a conflict by aggressive action. They were instructed to avoid this at all costs.[31] In the event of Indonesian aggression towards Australian troops, patrol leaders – usually lieutenants – were instructed to retaliate 'with only such force as may be necessary to enable him to ensure the safety of … [the] patrol'.[32] Soldiers were ordered to use their arms only if the patrol was directly threatened and there was no other course of action. In 1965, for instance, upon hearing of Indonesian soldiers in a village on the Australian side of the border, the commander of 2PIR, Lieutenant Colonel Donald Ramsay, ordered his patrol commander by radio to delay his approach until the Indonesians had departed. In doing so, a potentially volatile situation was avoided in which, Ramsay admitted, 'there could quite easily have been a firefight'.[33]

In providing an opportunity for realistic training, patrols were also fundamental in preparing the PIR for war. In many ways, patrolling was just like war, without the shooting. Patrols operated in the jungle by themselves for long periods of time, carrying all they needed between resupplies. The climate and the terrain were the same in which the unit would have to operate against Indonesia. Patrols were also an excellent

---

30   '1967/8 PNG Comd Patrol Programme', 18 May 1967, Papua New Guinea National Archives (PNGNA): 55 52/2/2; 'Papua and New Guinea Patrol and Exercise Programme 1971/1972', 7 April 1971, PNGNA: 1008 52/2/2; 'PNG Land Forces Patrol and Exercise Programme, July 1973 to June 74', n.d., PNGNA: 1008 52/2/2.
31   Defence Committee, Minute No. 74/1963, 'Border Crossings Papua – New Guinea/West Irian', 13 December 1963, NAA: A2031, 74/1963.
32   AHQ Operational Instruction 2/63 PIR, 25 February 1963, NAA: A6059 41/441/124.
33   Sinclair, *Keeping the peace*, 127–28.

means to develop and test physical fitness. In addition, patrols had a crucial cartographical function in the poorly mapped border region. Until the 1970s, when the Survey Corps completed a comprehensive mapping program, maps of many areas of PNG were poor. Aerial photos were often obscured by cloud and were less than satisfactory in picking out details such as tracks in the jungle. Some maps of the border region simply included large swathes of blank terrain, for which no topographical information existed. Patrols were therefore a crucial part of the Army's preparations for war and reported on the location of tracks, the 'going', villages and other features.

Patrols also had an important intelligence function and laid the foundations for the relationship with local peoples that would be crucial during wartime. Military–civil relationships were key here, with Army patrols working closely with Administration officers, who were scattered in small numbers around PNG, alongside around 3,100 police.[34] With good relationships between locals and Australian authorities, Papua New Guineans in crucial areas could provide information on Indonesian activity in the border region and on local geography. They could also be called on to provide fresh food and guides to patrols. Both the Army and the Administration took this relationship seriously lest poor relations lead to 'open hostility during times of peace or war', and troops were under strict instructions to approach locals with respect and not to damage property.[35] Patrols were also an opportunity to promote the Army in PNG, and to encourage recruits. The Army would often send 'prestige' patrols into certain regions; these were more elaborate affairs that could include the PIR Pipe Band. One such patrol, led by Lieutenant T Holland in 1963, was estimated to have been seen by tens of thousands of people.[36]

Plans for war

If war was to break out with Indonesia in PNG, it would have done so along the border, and patrols from the PIR would have been the tripwire. These forces were not initially intended to stop the Indonesians. Lacking heavy weapons, and able to trade space for time, the patrols were to

---

34 PNG Command, 'Papua New Guinea Force Operational Plan 1/66', August 1966, Australian War Memorial (AWM): AWM 122 68/4003.
35 ES Sharp to District Commissioner, 'Tabunomu Complaint – PIR', 29 May 1963, PNGNA: 55 52/2/2.
36 Sinclair, *Keeping the peace*, 93.

retire in the face of an Indonesian incursion. Only later, once it was determined that a hostile incursion was underway, would concerted action be launched. During war, PNG Command's principal role was to meet and repel border incursion or, if such action was beyond its capacity alone, to contain any threat until assistance could be provided from mainland Australia.[37] With the Indonesian takeover of West Papua, Australian plans for the defence of PNG became increasingly specific in focus and were meshed with the broader range of anti-confrontation plans being developed by Commonwealth forces (see Chapter 5, this volume). For PNG, the Defence Committee began developing Joint Service Plan Pygmalion in 1964, refining it over the next two years before the end of Confrontation caused it to be downgraded to a general contingency plan.

Plan Pygmalion focused on the threat of Indonesian raids across the border. At the height of Confrontation, PNG Command assessed that, at short notice, the Indonesians could deploy two companies of infantry, around 250 marines, and a company of police along the border area, from a total Indonesian force in West Irian of two infantry battalions, one police battalion and other support units. Intelligence officers believed that Indonesian forces would have two courses of action, alongside around 1,500 indigenous troops. The first, less overt, manner in which Indonesia might exert pressure was through the encouragement and support of subversive elements in PNG.

Planners feared that trained cadres in West Papua could cross the border to foment disaffection among Papua New Guineans. Indonesian forces might go further, and cross the border to mount raids and sabotage, as they had attempted to do in Borneo (and as Australian forces were doing in Kalimantan). Their options would be somewhat limited, given the scale of the border region, and the logistical difficulties of moving forces in that terrain. Moreover, planners assumed that any Indonesian action would be covert and small, as the country would be unlikely to risk war breaking out over PNG. Limited war was considered more likely to erupt because of action elsewhere, particularly Borneo, but in this scenario, Indonesia would be hard pressed to send additional troops to West Irian. Nonetheless, even small covert raids had the potential to have a significant strategic effect. Indonesia held the initiative, as it was able to choose the time and place of its incursions. Combined with subversive activities,

---

37 Cabinet Submission No. 118, 'Papua/New Guinea – Military Requirements', 8 April 1964, NAA: A4940 C3436.

such actions would require the deployment of a much larger Australian force than the Indonesians might field. This would tie up Australian forces needed in Malaysia, Borneo and, from 1965, Vietnam.[38]

Demonstrating that the PIR was now considered capable of performing operations similar to Australian units, the first draft of Plan Pygmalion called for the deployment of two companies of the PIR along the border, supported by an increased RAAF and RAN presence in and around the territory. The Special Air Service, which at the time consisted of a single company, would deploy to augment the PIR's long-range patrolling capability.[39] The two units had trained together for the first time in 1963, with the PIR giving a good account of itself in an exercise against the special forces unit along the Kokoda Track.[40] The two other companies of the PIR would be rotated with those resting and training in Port Moresby as necessary. A battalion of the Royal Australian Regiment was only to be sent to PNG if the situation deteriorated and reinforcements were necessary.[41] Experience fighting Indonesians in Borneo, and the expansion of the PNG Command to include a second battalion in 1965, led planners to expand the initial deployment of Pygmalion to consist of one battalion on either side of the central mountain ranges. This reinforced the plan to raise a third battalion, as this would allow PNG Command to rotate the units through the border without having to rely on infantry battalions from Australia.[42]

While addressing the potential for war in PNG, Plan Pygmalion was written in the broader context of Commonwealth defence and Confrontation; the plan both complemented planning in other theatres, such as Borneo, and also drew lessons from previous encounters with Indonesian forces.[43] Lieutenant General John Wilton, Chief of the General

---

38 PNG Command, 'Papua New Guinea Force Operational Plan 1/66', August 1966, AWM: AWM122 68/4003.
39 MF Brogan, 'Plan Pygmalion: Proposed conference at Port Moresby 19 – 21 July 65', 28 June 1965, NAA: A1946 1968/710; Department of Defence, 'Plan Pygmalion', 26 May 1966, NAA: A452 1972/4342.
40 DM Horner, *SAS: Phantoms of war, a history of the Australian Special Air Service*, 2nd ed. (Crows Nest: Allen & Unwin, 2002), 61.
41 Joint Service Plan 'Pygmalion', 9 April 1964, NAA: A452 1972/4342.
42 JPC Report No. 32/1968, 'Future Size and Role of the Pacific Islands Regiment', 10 May 1968, NAA: A8738 39; Cabinet Submission No. 118, 'Papua/New Guinea – Military Requirements', 8 April 1964, NAA: A4940 C3436.
43 Peter Dennis and Jeffrey Grey, *The official history of Australia's involvement in Southeast Asian conflicts 1948–1975*, vol. 5, *Emergency and Confrontation: Australian military operations in Malaya and Borneo 1950–1966* (St Leonards: Allen & Unwin in association with the Australian War Memorial, 1996), 194.

Staff in 1963, made a note of the applicability of lessons from Borneo to PNG, particularly in relation to the use of intelligence and coordination between the three services.[44] Similarly, the importance of cooperation with the civilian administration was emphasised in later command and control arrangements developed by the Joint Planning Committee.[45] Tactically, the operations envisaged on the border were similar, too. They were to take place at the company or platoon level, with troops patrolling from small bases close to the area of operations. Air support was to be vital, but the war itself was, at its core, an infantry fight. It was also, as in Borneo, a fight over the people. While Australian forces were to defend the border, in particular the 'vulnerable points' at which Indonesians might easily access Australian territory, the protection of Papua New Guineans was of equal importance.[46]

There was one final role for PNG Command. Unlike many other colonial forces, PNG Command had no internal security role. Prior to the Second World War, no military presence was considered necessary by Australian authorities; locally recruited police and armed European civilians had proved sufficient to counter any threats from Papua New Guineans. During the 1950s, broad fears of communist subversion – thought most likely to originate from agitation from European expats – worried authorities, but this constituted an intelligence and policing issue, rather than a military one. The advent of Confrontation and the threat from Indonesia gave the military more of an internal security role. However, this was only envisaged in terms of a war situation, during which specific government legislation would come into effect, specifically the Defence Regulations and the National Security Regulations, which covered threats such as sabotage, prohibited areas, the movement of people, and the control of photography and communications, including censorship.[47]

In 1966, the possibility of civil unrest in PNG led the government to explore the possibility of calling out the Army to support the police as a last resort. The suggestion was met with trepidation at all levels of Defence, due to the lack of training of PNG Command in such operations, and

---

44   Wilton to Sherger, 24 October 1963, NAA: A1946 1968/710.
45   Joint Planning Committee, 'Command and control of Operations in the Territory of Papua and New Guinea', 28 February 1964, NAA: A1946 1968/710.
46   Joint Planning Committee 'An outline plan to meet cover Indonesian activity in Papua/New Guinea', 10 April 1964, NAA: A1946 1968/710; Cabinet Submission No. 603, 23 March 1963, NAA: A5619 C174. Compare for instance the role of Australian forces in Borneo, as described in Dennis and Grey, *Emergency and Confrontation*, 253.
47   'Draft Plan to Safeguard Internal Security', n.d. [1966], NAA: A452 1964/5917.

the seriousness with which the use of the Army against civilians would be viewed at home and abroad.[48] There was also concern among some members of the Army that the Administration did not entirely understand the implications of calling out the military, or what constituted a serious enough internal security threat for this to occur.[49] While the Australian Government came extremely close to calling out the PIR in 1970 over riots in New Britain, troops were never used in this fashion during Australian rule in PNG.

Conclusion

As Australia became increasingly embroiled in Vietnam, the strategic importance of PNG and the threat of war breaking out there declined. The end of Confrontation with Indonesia in 1966 in particular heralded the lessening of the importance of PNG in Australia's strategic thinking. Although the border region continued to be a point of concern – and patrolling continued – tension dissipated sufficiently for PNG to be downgraded from an area of 'vital' interest, to simply an 'abiding' one by 1973.[50] Increasingly, the war in Vietnam occupied Australia's attention. While many were keen to do so, the troops of PNG Command were barred from participation in Vietnam, because New Guineans were not Australian citizens, but protected persons under the United Nations Trusteeship provisions governing Australian rule there.[51] Instead, a focus on preparing the military for independence increasingly occupied the attentions of PNG Command. In the nine years before independence was granted in 1975, the Australian Army embarked on a program of education among its Papua New Guinean soldiers, designed to fashion them into citizen-soldiers of an independent Papua New Guinean state. While the independence of PNG – and the serious problems facing the Papua New Guinean Defence Force subsequently – have dominated the history of this institution, for two decades the Army's units in PNG made a significant contribution to the defence of Australia.

---

48   CE Barnes, Cabinet Submission, 'Papua New Guinea – Threat to Internal Security', 4 July 1966, NAA: A1945 24/2/28.
49   'Plan to safeguard internal security in the Territory of Papua and New Guinea: Note of discussion in Port Moresby from 28th March to 2nd April 1966', 5 April 1966, NAA: A1945, 24/2/28.
50   'Strategic basis of Australian defence policy', June 1973 in Frühling, *A history of Australian strategic policy*, 464–75.
51   Lynch to Fox, 25 September 1968, NAA: A452 1966/4989; Ted Diro, interview with Tristan Moss, 31 July 2013; Jack Kukuma, interview with Tristan Moss, 3 August 2013.

Part 3.
Retrospective

9

The Australian way of war and the early Cold War

Peter J Dean

Is there an Australian way of war and, if so, how do Australia's military commitments in the early Cold War period map to this concept? These two questions form the fundamental basis of the concluding segment of this work. This chapter explores the conceptual notion of a 'way' or 'ways' of war in relation to Australia's strategic culture and military commitments in the period from 1945 until 1965. As the book has detailed, during this period Australia fought three conflicts – Korea, Malaya and Confrontation – and prepared to fight yet more in Indonesia, Papua New Guinea and across broader Southeast Asia. It demonstrates the importance of this period to Australia's, and the region's, security at a time of intense strategic competition.

This chapter will draw together these themes as well as situating the period of 1945–65 within the concepts of a strategic culture and a way of war. In particular, it will focus on exploring the genesis of British thinking in relation to their way of war. This is significant, not just in relation to Sir Basil Liddell Hart's pioneering work on the concept, but also due to the evolution of this concept in British strategic thinking and its parallels and applicability to the Australian context.

Context is critical. The manner in which Australia sought to achieve security during the early Cold War was part of a broader continuum of the Australian 'way(s) of war'. But like all epochs in history this was a period of both continuity and change. The period from 1945 to 1965 saw Australia's strategic circumstances alter as the country sought to address its contemporary security concerns. The onset of the Cold War, decolonisation in Asia, the advent of nuclear weapons and the continued advancement of military technology all helped to reshape Australia's strategic environment. At the same time, many aspects of Australia's approach to conflict – and the preparations for potential conflict – remained the same.

In attempting to reconcile the issues of strategic continuity, the Australian debate on a national way of war has, in many ways, paralleled many of the early debates on this concept that occurred in the United Kingdom. In particular, the traditional notion of an Australian way of war is overwhelmingly shaped by a false dilemma or dichotomy – the choice between either a continental defence (Defence of Australia, or DoA) or an expeditionary approach to Australian strategy – which similarly plagued early discourses on the British way of war.

Strategic culture and a way of war

Like any conceptual or theoretical approach, there is a plethora of criticism of attempts to outline a national way, or ways, of war and much ink has been spilt debating the relative merits of a way of war as a frame of analysis. Of particular note is the use of a way of war less often as a frame for historical analysis of complex events and more as a political tool grounded in a form of policy advocacy. This criticism casts its way back to the field's foundational work, Sir Basil Liddell Hart's *The British way in warfare*.[1]

While Liddell Hart's pioneering analysis dates from the 1930s, it was not until the 1970s that debate in international relations and strategic studies delved into a broader capstone concept: the idea that nation states have a strategic culture. Strategic culture has proven to be even more multifarious

---

1   Basil H Liddell Hart, *The British way in warfare* (London: Faber & Faber Ltd, 1932). Such debate is not restricted to Britain but occurs for each country on which studies have been based. For Australia some key texts include: Michael Evans, *The tyranny of dissonance: Australia's strategic culture and way of war 1901–2005*, Study Paper No. 306 (Canberra: Land Warfare Studies Centre, 2005), at: researchcentre.army.gov.au/sites/default/files/sp306_tyranny_of_dissonance-michael_evans.pdf; David Kilcullen, 'Australian statecraft: The challenge of aligning policy with strategic culture', *Security Challenges* 3, no. 4 (2007): 45–65; Peter J Dean 'The alliance, Australia's strategic culture and way of war', in *Australia's American alliance*, ed. Peter J Dean, Stephan Frühling, and Brendan Taylor (Melbourne: Melbourne University Press, 2016), 224–50.

than a national way of war, and in the academy even more controversial. Pioneered by the then Rand analyst Jack Snyder, and investigated deeply by scholars such as Ken Booth, Colin Grey and Alistair Ian Johnson,[2] this concept, like a way of war, has eluded precise definition and gone through various iterations of construction and theoretical interpretation. To choose just one, somewhat contemporary, definition, Kerry Longhurst has proposed that a strategic culture is:

> a distinct body of beliefs, attitudes and practices, regarding the use of force, which are held by a collective [usually a nation] and arise gradually over time through a unique protracted historical process.[3]

Scholars generally regard 'a way of war' as a subset of a nation's strategic culture.

Conceptually, a way of war is more grounded in military history. As Tony Echevarria has argued, 'we can only know a way of war historically by piecing together what has been done'.[4] Thus the concept can be conceived as a 'historical pattern or tradition reflecting how and why force has been used'.[5]

Thus the two concepts, strategic culture and a way(s) of war, are both useful in their own right but are better understood in terms of their interrelationship. As Lawrence Sondhaus has outlined:

> for the political scientist, the true utility of strategic culture lies in how it can help us understand observed behavior in the present (rather than to predict future behavior), for the historian of war and diplomacy [a way of war] offer[s] a useful framework for understanding the recent as well as the more distant past.[6]

---

2   See Ken Booth and Russell Trood, *Strategic cultures in the Asia-Pacific region* (London: MacMillan, 1999); Lawrence Sondhaus, *Strategic culture and ways of war,* Cass Military Studies (London: Routledge, 2006); Alastair Iain Johnston, 'Thinking about strategic culture', *International Security* 19, no. 4 (1995): 32; Alastair Iain Johnston, *Cultural realism: Strategic culture and grand strategy in Chinese history* (Princeton: Princeton University Press, 1995); Colin S Gray, 'Strategic culture as context: The first generation of theory strikes back', *Review of International Studies* 25, no. 1 (1999): 49–69, doi.org/10.1017/s0260210599000492; Colin Grey, 'Strategy and culture', in *Strategy in Asia: The past, present, and future of regional security,* ed. Thomas G Mahnken and Dan Blumenthal, Stanford Security Studies (California: Stanford University Press, 2014), doi.org/10.1515/9780804792820.
3   Kerry Longhurst, *Germany and the use of force: The evolution of German security policy 1990–2003* (Manchester: Manchester University Press, 2004), 17.
4   Antulio J Echevarria II, *Reconsidering the American way of war: US military practice from the Revolution to Afghanistan* (Washington DC: Georgetown University Press, 2014), 176.
5   Max Boot as cited in Echevarria, *Reconsidering the American way of war*, 19.
6   Sondhaus, *Strategic culture and ways of war*, 13.

Liddell Hart and the British way of war

Liddell Hart's original work was the conceptual birth of a 'way of war' in the academy.[7] Central to Liddell Hart's thesis was the case that strategic debates in the United Kingdom were best understood as a fundamental dilemma between continental and indirect (or navalist) approaches to strategy; whereby the British had to constantly balance European continental commitments against imperial commitments. For Liddell Hart, the one true approach to British strategy was the indirect approach. He argued that the 'misguided' decision during the First World War to purse a continental strategy over an indirect strategy was in contravention to the traditional British 'way of war'.[8]

Liddell Hart's argument was a direct response to the attrition-based warfare that characterised the Western Front from 1914 to 1918 and the subsequent losses suffered by Great Britain. This was a deeply personal experience for Liddell Hart who had served as a captain in the King's Own Yorkshire Light Infantry Regiment on the Western Front. Liddell Hart saw the British commitment of a large continental army to Europe and the subsequent loss of life as a result of 'shallow thought ... deformed by slavish imitation of Continental fashions' by the British Government. He worried that the movement away from a 'navalist' strategy based on the indirect approach was 'stunted by the consequences of that malformation are to be found in the years 1914–1918 and have been felt ever since'.[9]

---

7 The use of 'ways of war' relates to a nation's grand strategic approach to the use of military force. As such, this chapter defines a 'way of war' as the way and manner in which a military force is used by a nation state at the grand strategic level as part of its strategic culture. A way of 'warfare' is a type of military approach to operations adopted by a nation's military services to meet the strategic challenges it is faced with. A 'way of warfare' or 'warfighting' is, as David Horner has noted, the 'way a nation and its armed forces *fights* its wars' (emphasis added). See David Horner, 'The Australian way of warfighting', paper presented to the Australian Command and Staff College, Queenscliff, 24 June 1996. Such a view was standard in British Commonwealth doctrine and manuals: e.g. combined or amphibious operations are referenced to as a 'form of warfare'.
8 Liddell Hart, *The British way in warfare*.
9 Ibid., 7.

Liddell Hart and the conceptualising of the 'Australian way of war'

At the centre of Liddell Hart's analysis was the presentation of a dilemma between two approaches to strategy: a European continental strategy versus an indirect, maritime approach. A similar dichotomy has been the intellectual foundation from which debates on Australia's way of war have also evolved.[10] At the heart of the current Australian conceptualisation of a 'way of war' is a debate between those favouring an expeditionary approach to the use of military force in support of Australia's major power allies, versus those favouring a focus on the continental defence of the Australian mainland. While this Australian discourse has attracted only a small number of commentators and academics, the basic approach is characterised by this bifurcation. It is led by the two most prolific writers and policy advocates for each camp: Michael Evans (expeditionary) and Hugh White (continental or DoA).

The most prodigious writer on the Australian way of war has been Professor Michael Evans. In Evans's seminal work on the topic, *The tyranny of dissonance: Australia's strategic culture and way of war 1901–2005*,[11] he argued that the divide between expeditionary and continental approaches has personified Australian debates over strategy since Federation in 1901. Evans has argued even more directly and succinctly in the public sphere about the Australian way of war. In 2003, at the time of Australia's involvement in the controversial war against Iraq, he argued that:

> Effectively then, the Australian way of war has been based on fusing strategy and statecraft through the agency of expeditionary warfare using volunteer forces in coalition operations. In all of these struggles, the Anzac tradition has acted as an important conduit for the interpretation of Australian democratic national values – pragmatism, fairness, egalitarianism and mateship – within an alliance warfare setting.[12]

---

10   This debate in Australia has been driven by Australia's strategic circumstances, especially its geography, rather than a case of replicating a British strategic debate for antipodean needs.
11   Evans, *The tyranny of dissonance*.
12   Michael Evans, 'Values are our frontier', *The Australian*, 11 November 2003.

Former senior defence official, and one of the nation's leading public intellectuals on defence, Professor Hugh White agrees with Evans that the Anzac tradition has played a seminal role in the Australian way of war and defence policy. White noted in 2007 that Evans's interpretation was one also shared by the prime minister of the day, John Howard, whereby:

> our way of war is to send armed forces to support our allies in major land operations anywhere in the world in which our shared interests (often described as our 'values') are threatened ... [and that this approach] is supposed to guarantee that threats closer to home never emerge.[13]

To White, this way of war is one driven by a conceptualisation of Australia's alliances as a form of collective defence. White sees this approach to Australia's major power alliances as a particular form of collective security, one reminiscent of a type of security banking credit system – whereby Australia pays into a security account with a major ally. This is achieved by Australia supporting her great and powerful friends in distant offshore conflicts aligned with Australia's values in order to 'bank' security credits that Australia would be able to draw upon in conflicts or security concerns closer to home.[14]

White is, however, critical of this approach – seeing an expeditionary way of war as focused on the past rather than the future of Australia's security needs. In addition, he further refines this approach as being part of a tradition centred on the Australian Army's approach to warfare. This approach, he argues, is in opposition to the other tradition in Australian defence policy – continental defence.[15] From the period of the mid-1970s, the continental defence tradition was conceptualised as Defence of Australia (DoA), underpinned by the idea of self-reliance within the US alliance framework.[16] White's critique thus sits at the centre of the expeditionary versus continental divide that has dominated so many of the debates around Australian defence policy from the 1970s into the 2000s.

---

13   Hugh White, 'Anzac, our Achilles heel?', *The Age*, 24 May 2007.
14   This is not too different from the idea of past actions theory as a way of assessing military threats. See Daryl Press, *Calculating credibility: How leaders assess military threats*, Cornell Studies in Security Affairs (Ithaca: Cornell University Press, 2005).
15   White, 'Anzac, our Achilles heel?'.
16   Stephan Frühling, 'Australian defence policy and the concept of self-reliance', *Australian Journal of International Affairs* 68, no. 5 (2014): 531–47, doi.org/10.1080/10357718.2014.899310.

The one common feature of both Evans's and White's work is the centrality of Australia's alliance relationships to its way of war.[17] The alliance basis to the Australian way of war is widely recognised. One of Australia's leading political journalists and commentators, Paul Kelly, noted in 2002:

> for half a century the Australian way of war has been obvious: it is a clever, cynical, calculated, modest series of contributions as part of US-led coalitions in which Americans bore the main burden. This technique reveals a junior partner skilled in utilising the great and powerful in its own interest while imposing firm limits upon its own sacrifices. It is one reason the alliance is so popular.[18]

Agreement on this aspect of the Australian way of war is emblematic of the dominance of an alliance-based approach to Australia's strategic culture.

Australia's strategic culture

An alliance with a great and powerful friend has been the dominant approach to Australian strategic culture since the period before Federation. However, this is not to say that an alliance-based strategic culture is exclusive. The best way of understanding the dynamics of a strategic culture, especially when accounting for both continuity and change in this concept, is to understand it through the lens of a series of competing subcultures that vie for dominance over strategic policy.[19]

Throughout Australian history the competing subcultures in Australian strategy have included great power alliance, unarmed and neutral, armed neutrality (often also called 'armed and independent'), and a 'fortress Australia' approach.[20] These approaches to strategy have, at various times, battled for influence over Australian strategic policy – indeed, contemporary debates over the direction of Australian strategy in response

---

17   In his most recent work, White argues for 'strategic independence', i.e. the ending of the alliance with the United States and the movement to what could be termed armed neutrality. See Hugh White, *How to defend Australia* (Melbourne: Black Inc., 2019).
18   Paul Kelly, 'No lapdog, this partner has clout', *The Australian*, 28 August 2002.
19   Alan Bloomfield, 'Time to move on: Reconceptualizing the strategic culture debate', *Contemporary Security Policy* 33, no. 3 (2012): 437–61, doi.org/10.1080/13523260.2012.727679.
20   See Dean, 'The alliance, Australia's strategic culture and way of war'; and Peter J Dean, 'Armed neutrality: Dependence, independence and Australian strategy', in *After American primacy: Imagining the future of Australia's defence*, ed. Peter J Dean, Brendan Taylor and Stephan Frühling (Melbourne University Press, Melbourne, 2019).

to the rise of China and the relative decline of the United States has seen a resurgence of an argument advocating armed independence, led by Hugh White.[21]

However, despite the at times spirited debates over Australian strategy, the alliance subculture has dominated strategic policy. This dominance has been driven by a succession of governments, supported by policy elites, who have assessed Australia's relative position in the region and the world, as well as the material difficulties of self-defence, and have concluded that an alliance with a great and powerful friend is far and away the least costly approach economically, as well as providing materially more security. Thus, the main strategic debates in Australia since Federation have principally evolved around the balance between engagement and dependence with Australia's major alliance partners and the desired level of 'self-reliance' within the alliance (as opposed to self-sufficiency). This is what has largely driven the characterisation of the Australian way of war debate and the dichotomy between expeditionary versus continental defence approaches – both of which support the alliance-based strategic culture; a position deeply at play in the period of 1945–65 as Australia was engaged in Commonwealth defence efforts while also developing a new alliance with the United States.

Paralleling the British: The Australian 'dilemma'

Liddell Hart's thesis on the British way of war remained largely unchallenged until the 1970s, although international relations theorist John Mearsheimer has suggested that it was a 'short lived idea … lasting from around 1931–1933' as it paid little interest to changes in naval power in the latter half of the 1930s.[22] However, the popularity of Liddell Hart's thesis persisted well after its initial publication. The book was reprinted in 1941 and again in 1976 and, although Liddell Hart never revisited the concept in any other publication, it survives as a model and the genesis for subsequent conceptual works.

---

21 White, *How to defend Australia*.
22 Mearsheimer as quoted in Sondhaus, *Strategic culture and ways of war*, 2.

From the mid-1970s, Liddell Hart's work started to attract much greater academic attention and soon thereafter it was subjected to major criticism and revision by many leading British military historians of the time. One of the first major criticisms came from Sir Michael Howard. In a lecture at University College London in 1974, Howard was unstinting in his forensic analysis of Liddell Hart's work. Howard noted that Liddell Hart's

> analysis of British strategy was nothing more than a piece of brilliant political pamphleteering, sharply argued, selectively illustrated, and concerned rather to influence British public opinion and government policy rather than to illuminate the complexities of the past in any serious or scholarly way.[23]

Extrapolating on this line of analysis, Andrew Lambert noted in 2010 that Liddell Hart's thesis is 'a dogmatic prescription' of Julian Corbett's *Some principles of maritime strategy*, which itself should be only seen as 'the opening essay of an ongoing debate' and as a 'basic analytical tool'.[24] David French's 1990 monograph of a similar name, *The British way in warfare, 1688–2000*, argued that British governments had, in fact, concentrated on pursuing the country's strategic interests above all else, alternating between maritime and continental approaches to strategy as the circumstances dictated. The defining characteristic, he noted, was the emphasis on minimising cost.[25] Thus, the British way in warfare was neither navalist as Liddell Hart claimed, nor mixed in its approach as others have claimed, but 'essentially adaptive'.[26]

In a similar vein to Liddell Hart's original thesis, most commentators in Australia have applied the reductionist approach: posing a dilemma between expeditionary operations in support of distant allies versus the continental defence of Australia.[27] The parallel between the Australian debates and the original controversy over Liddell Hart's thesis is unmistakable. This is the key feature of both Evans's and White's assessments and it is core to

---

23   Michael Howard, *The causes of wars and other essays* (Cambridge, Massachusetts: Harvard University Press, 1983), 172.
24   Andrew Lambert, 'The naval war course', in *The British way in warfare: Power and the international system, 1856–1956: Essays in honour of David French*, ed. Keith Neilson and Greg Kennedy (Ashgate: Routledge, 2010), 250–51.
25   David French, *The British way in warfare, 1688–2000* (London: Routledge, 1990); see also Neilson and Kennedy, *The British way in warfare: Power and the international system, 1856–1956: Essays in honour of David French*.
26   French, *The British way in warfare, 1688–2000*, 23.
27   For the discussion of British defence policy in the twentieth century and his 'dilemma', see Hew Strachan, 'The British way in warfare revisited', *The Historical Journal* 26, no. 2 (1983): 447–61.

the ideas of other commentators in this debate such as Paul Kelly and John Birmingham, and academics such as Alan Bloomfield, Victor Nossal, Alex Burns and Ben Eltham.[28] Most significantly, both Evans and White used their characterisation of an Australian way of war as a foundation for their policy advocacy.

Evans, in the early 1990s, aimed to support the Australian Army's attempts to address what it saw as the limitations of the DoA policy. In the early 2000s, Evans also saw his interpretation of the Australian way of war as a way to support the Australian Government's commitments to the wars in the Middle East based, in part, on the continuity of this approach with Australia's traditional use of military force.

White's characterisation of an Australian way of war was used to highlight the expeditionary approach as outdated and relevant only to Australia's past rather than its strategic future. His focus was squarely on the centrality of the DoA concept. This binary divide and positioning of Australia's way of war as a core component of contemporary policy debates means that Australia's use of this concept has been largely captured in the same conceptual problems that beleaguered Liddell Hart's original work.

Moving beyond a binary approach has been the key to the modern British debate on their way of war. As Correlli Barnett has argued, 'it is a mistake to subscribe to either [British] school [maritime or continental] in its full doctrinal rigidity. All depends on particular cases'.[29] Brian Bond has noted that for the period in which Liddell Hart first outlined the concept, between the two world wars, continental and maritime strategies for the British were complementary not alternative strategies.[30] To Hew Strachan 'the choice [for the British] between the maritime and the continental strategies is, in historical terms, a false one'.[31]

---

28 John Birmingham, *A time for war: Australia as a military power*, Quarterly Essay No. 26 (Melbourne: Black Inc., 2005); Alan Bloomfield and Kim Richard Nossal, 'Towards an explicative understanding of strategic culture: The cases of Australia and Canada', *Contemporary Security Policy* 28, no. 2 (2007): 286–307, doi.org/10.1080/13523260701489859; Alex Burns and Ben Eltham, 'Australia's strategic culture: Constraints and opportunities in security policymaking', *Contemporary Security Policy* 35, no. 2 (2014): 187–210, doi.org/10.1080/13523260.2014.927672.
29 Correlli Barnett, *Britain and her Army, 1509–1970: A military, political and social survey* (London: Allen Lane, 1970), xviii as quoted in Strachan, 'The British way in warfare revisited', 455.
30 Brian Bond, *British military policy between the two world wars* (Oxford: Clarendon Press, 1981), 1.
31 Strachan, 'The British way in warfare revisited'.

For Michael Howard, the debate is actually about the nuances of strategy, and the 'British dilemma' should not be seen as a reductionist either/or strategic approach, but rather a relationship of interdependence between the command of the seas and the maintenance of a European balance of power.[32] Howard's nuanced assessment is equally applicable to Australia's way of war – it should not be seen as a doctrinally rigid choice between the defence of Australia or expeditionary approaches to strategy.

Beyond the false dilemma

The key to understanding Australia's way of war is to understand the complex set of calculations that drove the development, and constant revision, of Australia's strategic policy. This means it bears much more in common with the British way of war based on the analysis of French, Howard, Barnett and Strachan rather than the original, and rather limited, assessment of Liddell Hart. Ultimately, Australia's 'way of war' should be seen in terms of way*s* of war, in the plural sense. This is reflective of issues of both continuity and change in Australia's approach to strategy, which – like Great Britain's approach – has proven to be adaptive, defined by approaches to strategy that have been refined as circumstances dictated.

The key unifying element in the Australian example is its overriding preference for a strategic culture based on an alliance with a major power. Thus, Australia's ways of war are driven by a combination of the strategic circumstances of the country and its dominant strategic culture. In many senses, this too parallels the British experience. A defining feature of each country's ways of war is their relationship to respective major alliance partners. For the British, this was based around access to a continental-sized army in Europe to partner with its maritime power in order to affect the balance of power in Europe. During the First World War and 1939–40 this was France, thereafter it was a balance of France (1914–66) and the United States (1941–), then Germany (1966–) and the United States during the Cold War.[33]

---

32 Strachan, 'The British way in warfare revisited', 451.
33 Lawrence Freedman, 'Alliance and the British way in warfare', *Review of International Studies* 21, no. 2 (1995): 145–58.

Australia's 'ways of war', 1945–65

For Australia, material difficulties of continental defence, and the desire of a small to middle power to preserve the liberal international order in which it has prospered, has seen its major alliance partner shift from its colonial founder, Great Britain (1877–1942), to Great Britain and the United States (1942–68) and then the United States (1968–). As the introduction to this work notes, in contrast to popular imagination surrounding Prime Minister John Curtin's 1942 call to 'turn to America', Australian forces spent the best part of the following two decades closely integrated with the British and wider Commonwealth. From 1951, with the signing of the Australia, New Zealand and United States (ANZUS) Treaty, Australian strategy was built on balancing Australia's two great and powerful friends through a combination of Commonwealth defence, the US alliance and, for a short period, the Southeast Asia Treaty Organization (SEATO).

A key to understanding Australia's ways of war has been to understand the capabilities, interests and intents of its 'great and powerful friend(s)'. The vital element of this approach is to understand the role of Australia's major alliance partners in the context of global geopolitics and, especially, in their strategic approach to Australia's core areas of strategic interest: the South Pacific and Southeast Asia.[34]

Australian strategic history during 1945–65 amply demonstrates the need to move beyond the binary continental versus expeditionary debate. During this epoch, what emerges is the adaptability of Australian strategy, which derives a series of ways of war couched in the dominance of an alliance-based strategic culture.[35] In this system, Australian strategic culture is dominated by twin needs: the desire for a long-term alliance with great powers, and a regional defence strategy focused on the South Pacific and Southeast Asia – areas that are generally very low-priority geographic regions for Australia's major alliance partners.

As Stephan Frühling notes in Chapter 1, the interrelationship between Australia's strategic interests and those of its major power allies is key. The period from 1945 to 1965 is where:

---

34   Peter J Dean, 'A new strategic song? ANZUS, the 2020 Australian defence update, and redefining self-reliance', *War on the rocks*, 12 August 2020, at: warontherocks.com/2020/08/singing-a-new-strategic-song-anzus-the-2020-australian-defence-update-and-redefining-self-reliance/.
35   The notion of understanding a nation state's ways of war is outlined in Matthew S Muehlbauer and David J Ulbrich, *Ways of war: American military history from the colonial era to the twenty-first century* (New York: Routledge, 2018), doi.org/10.4324/9781315545691.

few certainties seemed to exist as Australia navigated its own particular version of the Cold War … [especially as] the centre of gravity of the global Cold War lay elsewhere … [and Australia's immediate geographic region] was nonetheless only of third-rate importance for Australia's [major power] allies.

During this period, the British Empire's intent and capabilities waned, while for the US peripheral theatres in the Cold War, like Southeast Asia, grew in importance as 1965 approached. As Tristan Moss demonstrates in Chapter 8, in the South Pacific meanwhile, both major powers showed little interest during a period of considerable Australian strategic concern. What is critical is the constant tension at the intersection of Southeast Asia and the South Pacific for Australia – the land border between Papua New Guinea and Indonesia and the constant tensions and difficulties in ANZUS over competing Australian and US interests.

A coalition-focused way of war

This means that Australia's ways of war during this period had two interrelated streams. The first is based around the use of force in coalition with Australia's great and powerful friends and generally consists of small (relative to the great powers), niche and largely single-service force commitments, generally dominated by the prominence of Australian land power. These forces are generally embedded into the forces of the larger ally and integrated into the larger ally's logistical system.

This approach has dominated Australian military history and seen the preponderance of Australian military power committed to the Middle East and Europe, but with episodic periods that focus on Asia, such as the period covered by this book.[36] In this approach, Australia largely operates at two levels of war:[37] strategic (decision to use force) and tactical (manoeuvres, engagements and battles that can be identified as a 'way of battle').[38]

---

36 See Douglas E Delaney, *The Imperial Army project: Britain and the land forces of the dominions and India, 1902–1945* (Oxford: Oxford University Press, 2018); Christopher Hubbard, *Australian and US military cooperation: Fighting common enemies* (Ashgate: Aldershot, 2005).
37 USAF College of Aerospace Doctrine, Research and Education (CADRE), 'Three Levels of War', in *Air and Space Power Mentoring Guide*, vol. 1 (Maxwell Air Force Base, Alabama: Air University Press, 1997), at: www.cc.gatech.edu/~tpilsch/INTA4803TP/Articles/Three%20Levels%20of%20War=CADRE-excerpt.pdf.
38 See Brian McAllister Linn, *The echo of battle: The Army's American way of battle* (Cambridge, Massachusetts: Harvard University Press, 2009).

This approach is symbolic of Australia's engagement in conflicts of the colonial period, in which it raised forces to support the British Empire in the Maori Wars, the Sudan War, the Boxer Rebellion and the Boer War. It is also reflective of the use of Australian military force from 1915 to 1918 in the Middle East and on the Western Front. This approach was replicated with the decision to send part of 2 Australian Imperial Force to the Middle East and Mediterranean between 1940 and 1943, the deployment of significant elements of the Royal Australian Navy to operations in those theatres, and the support for the British Empire Air Training Scheme that saw thousands of Australian airmen serve in Europe and the Mediterranean right through until 1945.

The same principle was applied to the Korean War, although this was closer to home than the conflicts in the Middle East and Europe. The assault on Korea came as a surprise but it was soon evident that there was a clarity of interests and alignment with the United States. As Tom Richardson highlights in Chapter 4, the 'political climate [for] Australian participation in the Korean War was by no means guaranteed', given the focus on Southeast Asia; however, the Australian foreign minister saw it as a 'golden opportunity' to build 'political goodwill in Washington' to clear the way for an alliance with the United States.

Thus, Australia's commitment to Korea was driven by both the consideration of regional security *and* alliance management. The Korean War, with its supporting UN Security Council Resolution, also accorded with another of Australia's long-term, post–Second World War approaches to its grand strategy: a liberal institutional approach to diplomacy used to support the institutions that framed the so-called 'rules-based international order'.[39]

This approach, of using military force in support of Australia's great power ally and global security concerns, continued after the period of the Vietnam War – namely through Australia's commitment to the defeat of Saddam Hussein's occupation of Kuwait in the UN-sanctioned operations of the First Gulf War, and the reprise in 2003 during which a 'Coalition of the Willing' supported the overthrow of Saddam Hussein's regime in Iraq during the Second Gulf War. The onset of the Global War on Terror

---

39   Andrew O'Neil, 'Conceptualising future threats to Australia's security', *Australian Journal of Political Science* 46, no. 1 (2011): 19–34, doi.org/10.1080/10361146.2010.544286.

after September 11, 2001 also saw Australia send military forces to fight in Afghanistan as well as forces to support the conflict against ISIS in Syria and Iraq.[40]

A regionally focused way of war

However, the limitations of Australia's alliance relationships, especially in its near region, have seen the development of a parallel approach to the Australian way of war built around the use of force by the Australian military in Southeast Asia and the South Pacific. This second stream approach is identified by the recognition that, for the majority of Australia's history, its two great and powerful friends have not shared the same levels of strategic interest in Australia's immediate geographical region.

This way of war has seen a lower frequency in the use of military force; however, given these regions' geographical proximity to Australia, the operations Australia has undertaken have arguably been of greater strategic importance than distant alliance deployments. This is largely due to these operations being undertaken in response to a perceived threat to the direct security of Australia and its immediate region, or in relation to Australia's unique strategic interests. The use of military force in these operations involves Australian commitment across all levels of war – strategic, operational and tactical – with a heavier emphasis in the South Pacific on joint operations, either independently, semi-independently or in coalition.

A number of exceptionally important conflicts and operations in these regions across Australian military history have illustrated this way of war. Notable in this approach has been Australia's commitment to securing the approaches to the continent from the north-east, in particular the island of New Guinea. Australia's first major military commitment of the First World War, an often-overlooked operation, was the capture of German New Guinea in 1914 by a wholly Australian joint expeditionary operation. While also driven by imperial requests, the location of a German colony on Australia's doorstep was a major concern to the fledgling nation at the outbreak of war in 1914. Thereafter the defence of Australian New

---

40   These latter conflicts saw significant promotion of Australian military efforts through the commitment of Royal Australian Navy and Royal Australian Air Force units, which at times made up the majority of Australia's commitment.

Guinea saw some of the most iconic battles of Australian military history fought on, above and around the island in 1942–44. Tristan Moss outlines in Chapter 8 the considerable commitment by the Australian military in the early Cold War to the defence of Australian territory in Papua New Guinea.

In the interwar period, Australia committed to the defence of both its immediate region and Southeast Asia via the Singapore strategy. With the advent of war with Nazi Germany and fascist Italy in 1939–40, Australia undertook multiple strategic approaches, including expeditionary deployments to the Middle East and Europe, regional deployments to Malaya, Singapore and the Dutch East Indies, and preparations for home defence.

The regional approach typifies the use of Australian military force during the early Cold War period. Early on, Australia assumed an expeditionary focus to strategic planning centred on the Middle East; but by the early 1950s, Australia left open the question of whether its forces would be sent to the Middle East or to Southeast Asia in the event of the Cold War turning hot. As Frühling notes in Chapter 1, by 1952–53 this emphasis had shifted to Asia and eventually Australia adopted an approach of seeking to have both Great Britain and the United States support the defence of Southeast Asia as a priority in a major global conflict.

Of course, preparation for conflict overseas was not the only thing on Australia's mind at the end of the Second World War. As John Blaxland and David Horner note in Chapters 2 and 3, Australia's largest-ever military commitment, the Pacific War, left a legacy that shaped the focus and direction of Australia's defence posture, force structure and military culture, and prompted an internal response through the establishment of the Australian Security Intelligence Organisation (ASIO) as the 'fourth arm of Australia's defence'.

Nevertheless, the ink was hardly dry on surrender documents with Japan before Australia was yet again involved in regional military operations. Australia's first postwar commitment was to the Malayan Emergency. As Thomas Richardson outlined in Chapter 6, the commitment of Australian forces to Malaya, followed up with Australia's work with Great Britain in the formation of the Far East Strategic Reserve (FESR), represented both Australia's attempts to resist communist aggression in the region and 'one of Australia's longest ... [regional] deployments'.

Southeast Asia was a major region of focus for this period – driven by the power of geographic proximity. In Chapter 5, Tristan Moss outlines the extent of planning for the Cold War turning hot in Southeast Asia, a decade-long enterprise that focused Australia's regional military efforts. Despite debates in the 1950s over the relative importance of the Middle East, it became increasingly apparent that Australia must focus on regional efforts. Inside these developments was a constant reprioritisation driven by regional geopolitical developments, global politics and the often conflicting and competing demands of Australia's defence policy and posture as well as the demands of ANZAM (the Australia, New Zealand and Malaya alliance), the FESR and SEATO.

Two key conflicts in the region would cement Australia's geographic focus and its attempts to ensure that its major power allies remained fixed on regional developments in Southeast Asia: Confrontation and Vietnam. While Vietnam is deliberately outside of the scope of this book, as Moss states 'for a decade before the Vietnam War, Australia prepared to fight a conventional war in Southeast Asia … [and] the FESR was ANZAM's contribution to SEATO … that allowed it a seat at the planning table'.

Confrontation with Indonesia, as Lachlan Grant and Michael Kelly outline in Chapter 7, was intricately linked to both the US alliance and Australia's involvement in the war in South Vietnam. It also highlighted the fragility of over-reliance on great and powerful friends, as the United States consistently refused Australia's attempts to get clear commitments over Indonesia through the ANZUS Treaty. As James Curran's work *Unholy fury* highlights, 'perhaps the most dramatic manifestation of the limits to rhetoric of shared values and common interests [in the ANZUS alliance] was made over the question of Indonesia'.[41] Australia's constant search for reassurances from the United States over Indonesia were rebuffed. While ambiguity within the wording of the ANZUS Treaty provided reassurance to the United States over possible entrapment by Australia in a conflict with Indonesia, it consequently stoked Australian fears of abandonment. Australian persistence was eventually met with a striking blow by President Kennedy, who noted to the Australian Minister of

---

41   James Curran, *Unholy fury: Whitlam and Nixon at war* (Melbourne: Melbourne University Press, 2015), 40.

External Affairs Garfield Barwick that 'people have forgotten ANZUS and are not at the moment prepared for a situation which would involve the United States'.[42]

The US response had far-reaching strategic consequences, helping to drive Australian engagement with the United States in the Vietnam War, while hedging through

> substantially increased military expenditure, raising the strength of the regular army, purchasing 40 additional Mirage fighters, a third DDG, and ordering 24 F-111 bombers ... [to develop an] Australian capability to act independently of allies against Indonesia.[43]

As Grant and Kelly note, while ultimately the Australian and British response to Confrontation through Operation Claret 'remains a model of conducting a successful low-intensity conflict while maintaining diplomatic relations with the opposing nation', strategically it struck at the heart of Australian fears of US abandonment and thus the need for greater regional self-reliance.

This in turn shaped Australia's response to Vietnam. The Menzies Government aimed to provide a prompt gesture of combat support for Vietnam to generate goodwill towards Australia in Washington and to keep the United States engaged in the region. In addition, the provision of strong Australian diplomatic support to the United States and South Vietnam was aimed at hopefully 'obscur[ing] how small a military contribution Australia was capable of making'.[44]

Justified by SEATO and ANZUS, and spurred on by concerns stoked by the US response to Confrontation, the Australian Government committed advisers and later combat troops to Vietnam, premised on the idea that for a modest financial cost and a small commitment of forces Australia could draw the United States further into the defence of Southeast Asia. This strategy overlooked the nature of the conflict in South Vietnam, including the difficulties the United States would have in achieving a military outcome. Ultimately, the course of the war in Vietnam would lead to a US withdrawal from continental Southeast Asia, personified

---

42　Kennedy as quoted in Curran, *Unholy fury*, 44.
43　Stephan Frühling, *A history of Australian strategic policy since 1945* (Canberra: Defence Publishing Service, 2009), 21.
44　Frank Frost, *Australia's war in Vietnam* (Sydney: Allen & Unwin, 1987).

by the declaration of the Nixon Doctrine in 1969 and the increasing Vietnamisation of the war in South Vietnam. These moves undermined the very basis of Australia's approach to regional security.

While Australia may have been largely focused on Southeast Asia in 1945–65, this did not stop the government from placing a high importance on the defence of the Australian mainland and the South Pacific. The South Pacific presents as peripheral to the bifurcation of the Australian way of war; however, it is exceptionally easy to view this region in a different light given the level of military commitment to the area throughout Australia's history. This is illustrated by major operations in New Guinea in the Second World War and deployments in the Cold War: operations Morris Dance (1987), Quick Step (2006) and Operation Fiji Assist (2016) in Fiji, deployments and operations in East Timor (1941–42, 1999, 2006), plus various deployments from the end of the Second World War through to today for humanitarian and disaster relief operations and peacekeeping/peace enforcement operations.[45] The South Pacific has returned to focus through strengthened bilateral defence partnerships, the Pacific Patrol Boat Program and, from 2019, with the much-hyped federal government 'Pacific Step Up'.[46]

Reconceptualising the Australian 'way of war'[47]

These reflections on Australia's ways of war, concentrated on the period of the early Cold War, highlight the redundancy of the focus on a binary divide between the expeditionary and DoA schools of thinking on Australian strategy. Such a dualistic approach ignores the complexity and constant adaptability of Australia's approach to strategic policy. Conceptually, many of the operations in Southeast Asia in the period from 1945 to 1965

---

45 See Joanne Wallis, *Pacific power? Australia's strategy in the Pacific Islands* (Melbourne: Melbourne University Press, 2017); see also Dean, 'The alliance, Australia's strategic culture and way of war', 242.
46 Prime Minister, Minister for Foreign Affairs, and Minister for Defence, 'Strengthening Australia's commitment to the Pacific', media release, 8 November 2018, at: www.pm.gov.au/media/strengthening-australias-commitment-pacific.
47 This argument has been outlined by the author in two other key assessments. See Dean, 'The alliance, Australia's strategic culture and way of war'; and Peter J Dean, 'Towards an Australian Marine Corps? Australian land power and the battle between geography and history', in *A new strategic environment and roles of ground forces: NIDS international symposium* (Tokyo: National Institute for Defense Studies, 2019).

sit at the intersection of the expeditionary and DoA approaches, mixing together elements of both and forming what arguably could be labelled a third way of war for Australia: one focused on a regionalist approach.

In contemporary discussions of Australian strategy, some commentators have argued that a maritime strategy with a focus on the region is relatively new phenomenon: a 'third way' of thinking in Australian strategic policy, as manifested through the adoption of a maritime strategy for the Australian Defence Force and the revised focus of the 2009, 2013 and 2016 defence white papers.[48] But as the chapters in this book have outlined, the period from 1945 to 1965 makes it clear Australia has a much longer and richer tradition in regional operations: it has always been there, as a consequence of the interplay of Australia's geopolitical circumstances and the fundamental tensions between Australia's interests in its region and those of its great and powerful allies.

The more regionalist approach placed a premium on Australia's middle power status with a pragmatic focus on the use of force not just for continental defence or expeditionary operations but throughout Australia's 'areas of direct military interest' – Southeast Asia and the South Pacific. Such an approach does not deride expeditionary concerns about the global balance of power, but is more pragmatic in its view of Australia's strategic weight and influence. Nor is it totally divorced from the idea of DoA – focusing as it does on operations closer to Australia's geographic centre of gravity. At times, it has provided for a more balanced approach to Australia's military structure and organisation, with an emphasis on capabilities that can be used throughout the region; an approach that was particularly influential in the late 1950s and 1960s and again during strategic guidance in the 1990s until the events of September 11, 2001.

These three ways of war have each held sway at different stages of Australian strategic history. However, what is critical to understand is that they were not rigidly adhered to in any one era and have been evident, in various forms, in all eras. What is central to understanding each of these

---

48 Michael Evans, *The third way: Towards an Australian maritime strategy for the twenty first century*, Australian Army Research Paper, no. 1 (Canberra: Australian Army, 2014). While Evans correctly positions the difficulties for Australia in developing a maritime strategy being a result of 'sea blindness' and Australia's reliance on the maritime supremacy of its great and powerful friends, he also attributes it to the 'schism between continental and expeditionary approaches in strategic behaviour' in Australia.

conceptual approaches is the fundamental adaptability of Australian strategy, reflective of the pragmatic approach Australia takes to alliance management and regional and global security concerns.

Depending on dictates provided by Australia's strategic environment, each of these different ways of war have taken on different roles and places in Australian defence thinking. The period of 1945–65 is not only fascinating in its own right, but also informs contemporary debates. Then, as now, 1954–64 was a period defined by uncertainty, changing alliance structures, evolving threats, geopolitical change and great power competition.

Since the turn of the century, a layered approach, reflective of these three ways of war, has been evident in formal policy through the strategic objectives laid out in the 2000, 2009 and 2013 Defence white papers. These documents provided for a hierarchy of priorities based on DoA, then regionalism and finally global concerns. In the 2016 Defence white paper, these three strategic objectives continued to coexist but were placed on an equal footing.[49]

In response to the rise of China and the changing regional balance of power, Australian defence policy continues to adapt. The 2020 Defence Strategic Update outlined new strategic objectives: shape, deter and respond. In this approach, the centrality of the US alliance remains; however, the focus geographically is now the Indo-Pacific, defined as the region from the north-west Indian Ocean, through Southeast Asia to the South Pacific. Regionalism, it seems, is back in the ascendency in Australian strategic policy – just like it was in the period covered in this book. However, this does not totally ignore global security concerns, while at the heart of all Australian strategic policy documents sits the fundamental bedrock of the defence of Australia. The period of 1945–65 thus holds many important lessons for contemplation, for, as Mark Twain noted, while history may not repeat itself, it does rhyme.

---

49   Commonwealth of Australia, *Defence white paper 2016* (Canberra: Australian Government Department of Defence, 2016), 69.

Index

ACP. *see* Australian Communist Party (ACP)
anti-communism
   ASIO (Australian Security Intelligence Organisation), 60–63, 65–66, 67–72
   legislation, 62–63, 65–66, 67–69, 117
   referendum against communism, 67–69
ANZAM (Australia, New Zealand and Malaya) agreement, 30, 31
   Far East Strategic Reserve (FESR), 96–98, 100, 113
   planning force, 21, 24, 107–109, 191
ANZUS (Australia, New Zealand and United States) treaty, 92, 98
   Australian strategic approach, 186
   concerns about US commitment, 30–31, 141
   drafting, 66
   limitations, 191–192
   origins, 17–18, 41
ASIO (Australian Security Intelligence Organisation), 190. *see also* espionage
   anti-communism activities, 60–63, 65–66, 67–72
   counterespionage role, 64
   criticisms, 71–72
   formation, 57–59
   internment planning, 65, 69–70
   origins, 53–54
   Reed, Geoffrey, 59
   Spry, Charles, 64, 68, 70
   structure, 59
Attlee, Clement, 58, 66
Australia
   allies, 11–12, 28, 180–182, 185
   Commonwealth Investigation Branch (CIB), 55–56
   Commonwealth Investigation Service (CIS), 56, 58
   Commonwealth Police, 54–55
   Commonwealth Security Service, 55
   Commonwealth war book, 65
   defence expenditure, 26, 31–32, 163
   diplomacy, 138, 139–140, 156, 188, 192
   military priorities, 16–17, 19–20, 26
   referendum against communism, 67–69
   regional influences, 11–12, 16
   regional significance, 15
   relationship with Indonesia, 138, 139–140, 156
   Special Intelligence Bureau (SIB), 54–55
   strategic approach, 25–28, 33–34, 139, 157–158
   strike-breaking, 61
   way of war, 179, 184, 186–195

Australia, New Zealand and Malaya agreement. *see* ANZAM (Australia, New Zealand and Malaya) agreement
Australia, New Zealand and United States treaty. *see* ANZUS (Australia, New Zealand and United States) treaty
Australian Army, 39, 44–46. *see also* Pacific Islands Regiment (PIR)
   artillery, 153
   counterinsurgency, 115–116
   Directorate of Intelligence, 54
   engineers, 153
   jungle warfare, 115, 124, 128, 131, 133, 158
   Korean War, 78–83
   Malayan Emergency, 99, 123
   PNG Command, 165, 169, 171–172
   signallers, 153
   Special Air Service (SAS), 150–152, 170
   training, 100–102, 129
   Vietnam War, 134
Australian Communist Party (ACP), 57. *see also* communism; Communist Party of Australia (CPA)
   government actions, 60–63, 64, 65–66, 67–72
   links with Soviet Union, 61–62, 63–64
   membership, 68
   name change, 57, 69
   police activities, 66
   relationship with Labor Party, 68, 71
   response to ASIO, 61
   Sharkey, Lance, 60
Australian military. *see also* Royal Australian Regiment (RAR)
   2020 Defence Strategic Update, 195
   Anzac tradition, 180
   Australian Imperial Force, 19, 44–45
   British influence, 36, 41, 48–50, 51–52
   Citizen Military Forces, 26, 44–45, 160
   colonial period, 188
   conscription, 26, 32, 64, 143
   demobilisation, 37, 41–42
   deployment, 1
   Global War on Terror, 188–189
   Gulf War (First and Second), 188
   identity, 36
   independence, 28
   Interim Army, 37
   Iraq, 179
   Korean War, 76–77
   Middle East, 17, 18–19
   national service, 26, 32, 64, 143
   official histories, 3
   Pentropic military structure, 26, 102
   Permanent Military Force (PMF), 44–46
   political influences on, 75, 87, 91–92
   professionalisation, 2, 35
   regional strategy, 189–193
   service families, 104–105
   size, 36–37, 44, 51
   Southeast Asia commitments, 30–31, 163, 170
   strategic approach, 187–188
   technology, 31–32
   uniforms, 36
   Vietnam War, 2, 29, 30–31, 32
Australian relationship with Britain. *see also* ANZAM (Australia, New Zealand and Malaya) agreement; Far East Strategic Reserve (FESR)
   air force cooperation, 47–48
   alliance partner, 186
   colonial warfare, 188

INDEX

competing priorities, 110, 140, 189
Empire Air Training Scheme, 46
impact of espionage, 57
independence, 40, 49, 95
limitations of, 33–34
Malayan Emergency, 18, 123–124
military forces, 2, 46, 47, 103–104, 142
Singapore strategy, 15, 190
Statute of Westminster, 40, 49
tensions with United States, 18–19, 97
Venona program, 57–59, 60, 61
weapons testing in Australia, 56–57, 58
Australian relationship with United States. see also ANZUS (Australia, New Zealand and United States) treaty
alliance partner, 186
Coalition of the Willing, 188–189
competing priorities, 189
defence commitment, 15
impact of espionage, 57
Korean War, 17–18, 75, 188
limitations of, 27–28, 30, 33–34, 191–192
military forces, 79–80, 82, 85–86, 90–91
prioritisation, 26
Radford–Collins agreement, 18
tensions, 24
tensions with Britain, 40–41
Venona program, 57–59, 60, 61
Australian Security Intelligence Organisation. see ASIO (Australian Security Intelligence Organisation)

Barwick, Garfield, 140, 192
Borneo
Australian deployment, 32, 137, 144–147, 149–150, 151–152, 153
precedent for Papua New Guinea, 171
Bradley, Omar, 18
Briggs, Harold, 120–122
Britain. *see also* Australian relationship with Britain
alliance with France, 13
Anglo–Malayan Defence Agreement, 139
Far Eastern Land Forces Training Centre (FTC), 125
MI5, 58
military deployment, 25
military priorities, 16–17, 19–20
pound sterling economic area, 41
presence in Malaya, 116–117
way of war, 178, 182–183, 185
British Commonwealth Occupation Force (BCOF), 75
in Japan, 43, 46, 50, 96, 103
British Defence Coordinating Committee (Far East) (BDCC(FE)), 99–100
Brunei, 138

Canada, 48, 49
Chiefs of Staff Committee (Australia), 16, 42
Chifley, Ben, 58–59
China, People's Republic of, 195
in Korean War, 77, 79, 80–81
proclamation of, 60
support of Democratic People's Republic of Korea, 74
support of Indonesia, 143
Cold War. *see also* espionage; Soviet Union
origins, 12–14, 56–57
security, 1
threat of global war, 12, 19, 66–67, 70, 95
trends in Australia, 5–6, 175–176
US strategy, 21
war planning, 191

Commonwealth Prime Ministers' Conference (1946), 16
Commonwealth Prime Ministers' Conference (1951), 66
Commonwealth Strategic Reserve, 20, 24, 30
communism. *see also* Australian Communist Party (ACP); Communist Party of Australia (CPA)
  Communist Party Dissolution Act (Australia), 65–66
  domino theory, 33, 34
  in Europe, 13, 22–23
  as global threat, 123–124
  Industrial Workers of the World (IWW), 54
  labour movement, 57, 61, 71
  legislation against, 62–63, 65–66, 67–69, 117
  referendum against communism, 67–69
  in Southeast Asia, 12, 107, 115, 123–124, 143
  spread, 29
  threat to Western nations, 72, 75
Communist Party of Australia (CPA), 55. *see also* Australian Communist Party (ACP)
  ASIO activities against, 69–70
  membership, 55
  name change, 57, 69
Council of Defence (Australia), 16–17
Curtin, John, 2, 186

Defence Committee (Australia)
  ANZAM agreement, 97–98
  Australian policy objectives, 28
  Korean War, 77
  Pacific Islands Regiment (PIR), 164
  Papua New Guinea, 159, 169
  size of Australian forces, 30–31
  Soviet Union aims, 70
Democratic People's Republic of Korea (DPRK), 73
diplomacy, 138, 139–140, 156, 188, 192

espionage, 54, 56–58, 60, 61–62. *see also* ASIO (Australian Security Intelligence Organisation)
  Gouzenko, Igor, 40, 56
  Petrov, Vladimir, 60
  Venona program, 57–59, 60, 61
Europe, 12–13
Evatt, Herbert (Doc), 39–40, 57, 68–69

Fadden, Arthur, 76
Far East Strategic Reserve (FESR), 95, 142, 190. *see also* ANZAM (Australia, New Zealand and Malaya) agreement
  ANZUK (Australia, New Zealand and United Kingdom) Division, 108–109, 114
  in Indonesian Confrontation, 109–114
  origins, 96–99
  purpose, 97–98
  role of United States, 107
  shortages, 106–107
  structure, 98, 99–100
  training, 100–102
  war planning, 105–109, 110–114
Far Eastern Land Forces (FARELF), 100, 127–128
First World War, 158, 178
  internal security, 54
Five Power talks, 20

Global Agreement on Tariffs and Trade. *see* World Trade Organization (WTO)
Gouzenko, Igor, 40, 56

Hasluck, Paul, 143
historiography, 2–5
HM Ships
    Albion, 145
    Belfast, 89
    Glory, 76
    Ocean, 88
HMA Ships
    Anzac, 88
    Arunta, 99
    Bataan, 75, 87, 88, 89
    Duchess, 154
    Melbourne, 44, 101, 102
    Murchison, 88, 89, 90, 91
    Shoalhaven, 75, 87, 88
    Sydney, 44, 76, 91, 102, 154
    Teal, 154
    Tobruk, 88
    Vampire, 154
    Vendetta, 154
    Warramunga, 76, 88, 99
    Yarra, 154–155
HMC Ships
    Athabaskan, 88
    Cayuga, 88
    Sioux, 88
HMNS *Piet Hein*, 91
Hughes, William, 54, 158

Indonesia
    air force, 111–112
    decolonisation, 12
    independence, 37–38
    military actions, 110–111
    relationship with Australia, 138, 139–140, 156
    response to Federation of Malaysia, 138–139
    Suharto, 33, 155
    Sukarno, 137, 138, 140, 143, 155–156
    West Papua, 28, 30, 157, 162
Indonesian Confrontation, 33, 109–113, 191–192
    Australian casualties, 146, 149, 150, 152
    Australian response, 139–144
    Australian troop commitment, 142–143
    Clandestine Communist Organisation, 146
    Claret operations, 145, 147–150, 192
    diplomacy, 138, 139–140, 156
    Director of Borneo Operations (DOBOPs), 144, 147–148
    hearts and minds operations, 151, 153
    peace treaty, 156
    resolution, 155–156
    Sarawak incursions, 144, 145–150
    threat towards Papua New Guinea, 162–166, 169–170
Industrial Workers of the World (IWW), 54
International Bank for Reconstruction and Development. *see* World Bank
International Monetary Fund, 14

Japan
    British Commonwealth Occupation Force (BCOF), 43, 46, 50, 96, 103
    occupation, 1, 37, 41
    presence in Korea, 73
Joint Chiefs of Staff (United States), 18, 20, 24, 107
jungle warfare, 115, 124, 128, 131, 133, 158

Kim Il Sung, 73
Konfrontasi. see Indonesian Confrontation
Korea, North. *see* Democratic People's Republic of Korea (DPRK)

Korea, South. *see* Republic of Korea (ROK)
Korean War
   Australian casualties, 92
   Australian participation, 188
   ceasefire, 82–83
   Chinese participation, 79, 80–81
   history, 2
   Maryang-San, 81
   origins, 14, 73–74
   role of RAAF (Royal Australian Air Force), 83–87
   role of RAN (Royal Australian Navy), 87–91
   static phase, 82, 84
   United Nations resolution, 74
   US participation, 74

Laos, 29, 108
Liddell Hart, Basil, 176–179, 182–183

MacArthur, Douglas, 36, 51, 55, 77
Makin, Norman, 57
Malay Peninsula, 105
   Kra Isthmus, 105, 106, 113
   strategic significance, 16, 23–24
Malayan Communist Party (MCP), 116–120, 122, 126, 127, 131, 132–133
Malayan Emergency, 190
   ambushes, 129–130, 135
   Australian casualties, 134
   Australian commitment, 106–107, 115, 123–133, 134–135
   Australian involvement, 32, 99
   Briggs Plan, 120–122, 125, 127, 131
   British response, 118–119, 120–122, 125–126
   Communist Terrorists (CTs), 118, 127–129, 132, 133, 145, 153
   The conduct of anti-terrorist operations in Malaya (ATOM), 125–126, 134
   Far Eastern Land Forces (FARELF), 100, 127–128
   Far Eastern Land Forces Training Centre (FTC), 125
   hearts and minds operations, 121, 122, 125, 127
   impact on Vietnam War operations, 134–135
   independence, 122
   jungle warfare, 115, 124, 128, 131, 133
   legacy, 134–135
   Orang Asli, 131, 133
   Royal Australian Air Force (RAAF) participation, 18
Malayan Peoples' Anti-Japanese Army (MPAJA), 116
Malayan Races Liberation Army (MRLA), 115, 118–120, 122, 126, 131, 133
Malaysia
   Federation of, 138–139
   Tunku Abdul Rahman, 138
Mao Zedong, 60, 74
McKell, William, 62
Menzies, Robert, 63
   Cold War perspective, 61–62, 66–67
   international alliances, 18, 24, 26, 75–76, 141
military discipline, 79–80
military history, 2–5
military morale, 85–86, 103–104
military strategy, 130, 135, 146–147, 149, 150, 151
   ambushes, 149, 150, 151
   Claret operations, 147–150
   conflict deterrence, 5
   continental approach, 178
   deployment in Asia, 11
   indirect (navalist) approach, 178

patrols, 166–168
study of, 178–181
military technology, 2, 39, 47
   aircraft carriers, 43, 91, 99, 145
   British *versus* US, 48–49
   helicopters, 155
   mines, 89, 146, 149
   nuclear, 21–23, 25–26, 29, 60, 66, 102
   planes, 83, 84–87, 111–112
   ships, 76
   submarines, 43
   weaponry, 161–162, 165–166
mutually assured destruction, 29

NATO (North Atlantic Treaty Organization), 70
   established, 60
   nuclear armament, 22–23, 26
   origins, 13–14
   United States–British tensions, 18–19
Netherlands, 30, 38, 162
New Zealand, 20, 98, 106. *see also* ANZAM (Australia, New Zealand and Malaya) agreement; ANZUS (Australia, New Zealand and United States) treaty
North Korea. *see* Democratic People's Republic of Korea (DPRK)
nuclear technology, 21–23, 25–26, 29, 60, 66, 102

OECD (Organisation for Economic Co-operation and Development), 14

Pacific Islands Regiment (PIR), 159. *see also* Papua New Guinea
   barred from participation in Vietnam, 172
   expansion, 164–165
   jungle warfare, 165–166
   patrols, 166–168

   PNG Command, 165, 169, 171–172
   relationship with police, 162, 171–172
   reraising, 161–162
   restrictions, 162
   role, 116, 165–168
   structure, 165–166
   training, 170
   weaponry, 165–166
Pacific region
   ANZUS treaty, 141
   Australia in, 15, 18, 33, 43, 186–187, 193–194
   warfare, 35–36, 51, 55
Papua New Guinea. *see also* Pacific Islands Regiment (PIR)
   Australian presence in, 28, 110, 158–160, 162, 189–190
   defence against Indonesia, 163–164, 166–167
   First World War, 189
   independence, 172
   Indonesia in West Papua, 30
   influence of Malayan Emergency, 171
   military–civil relationships, 168, 171
   New Guinea Infantry Battalion, 159
   Papua New Guinea Volunteer Rifles, 160
   Papuan Infantry Battalion, 158–159
   race relations, 162, 165
   vulnerability, 160
   war planning, 168–172
peacekeeping, 38
Pentomic military structure, 22, 26
Pentropic military structure, 26, 102
Petrov, Vladimir, 60
prisoners of war, 37, 92

RAAF (Royal Australian Air Force), 38–39, 46–48
　Far East Strategic Reserve (FESR), 99
　in Indonesian Confrontation, 155
　in Korean War, 83–87
　in Malayan Emergency, 114, 123, 131–132
　No. 77 Squadron, 83–87, 92
　size, 36
　technology, 47
racism, 105, 162, 165
RAN (Royal Australian Navy), 43–44. *see also under* individual ship's names
　conflicts, 154–155
　Far East Strategic Reserve (FESR), 98–99
　in Indonesian Confrontation, 142, 154–155
　in Korean War, 87–91
　in Malayan Emergency, 123, 154
　in Papua New Guinea, 159–160, 163
　size, 36–37
　training, 101
regional security, 16, 186, 188, 189–193, 194–195
repatriation, 37–38
Republic of Korea (ROK), 73
Returned and Services League (Australia), 51
Royal Australian Air Force. *see* RAAF (Royal Australian Air Force)
Royal Australian Navy. *see* RAN (Royal Australian Navy)
Royal Australian Regiment (RAR)
　in Indonesian Confrontation, 137, 142, 144–147, 148, 149–150
　in Korean War, 78–79, 80–83
　in Malayan Emergency, 98, 123, 126–130, 132–133
Russia. *see* Soviet Union

SEATO (Southeast Asia Treaty Organisation), 20, 27, 96, 186, 191
　war planning, 107–109, 113–114
Second World War, 35, 190
　Australian participation, 1
　internal security, 55
　Papua New Guinea, 158–159
　postwar period, 39
　postwar planning, 42–43, 52
　trauma, 51
South Korea. *see* Republic of Korea (ROK)
Southeast Asia
　decolonisation, 11
　economic upheaval, 116
　US interest in, 21, 27
Southeast Asia Treaty Organisation. *see* SEATO (Southeast Asia Treaty Organisation)
Soviet Union, 12. *see also* Cold War; espionage
　allegiance with Democratic People's Republic of Korea, 73–74
　allegiance with Hitler's Germany, 55
　Berlin blockade, 47, 60
　Communist Information Bureau (Cominform), 57
　espionage, 40, 56–59
　KGB, 57
　military threat, 13–14, 21, 70
　support of Indonesia, 30, 141
Spender, Percy, 66, 75–76
Stalin, Josef, 74
State Department (United States), 18, 66
Statute of Westminster, 40, 49
strategic culture, 176–177, 186–187, 193–195. *see also* way of war
　2020 Defence Strategic Update (Australia), 195

INDEX

Australia, 181–182, 183–184
Britain, 182–183, 184–185
The British way in warfare, 176, 178
influences on Australia, 176
strategy, 130, 135, 146–147, 149, 150, 151
  ambushes, 149, 150, 151
  Claret operations, 147–150
  conflict deterrence, 5
  continental approach, 178
  deployment in Asia, 11
  indirect (navalist) approach, 178
  patrols, 166–168
  study of, 178–181
subversion, 54–55, 60, 171
  countersubversion, 61–62, 71–72
Suez Crisis, 28, 52
Suharto, 33, 155
Sukarno, 137, 138, 140, 143, 155–156
Syngman Rhee, 73

Tange, Arthur, 32
technology, 2, 39, 47
  aircraft carriers, 43, 91, 99, 145
  British *versus* US, 48–49
  helicopters, 155
  mines, 89, 146, 149
  nuclear, 21–23, 25–26, 29, 60, 66, 102
  planes, 83, 84–87, 111–112
  ships, 76
  submarines, 43
  weaponry, 161–162, 165–166
Thailand, 105–106, 109
trade unionists
  and communism, 55, 61, 62, 71, 117
  strike-breaking, 61
Truman, Harry S, 13, 74, 77

United Kingdom. *see* Britain
United Nations, 40, 42
  Good Offices Committee for Indonesia, 38
  Korean War resolution, 77
  Security Council, 74, 143, 188
United States
  Air Force (USAF), 83–87
  deployment in Vietnam, 29
  Eisenhower Administration, 21–27, 28
  Kennedy Administration, 27, 29, 141, 191–192
  Marshall Plan, 57
  military priorities, 21
  military strategy, 26
  Nixon Doctrine, 193
  Pentomic military structure, 22, 26
  perspective on Southeast Asia, 12
  presence in Europe, 13
  and Soviet Union, 12
  Strategic Air Command, 22
USSR. *see* Soviet Union

Venona program, 57–59, 60, 61
Vietnam War, 1–2, 137–138, 192–193
  Australian casualties, 134
  Australian troop commitment, 143
  The division in battle, 134
  history of, 2
  impact of Malayan Emergency, 134–135

war crimes, 38
war planning, 105–109, 110–113, 175, 191
way of war, 176–177. *see also* military strategy; strategic culture
  adaptive, 185
  alliances, 180–182, 185, 186–189
  British, 178, 182–183, 185

coalition approach, 187–189
Defence of Australia (DoA) approach, 179, 184, 194
Evans, Michael, 179–180, 184
expeditionary approach, 179, 184, 190, 194
regionalist approach, 193–195
White, Hugh, 180–181
Woomera weapons testing, 56
World Bank, 14
World Trade Organization (WTO), 14

www.ingramcontent.com/pod-product-compliance
Lightning Source LLC
Chambersburg PA
CBHW061251230426
43664CB00025B/2932